LIFE AND LETTERS OF HERBERT SPENCER

VOLUME II

Herbert Spencer
When 73

LIFE AND LETTERS OF HERBERT SPENCER

BY

DAVID DUNCAN, LL.D.

WITH ILLUSTRATIONS

IN TWO VOLUMES

VOLUME II

D. APPLETON AND COMPANY
NEW YORK   MCMVIII

Published May, 1908

CONTENTS

VOL. II

v

CONTENTS

LIST OF FULL-PAGE ILLUSTRATIONS

VOL. II

vii

LIFE AND LETTERS
OF HERBERT SPENCER

VOLUME II

CHAPTER XXI

ALTRUISM AS A FACTOR IN SOCIAL EVOLUTION

(*January*, 1892—*June*, 1893)

THE several parts of the *Principles of Ethics* were not written with that adherence to the order laid down in the original programme which had characterised the earlier volumes of the series. '' The Data '' had been given to the world in 1879, under the fear that his health might give way completely before he could reach it in ordinary course. Ten years after he again turned aside from the *Sociology* to write '' Justice.'' Many things had happened during the decade showing how crude and distorted were the ideas entertained on this subject. Moreover, coinciding as it did to a large extent with the more systematic part of *Social Statics,* respecting parts of which his opinion had changed, the publication of '' Justice '' was desirable, both in vindication of his consistency, and as a corrective to the conclusions which, rightly or (as he thought) wrongly, were being drawn from the earlier work. This Part being

1

off his hands about midsummer, 1891, he set about writing the remaining Parts. " The Inductions of Ethics " and " The Ethics of Individual Life " were issued in June, 1892, thus completing the first volume; " Negative Beneficence " and " Positive Beneficence "—the concluding parts of the second volume—being published by midsummer of the following year.

To guard himself " from those errors of judgment that entail mischievous consequences " he solicited the criticisms of married lady friends on whose judgment he could rely—Mrs. Lecky, Mrs. Leonard Courtney, Mrs. Lynn Linton and Mrs. Meinertzhagen.

To Mrs. Lecky.

18 *February*, 1892.

I want one or two ladies to act as Grundyometers, and I have thought of you as an appropriate one. Would you be kind enough to tell me what you think of the enclosed: bearing in mind that I am compelled by the scheme of my " Inductions of Ethics " to give a large amount of this detail, objectionable though it is.

28 *February*.—Thank you very much for your letter and its criticisms. I will attend to the points you name, and by so doing avoid giving handles against me. I am glad to find that you do not think the general presentation of the subject objectionable.

27 *May*.—Again I put your function of Grundyometer in requisition. Here are two chapters on " Marriage " and " Parenthood," in respect of which I should like the opinion of some ladies.

The *Standard* (1 July) embraced the occasion of the appearance of the completed first volume to give an outline of the work he had accomplished during the past fifty years. Though during the past decade he had " been absolutely at issue on fundamental principles with what still describes itself as the Liberal Party," he would not, said the *Standard*, find much comfort in calling himself a Conservative, " for there, too, he would find what he regards as the socialistic poison at work with undeniable, if not equal activity." Unqualified acceptance of his views he did not value very highly. As he said in March, 1892, when thanking Count Goblet d'Alviella for a copy of the Hibbert Lectures on *L'Idée de Dieu:*—

That there should be a considerable amount of community of thought between us is, of course, satisfactory to me, and that there should be also some points of difference is quite natural. One who adheres to a doctrine in all its details is commonly one who has not much independence and originality of thought, and whose adhesion therefore is of less significance.

The *Ethics* were laid under contribution for what he calls " a remarkable tribute of appreciation "—a calendar of quotations from his works for every day in the year, compiled by Miss Julia R. Gingell, and afterwards published as a volume of *Aphorisms*.

The unauthorised publication of biographical details by those who came in contact with him in home life or in business was naturally looked upon as a breach of confidence. This will explain the earlier portions of the following letter to a former secretary.

To W. H. HUDSON.

27 *May*, 1892.

When some time since I saw in the *Review of Reviews* extracts from your article in the *Arena,* I felt inclined

3

to write to you disapprovingly, expressing the opinion that you ought not to have published these biographical details, reproduced here, without my assent. I did not carry out my intention, however.

And now that I have met in the *Popular Science Monthly* with the report of your lecture delivered at Ithaca, I find myself called to write rather in the opposite sense; feeling that what I had before to say in the way of disapproval is now more than counter-balanced by what I have to say in the way of approbation. . . . I did not know, until I came to read this article, that you had so thoroughly grasped the Synthetic Philosophy in its nature and bearings. . . . You have decidedly done me a service in putting forward so clearly the origin and development of the doctrine of evolution, and by correcting, so far as correction is possible, the erroneous views that are current respecting my relations to Darwin.[1]

Notwithstanding a formal refusal to write a leaflet for the Ratepayers' Defence League he eventually yielded and prepared a short paper on " County Council Tyranny " in carrying out the Public Health Act. The League had played an active and successful rôle in the School Board elections held towards the end of 1891. He himself was invited to allow himself to be nominated as an Alderman by the Moderate Party in the London County Council. Though the invitation expressly stated that he was not to be asked " for any promise of regular attendance," he regretted that neither his work nor his health would permit of acceptance. " To sit out a debate, even were I to take no part in it, would make me ill for a month." The proposed nomination having

---

[1] See Hudson's *The Philosophy of Herbert Spencer*, chaps. i. and ii.

4

been announced in the Press he wished equal publicity
to be given to his refusal. The publication of his letter
in the *Standard* (March 14, 1892) afforded the text
for a skit, headed, "The Philosopher and the Sufficient
Reason," in the *Saturday Review*.

He was opposed to the extension through St. John's
Wood of the Manchester, Sheffield and Lincolnshire Railway (now the Great Central), unless safeguards were
adopted to protect residents from the usual railway
nuisances.

To the Earl of Wemyss.

1 *June*, 1892.

I have decided to put down in writing the essential
things I have to say apropos of this new line through St.
John's Wood.

For a generation past the stupid English public have
tamely submitted to the enormous evil inflicted upon
them by railway companies at every large town in the
kingdom—the evil of peace disturbed day and night by
the shrieks of railway whistles. With their dull, bovine
unintelligence they have let it be tacitly assumed that
railway companies, and even private manufacturers,
have a right to make noises of any degree of loudness,
with any degree of frequency, at whatever times they
please. . . . These daily aggressions on hundreds of
thousands of people—to some serious and to all annoy-
ing—ought to be peremptorily forbidden, even had railway companies to suffer in consequence considerable
inconvenience and cost. But they need suffer no inconvenience and no cost. This immense nuisance is wholly
superfluous—nay more than that, it is continued at
the same time that there might be a signalling system
far more efficient, while entailing relatively little annoyance.

5

In a note to Lord Wemyss (30 October, 1892) declining an invitation to preside at the annual meeting of the Ratepayers' Defence League, he refers again to the " dull, bovine unintelligence " of his countrymen.

I quite agree with you in your belief that little or nothing can be done to check the increasing drift towards socialism, unless the ratepayers can be roused to action. But unhappily the English people, and perhaps more than others the middle classes, are too stupid to generalize. A special matter immediately affecting them, like the Trafalgar Square meeting, may rouse them to action, but they cannot be roused to action by enforcing upon them a general policy. The results are too remote and vague for their feeble imaginations.

His rooted objection to giving bodies of men powers that may be exercised to the detriment of individuals and ultimately to the injury of the public comes out in a letter to Dr. T. Buzzard, who had asked for his signature to a petition then being signed with a view to obtain a charter for what is now the Royal British Nurses Association.

To T. Buzzard.

15 *March,* 1892.

I greatly regret that I cannot yield to your request, but I cannot do so without going contrary to my well-established beliefs.

If the proposed measure were likely to end where it is now proposed to end I should not object, but I feel a strong conviction that it will not end there, but will be a step towards further organization and restriction, ending in a law that no hired nurse may practice without a certificate—a restriction upon individual liberty to which I am strongly opposed.

I have been for many years observing how changes, which it was supposed would stop where they were intended, have gone on to initiate other changes far greater than the first. . . .

The certificating of a nurse can insure only that she has a due amount of technical knowledge. It cannot secure sympathy and cannot secure unwearying attention. . . .

At the present time there is a mania for uniformity, which I regard as most mischievous. Uniformity brings death, variety brings life; and I resist all movements towards uniformity.

Not only did he object to the obstruction by the Irish party of useful legislation until Home Rule had been granted,[1] but he objected also to Home Rule itself.

To the Earl of Dysart.

27 *May*, 1892.

I regret to see by the papers that you have become a Home Ruler. In my early days I held the unhesitating opinion that self-government was good for all people, but a life passed in acquiring knowledge of societies in all stages has brought a decided change of opinion. The goodness of these or those institutions is purely relative to the natures of the men living under them.

3 *June.*—The political question I must leave untouched, but I enclose you some paragraphs recently taken from an American publication respecting the administration of justice in Chicago, which will serve to illustrate the truth I before pointed out that political arrangements are of small value where there does not exist a character adapted to them.

A memorandum dated June, 1892, describes a project he had entertained since 1865, when he wrote the article

---

[1] See vol. i., chap. xvii., p. 329.

7

on " Political Fetichism." It seemed to him " that immense advantage would be derived if the Acts of Parliament that have been tried and repealed during all these past centuries could be brought together in such wise as that any one could easily see what they were passed for, what evils they were to meet, what provisions were made, what effects were produced, and what are the reasons given for repeal, joined of course with the dates." Mr. Wordsworth Donisthorpe had already made an experiment in this way, but the thing could be done satisfactorily only if some one would furnish means of defraying the great cost. The matter fell through owing to the financial support Spencer had hoped for not being forthcoming.[1] How reluctant he was to abandon it may be gathered from the following letters.

To W. DONISTHORPE.

30 *May,* 1892.

I should like to see these sample pages in a finished form, with the corrections and additions made as you have written them in red ink. I am quite prepared to be at any such extra cost as is entailed by making these alterations, for I am very desirous to preserve a finished sample of the proposed tables. I do not think I have named before what would be an essential part of the thing when completed—a Subject-Index, so drawn up as to make it easy to find, under each division and sub-division and sub-subdivision, all the various Acts of Parliament referring to any one particular topic. The enclosed sketch will show what I mean.

17 *June.*—Thanks for the final impression of the table. I think before the type is distributed you should cer-

---

[1] *Various Fragments,* p. 137.

tainly have a considerable number of extra proofs. . . . I suggest this, because I have still hopes that something may be done. The thing is so manifestly important— would be so immensely instructive and so immensely useful, that I think if it is properly put before those interested there may be the needful funds raised. . . . It might be not amiss to send one of these final copies with the additional columns to Mr. Carnegie, along with some explanation of the index and mode of reference. I wish you would speak to Lord Wemyss and the Earl of Pembroke, saying that you have been doing the thing at my suggestion and that I think it is supremely important. Pray let me have the printer's bill.

Life among the trees and the birds, and the companionship of Mr. and Mrs. Potter's grandchildren, had been looked forward to long before the time came for the annual holiday of 1892. From Pewsey he wrote to Miss Baker in July :—

I get a good deal of sitting out of doors under the trees bordering the croquet lawn, where I do the greater part of my work. . . . Yesterday, as I sat there, hearing from time to time the cooing of a wild dove which had a nest close at hand, I heard singing at the same time two skylarks, one woodlark, two chaffinches, a goldfinch, and a linnet, and at other times there are frequently singing blackbirds, thrushes, robins, besides other birds of which I do not know the names.

The return home of Mrs. Meinertzhagen's children, who had spent a few weeks with him at Pewsey, afforded an opportunity for setting forth one of the applications of what he regarded as an important, but neglected subject—the Physics of Physiology.[1]

---

[1] See vol. i., chap. viii., p. 125.

To MRS. MEINERTZHAGEN.

PEWSEY, 20 *August*, 1892.

I was glad to get your note and to find from it that you all thought that the children were looking *very* well. We all thought here that they had greatly improved during their stay.

May I make a suggestion with respect to clothing? . . . There is an enormous amount of mischief consequent upon the *uneven circulation* which is caused by uneven covering. The *rationale* of the matter is a very simple one. The vascular system constituted by the heart and by the ramifying system of blood vessels is a closed cavity having elastic walls. Of necessity, if you constrict the walls of any part of this cavity, the blood has to go somewhere, and it is thrust into some other parts of the cavity. If the constriction is great and extends over a considerable area, the pressure of blood throughout the unconstricted vessels becomes great and if any of them are feeble they dilate, producing local congestion. . . . This, if the cold and consequent constriction are long continued, is productive of mischief—in some cases extreme mischief. This is very well shown by the effects of wading among salmon-fishers when they are not extremely strong. I have myself experienced the result in producing increased congestion of the brain. . . . A friend of mine, the late Prof. Sellar, also a nervous subject had to leave off wading when salmon fishing, because it forthwith produced palpitation of the heart. . . . The internal organs of the body are the parts which have their blood-vessels unduly distended by the pressure, and if any of them are feebler than the rest, more or less disturbance of function results. In one case, and a most common one, there may be congestion of the respiratory membranes and a cold or a cough, but in other cases the congestion is in the alimentary canal and some bowel attack results. . . . The thing to be aimed at in clothing is such a distribution of covering as shall keep all parts evenly warmed. . . .

10

Excuse my long lecture, but whenever I see what seems to me an evil I cannot avoid making an effort to rectify it.

Leading Japanese statesmen, resident in or visiting London, were wont to consult him on matters bearing on the changes their country was passing through. He was not without misgivings when he thought of the risks incident to the coming together of an oriental and an occidental civilisation. As regards internal affairs he was impressed with the danger of granting political power at once to a people hitherto accustomed to despotic rule. With reference to external or international affairs, he counselled a policy, not of isolation, but of resistance to interference by foreigners. This, it must be remembered, was long before Japan had proved herself able to hold her own against a European power. What was present to his mind was the danger that, by means of treaties or other agreements, Japan might give foreigners a foothold on her territory, such as China had given.

On his way to a meeting of the Institut de Droit International at Geneva, Mr. Kentaro Kaneko sought to renew the intercourse he had enjoyed with Spencer two years before.

To KENTARO KANEKO.

PEWSEY, 21 *August*, 1892.
Probably you remember I told you that when Mr. Mori, the then Japanese Ambassador, submitted to me his draft for a Japanese Constitution, I gave him very conservative advice, contending that it was impossible that the Japanese, hitherto accustomed to despotic rule,

should, all at once, become capable of constitutional government.

My advice was not, I fear, duly regarded, and so far as I gather from the recent reports of Japanese affairs, you are experiencing the evils arising from too large an instalment of freedom.

23 *August*.—Since writing to you on Sunday it has recurred to me, in pursuance of my remarks about Japanese affairs and the miscarriage of your constitution, to make a suggestion giving in a definite form such a conservative policy as I thought should be taken.

My advice to Mr. Mori was that the proposed new institutions should be as much as possible *grafted* upon the existing institutions, so as to prevent breaking the continuity—that there should not be a *replacing* of old forms by new, but a modification of old forms to a gradually increasing extent. I did not at the time go into the matter so far as to suggest in what way this might be done, but it now occurs to me that there is a very feasible way of doing it.

You have, I believe, in Japan still surviving the ancient system of family organization. . . . Under this family or patriarchal organization it habitually happens that there exists in each group an eldest male ascendant, who is the ruling authority of the group—an authority who has in many cases a despotic power to which all descendants of the first and second generations unhesitatingly submit. This organization should be made use of in your new political form. These patriarchs or heads of groups should be made the sole electors of members of your representative body. . . . Several beneficial results would arise. In the first place, your electorate would be greatly reduced in number, and therefore more manageable. In the second place, the various extreme opinions held by the members of each group would be to a considerable extent mutually cancelled and made more moderate by having to find expression through the patriarch who would in a certain measure be influenced by the opinions of his descendants. And then, in the third place, and chiefly, these patriarchal electors, being all aged men, would have more conservative leanings than the younger members of their groups—would not be in favour of rash changes.

In pursuance of the principle for which I have contended, that free institutions, to which the Japanese have been utterly unaccustomed, are certain not to work well, and that there must be a gradual adaptation to them, I suggest that, for three or four generations, the assembly formed of representative men elected by these patriarchal heads of groups should be limited in their functions to making *statements* of *grievances,* or of evils or what they think evils, which they wish to have remedied—not having any authority either to take measures for remedying them, or authority even for suggesting measures, but having the function simply of saying what they regard as grievances. This would be a function completely on the lines of the function of our own representative body in its earliest stages. . . .

After three or four generations during which this representative assembly was powerless to do more than state what they thought were grievances, there might come three or four other generations in which they should have the further power of suggesting remedies—not the power of passing remedial laws, such as is possessed by developed representative bodies, but the power of considering in what way they thought the evils might be met, and then sending up their suggestions to the House of Peers and the Emperor.

And then, after this had been for generations the function of the representative body, there might eventually be given to it a full power of legislation, co-ordinate with that of the other two legislative authorities. Such an organization would make possible the long-continued discipline which is needful for use of political power, at the same time that it would at once do away with the possibilities of these quarrels from which you are now suffering.

The Japanese Constitution, Mr. Kentaro Kaneko assured him, had been drawn upon conservative lines, owing largely to advice given by Spencer and others. While seeking permission to forward Spencer's two letters to Count Ito, Mr. Kaneko reminded him (24 August) that Japan was now negotiating with the Treaty Powers of Europe and America to revise the existing treaty. By the revision Japanese statesmen expected to open the whole Empire to foreigners and foreign capital, and there was much difference of opinion in regard to the restrictions to be put on foreigners (1) holding land, (2) working mines, and (3) engaging in the coasting trade. Mr. Kaneko then goes on to say:

One interesting question—viz., inter-marriage of foreigners with Japanese—is now very much agitated among our scholars and politicians. This question is one of the most difficult problems, and it falls within the scope of social philosophers; therefore, your opinion will decide the case. Can I be permitted to have the privilege to know your opinion on this question?

To KENTARO KANEKO.

26 *August*, 1892.

Your proposal to send translations of my two letters to Count Ito, the newly-appointed Prime Minister, is quite satisfactory. I very willingly give my assent.

Respecting the further questions you ask, let me, in the first place, answer generally that the Japanese policy should, I think, be that of *keeping Americans and Europeans as much as possible at arm's length*. In presence of the more powerful races your position is one of chronic danger, and you should take every precaution to give as little foothold as possible to foreigners.

It seems to me that the only forms of intercourse which you may with advantage permit are those which are indispensable for the exchange of commodities and exchange of ideas—importation and exportation of physical and mental products. No further privileges should be allowed to people of other races, and especially to people of the more powerful races, than is absolutely needful for the achievement of these ends. Apparently you are proposing by revision of the treaty powers with Europe and America "to open the whole Empire to foreigners and foreign capital." I regard this as a fatal policy. If you wish to see what is likely to happen, study the history of India. Once let one of the more powerful races gain a *point d'appui* and there will inevitably in course of time grow up an aggressive policy which will lead to collisions with the Japanese; these collisions will be represented as attacks by the Japanese which must be avenged; forces will be sent from America or Europe, as the case may be; a portion of territory will be seized and required to be made over as a foreign settlement; and from this there will grow eventually subjugation of the entire Japanese Empire. I believe that you will have great difficulty in avoiding this fate in any case, but you will make the process easy if you allow any privileges to foreigners beyond those which I have indicated.

In pursuance of the advice thus generally indicated, I should say, in answer to your first question, that there should be, not only a prohibition to foreign persons to hold property in land, but also a refusal to give them leases, and a permission only to reside as annual tenants.

To the second question I should say decidedly, prohibit to foreigners the working of the mines owned or worked by Government. Here there would be obviously liable to arise grounds of difference between the Europeans or Americans who worked them and the Government, and these grounds of difference would immediately become grounds of quarrel, and would be followed by invocations to the English or American Governments or other Powers to send forces to insist on whatever the European workers claimed, *for always the habit here and elsewhere among the civilised peoples is to believe what their agents or settlers abroad represent to them.*

In the third place, in pursuance of the policy I have indicated, you ought also to keep the coasting trade in your own hands and forbid foreigners to engage in it. This coasting trade is clearly not included in the requirement I have indicated as the sole one to be recognised—a requirement to facilitate exportation and importation of commodities. The distribution of commodities brought to Japan from other places may be properly left to the Japanese themselves, and should be denied to foreigners, for the reason that again the various transactions involved would become so many doors open to quarrels and resulting aggressions.

To your remaining question, respecting the inter-marriage of foreigners and Japanese, which you say is " now very much agitated among our scholars and politicians," and which you say is " one of the most difficult problems," my reply is that, as rationally answered, there is no difficulty at all. It should be positively forbidden. It is not at root a question of social philosophy. It is at root a question of biology. There is abundant proof, alike furnished by the inter-marriages of human races and by the inter-breeding of animals, that when the varieties mingled diverge beyond a certain slight degree *the result is invariably a bad one* in the long run. I have myself been in the habit of looking at the evidence bearing on this matter for many years past, and my conviction is based upon numerous facts derived from numerous sources. This conviction I have within the last half hour verified, for I happen to be staying in the country with a gentleman who is well known as an authority on horses, cattle and sheep, and knows much

16

respecting their inter-breeding; and he has just, on inquiry, fully confirmed my belief that when, say of different varieties of sheep, there is an inter-breeding of *those which are widely unlike,* the result, especially in the second generation, is a bad one—there arises an incalculable mixture of traits, and what may be called a chaotic constitution. And the same thing happens among human beings—the Eurasians in India, and the half-breeds in America, show this. The physiological basis of this experience appears to be that any one variety of creature in course of many generations acquires a certain constitutional adaptation to its particular form of life, and every other variety similarly acquires its own special adaptation. The consequence is that, if you mix the constitutions of two widely divergent varieties which have severally become adapted to widely divergent modes of life, you get a constitution which is adapted to the mode of life of neither—a constitution which will not work properly, because it is not fitted for any set of conditions whatever. By all means, therefore, peremptorily interdict marriages of Japanese with foreigners.

I have for the reasons indicated entirely approved of the regulations which have been established in America for restraining the Chinese immigration, and had I the power would restrict them to the smallest possible amount, my reasons for this decision being that one of two things must happen. If the Chinese are allowed to settle extensively in America, they must either, if they remain unmixed, form a subject race in the position, if not of slaves, yet of a class approaching to slaves; or if they mix they must form a bad hybrid. In either case, supposing the immigration to be large, immense social mischief must arise, and eventually social disorganization. The same thing will happen if there should be any considerable mixture of the European or American races with the Japanese.

You see, therefore, that my advice is strongly conservative in all directions, and I end by saying as I began—*keep other races at arm's length as much as possible.*

I give this advice in confidence. I wish that it should not transpire publicly, at any rate during my life, for I do not desire to rouse the animosity of my fellow-countrymen.

P.S.—Of course, when I say I wish this advice to be in confidence, I do not interdict the communication of it to Count Ito, but rather wish that he should have the opportunity of taking it into consideration.

Though he did not wish this letter made public during his life, Spencer has endorsed on the copies of the correrespondence—'' My letters of advice contained in this batch should be read and published.'' Shortly after his death the letter of August 26 was sent from Tokio for publication in the *Times* (18 January, 1904), which wrote of it as giving '' advice as narrow, as much imbued with antipathy to real progress, as ever came from a self-sufficient, short-sighted Mandarin, bred in contempt and hatred of barbarians.''

The correspondence makes little mention of the *Ethics,* the concluding chapters of which were being written before he left town in December.

To FREDERIC HARRISON.

4 *December,* 1892.

In your reply to Huxley [1] I have just come upon a passage (p. 716) which startled me by showing a degree of agreement between your view and my own concerning certain ultimate questions much greater than I had supposed. . . .

I am in the middle of the last chapter of the *Ethics.* . . . I have been so ill that during the last fortnight I

---

[1] *Fortnightly Review,* December.

have been obliged to suspend work altogether, but when lying in bed have from time to time made memoranda of thoughts to be expressed in this closing chapter of the Synthetic Philosophy: the most significant of these sentences . . . belonging to the last section of this last chapter. Of the three relevant sentences here are copies:—

" A transfigured sentiment of parenthood which regards with solicitude not child and grandchild only, but the generations to come hereafter—fathers of the future creating and providing for their remote children.''

" May we not say that the highest ambition of the truly beneficent will be to have a share—even but an infinitesimal share—in the making of man.''

" While contemplating from the heights of thought that far-off life of humanity never to be enjoyed by them, but only by a remote posterity, they will feel a calm pleasure in the consciousness of having aided by conduct or by teaching the advance towards it.''

I send you these copies of memoranda, partly because, if I do not, you will, when the book is published, suppose that I have been plagiarizing on you; and partly because they show, as I say, a degree of agreement greater than I supposed. The chief difference between us is evidently a matter of names. . . . I regard the ideas and sentiments contained as belonging to ethics. You regard them as belonging to religion. . . . You do not apparently recognise the fact that ethics and religion, originally one, have been differentiating from the beginning, and have become in modern times quite distinct; so that ethics is being secularised (as we see even in the teachers of Christianity, who more and more are unawares separating morality from religion), and you do not infer that they [ethics and religion] will never again be reunited. Nor do you admit that as religion originally implied belief in a supposed anthropomorphic power, it remains, when the anthropomorphic character gradually disappears, as a belief in a Power as unknown

19

and transcending knowledge. As I say, this difference is after all very much a difference of names, save, indeed, that while I consider that there will be a persistent recognition of this unknown Power, you apparently do not think the recognition of it will continue.

Just before Christmas he went to St. Leonards, and never afterwards spent a winter in London.

To Sir William H. Flower.

St. Leonards, 17 *January*, 1893.

I am sorry that I cannot join the Committee of the Owen memorial. Two obstacles stand in the way.

For a long time past I have held that the getting up of testimonials and memorials is becoming an abuse and should be resisted. . . .

The second obstacle is that, large though Owen's claims may be in the way of achievement, he lacked a trait which I think essential—he was not sincere. He did not say out candidly what he believed, but tried to please both parties, the scientific world and the religious world. This is not my impression only, but that, I believe, of many.

After some reflection he changed his mind and wrote requesting his name to be added to the Committee.

As he grew older his dissatisfaction with the trend of political and social affairs at home and abroad became more acute.

To John Tyndall.

30 *January*, 1893.

You are doubtless looking forward with eagerness and anxiety to the opening of Parliament and the disclosure of this great scheme of national dissolution. What a state of the world we are living in, with its socialism and

20

anarchisms, and all kinds of wild ideas and destructive actions! The prophesies I have been making from time to time ever since 1860, as to the results of giving to men political power without imposing on them equivalent political burdens, are becoming true faster than I had anticipated.

3 *April.*—I, in common with you, look at the state of the world in dismay; but I have for a long time past seen the inevitableness of the tremendous disasters that are coming. . . . But you and I will not live to see it. Happily—I think I may say happily—we shall be out of it before the crash comes.

To H. R. Fox Bourne.

2 March, 1893.

Has anything been done by the Aborigines Protection Society in respect of this division of Queensland? Surely some very strong protest should be made. It has been all along conspicuous enough that the proposals for division arise among sugar planters, who are anxious to be able to import Kanakas without any restraint, and to reduce them, as they inevitably do, to a state of slavery. As to any safeguards due to contract and appeal to magistrates for protection, the thing is simply absurd.

It seems to me that while we are pretending to be anxious to abolish slavery in Africa, we are taking measures to establish slavery under another name in Australia.

In his letter to Professor Tyndall of April 3, quoted above, mention is made of " a domestic crisis, due to the allegation made by the ladies of my household, that their means would not enable them to carry out our agreement any longer, easy as it is for them. This entailed on me dreadful worry, and an amount of both intellectual and emotional perturbation that knocked me

21

down utterly, so that a few days ago I was worse than I had been these six years.'' This was a grievous upsetting of the arrangement entered into so hopefully in 1889. From the beginning he had made no secret that his reason for setting up a house of his own was his craving for the social comforts and pleasures of domestic life. It is difficult, therefore, to understand how it could have been assumed by these ladies that in his own house he would live almost entirely by himself, leaving the other members of the household to go their own way. For such a solitary life there was absolutely no reason why he should have exchanged the conveniences and comforts of Queen's Gardens, saddling himself also with greatly increased expenditure. When the arrangement was first proposed some of his friends felt that unless carried out with more than ordinary prudence on both sides it would not work smoothly, there being so many points on which misunderstanding might arise. Instead of the household partaking of the unity of one family, there were really two family interests, and these two interests could not be counted upon to pull always in the same direction. Union of interests in certain things and separation of interests in others could only be carried on with the utmost forbearance on both sides and the most generous interpretation of the terms of the agreement. In both these respects it speaks well for those concerned that it worked so harmoniously as it did for some years. When differences at length arose his principal concern was to get at the facts, so that the ladies might be in a position to satisfy themselves as to whether it was or was not in their interests to continue the arrangement. While doing all he could to meet their views of economy

22

and his own views of equity, and thus to allow of the arrangement being continued, he did not look upon its termination as a calamity that must be averted at almost any cost. There was a point beyond which he would not go in the matter of concession. " You and your sisters have to accept or reject my proposals—generous proposals, I think them. . . . I do not wish any further letters or proposals or correspondence, and would willingly have given £500 rather than suffer the illness which the business has brought upon me . . . and will have no more trouble about the matter. You have simply to say ' yes ' or ' no ' to the agreement I have proposed." After some hesitation his terms were accepted and a new agreement drawn up.

The settlement of this disagreeable matter enabled him to leave town with an easier mind.

To SIR JOHN LUBBOCK.

PEWSEY, 18 *May*, 1893.

Thanks for your invitation, but you see by the address that I am out of reach. An old friend of mine went over to Brussels to make a morning call and came straight back, but you would hardly expect me to emulate him. . . . I fear that now the X. is dead there is but little chance of our meeting, save by accident at the Club. I wish it were otherwise.

To JOHN HAWKE.

PEWSEY, 29 *May*, 1893.

Having, as you say, expressed myself strongly on the subject of gambling and betting, I feel bound to give some little aid to your society, which aims, if not to suppress it (which is hopeless), yet to diminish it, and herewith I enclose cheque. . . .

23

As to giving my name as one of the Vice-Presidents, I should have no objection were it not that the association of my name with a body so largely clerical in its character would lead to adverse criticisms. It is not that I in the least object to such an association, and it may be that the clergymen named are sufficiently liberal to work with one whose religious opinions are so obviously at variance with their own. But experience in another case has led me to see that I shall be liable to adverse interpretation of my motives. Change in my opinions concerning land-tenure has been ascribed to a desire to ingratiate myself with the land-owning class, and I doubt not that if I were, as you suggest, to accept the position of vice-president along with so many members of the Church, it would be ascribed to a desire to ingratiate myself with the clergy.

Neither imperialism nor athleticism found favour with him; one reason for his objection to the latter being the vice of betting associated with it. An invitation to join the general committee being formed to carry out the Pan-Britannic Idea, expounded in *Greater Britain*, was declined.

To J. ASTLEY COOPER.

PEWSEY, 20 *June*, 1893.

I fear I cannot yield to your suggestion, and for the reason that I entertain grave doubts respecting the aims of the organization to which *Greater Britain* points.

A federation of Great Britain with her colonies would in my opinion have the effect of encouraging aggressive action on the part of the colonies, with a still more active appropriation of territories than is at present going on, and there would be continued demands upon the mother-country for military and financial aid.

24

28 *June.*—Though your explanation serves to remove the objection I made, it does not remove another objection which I did not name.

I have long held that athleticism has become an abuse, and occupies far too much space in life and in public attention; and I should be very much averse to any arrangement like that you propose which would tend to render it more prominent than it is already.

When I tell you that in the space of nearly 50 years spent in London I have never once been to see the University Boat Race, and have never witnessed a cricket match at Lord's, and that for many years past I have intentionally refrained from doing so, you will see that my views on the matter are such as to negative the cooperation you suggest.

CHAPTER XXII

LATTER DAY CONTROVERSIES

(*November,* 1889—*October,* 1895)

(i.)

Soon after taking up residence in Avenue Road in the autumn of 1889 he was plunged into a controversy, which not only interrupted his work and embittered his life for several months, but broke up for a time an intimate and valued friendship of nearly forty years' standing. This most unfortunate event had its origin in a meeting Mr. John Morley had at Newcastle with his constituents, one of whom urged the nationalisation of the land, Spencer being quoted in favour of the resumption of ownership by the community (*Times,* November 5). In a letter to the *Times* (November 7) Spencer pointed out that the book referred to was published forty years ago, and that, while still adhering to the general principles, he now dissented from some of the deductions. The land question had been discussed in *Social Statics* in the belief that it was not likely to come to the front for many generations; but it had been pointed out that when it did come up " the business of compensation of landowners would be a complicated one." " Investigations made during recent years into the various forms of social organization, have in part confirmed and in part changed the views published in

26

1850." " I have no positive opinion as to what may hereafter take place. The reason for this state of hesitancy is that I cannot see my way towards reconciliation of the ethical requirements with the politico-economical requirements." Nothing was said by Spencer in this letter about the opinion attributed to him at Newcastle that " to right one wrong it is sometimes necessary to do another." He now (*Times*, November 11) wrote to say that as he could not remember everything he had written during the last forty years, it would be unsafe to assert positively that he had nowhere expressed such an opinion. " But my belief is that I have not said this in any connection, and I certainly have not said it in connection with the question of landownership." The only change of view was " that whereas in 1850 I supposed that resumption of landownership by the community would be economically advantageous, I now hold that, if established with due regard to existing claims, as I have always contended it should be, it would be disadvantageous."

Professor Huxley now entered the lists, writing (*Times*, November 12) " in the name of that not inconsiderable number of persons to whom absolute ethics and *à priori* politics are alike stumbling-blocks." " I have long been of opinion that the great political evil of our time is the attempt to sanction popular acts of injustice by antiquarian and speculative arguments. My friend, Mr. Spencer, is, I am sure, the last person willingly to abet this tendency." Professing himself unable to see in what respect his friend and he disagreed on the land question, Spencer, in his reply, took up the comments made by Professor Huxley on absolute political ethics.

" However much a politician may pooh-pooh social ideals, he cannot take steps towards bettering the social state without tacitly entertaining them. . . . The complaint of Professor Huxley that absolute political ethics does not show us what to do in each concrete case seems to me much like the complaint of a medical practitioner who should speak slightingly of physiological generalizations because they did not tell him the right dressing for a wound, or how best to deal with varicose veins " (*Times,* November 15).

Having intimated that the above letter was to be his last, he did not reply to the rejoinder from Professor Huxley (*Times,* November 18), in which reference is made to Spencer's " remarkable inability to see that we disagree on the land question," and to the physiological argument which " is hardly chosen with so much prudence as might have been expected." " Mr. Spencer could not have chosen a better illustration of the gulf fixed between his way of thinking and mine. Whenever physiology (including pathology), pharmacy and hygiene are perfect sciences, I have no doubt that the practice of medicine will be deducible from the first principles of these sciences. That happy day has not arrived yet." And if at present it would be unsafe for the medical practitioner to treat bodily diseases by deduction what is to be said of the publicist who " seeks guidance not from the safe, however limited, inductions based on careful observation and experience, but puts his faith in long chains of deduction from abstract ethical assumptions, hardly any link of which can be tested experimentally ? "

THOMAS HENRY HUXLEY AND HIS GRANDSON.

On being reminded by Mr. Frederick Greenwood that he had not yet repudiated the doctrine that "to right one wrong it is sometimes necessary to do another," Spencer wrote (*Times*, November 19): "It never occurred to me that, after what I said, this was needful. But as he thinks otherwise, I very willingly repudiate it, both for the past and the present. Even did I wish to continue my discussion with Professor Huxley, it would be ended by his letter. From it I learn that the principles of physiology, as at present known, are of no use whatever for guidance in practice, and my argument, therefore, collapses." A week later (*Times*, November 27) he wrote again: "I cannot allow the late controversy to pass without disclaiming the absurd ideas ascribed to me. . . . The suggestion that an ideal must be kept in view, so that our movements may be towards it and not away from it, has been regarded as a proposal forthwith to realise the ideal."

The breach thus brought about was a matter of much concern to their intimate friends, specially so to Professor Tyndall, Sir Joseph Hooker, Dr. Hirst, and other members of the X Club. It came as a surprise to Professor Huxley, who was not aware of having said anything sharper than he had said before, both privately and publicly.

FROM JOHN TYNDALL.

25 November, 1889.

You may well believe that this newspaper controversy has been a source of mourning to my wife and me. Many a time since it began have I wished to be at your side or, better still, to have you and Huxley face to face. With a little tact and moderation the difference between

29

you—if a difference exist at all—might have been easily arranged. When I read the concluding part of your first long letter, where you speak of state ownership as resulting in disaster, I exclaimed, " Bravo Spencer! "; but on reading the whole letter, it seemed to me that you were too anxious to prove your consistency. Relying upon merits which the whole world acknowledges, you ought, I think, to be able to say, " Damn consistency! " in regard to these scraps and fragments of your views. . . . From a public point of view, and with reference solely to the questions discussed, I thought Huxley's letters excellent. From another point of view, he might, I think, have kept more clearly in mind that he was dealing not with an ordinary antagonist, but with a friend who had such just and undeniable claims upon his admiration and affection. . . . It is a monstrous pity that you and he should appear to stand before the public as antagonists, to an extent far beyond what the facts would justify. *You* deal with political principles; *he* deals with the problems of the hour—the problems, that is to say, that have to shape the course of the practical statesman. There is no necessary antagonism here.

The breach might have been repaired before the end of the year had Spencer talked the matter over with his friends, instead of shutting himself up and seeing no one. The friendly offices of the other members of the X Club were offered for the adjustment of the difference; but instead of availing himself of these, he wrote a letter withdrawing from the Club—a letter which, on Sir Joseph Hooker's advice, was kept back. Professor Huxley was quite ready to meet him more than half-way: intimating in a letter to Sir Joseph Hooker, intended for Spencer's perusal, that he had not the slightest intention of holding Spencer up to ridicule; that nothing astonished him more and gave him greater pain than Spencer

30

taking the line he did; that his wish was, if needs be, to take all the wrong on his own shoulders and to assure Spencer that there had been no malice; and that if he had been in Spencer's estimation needlessly sharp in reply, he was extremely sorry for it. It is a pity that the olive branch thus held out was not accepted. In explanation of his attitude Spencer wrote to Professor Tyndall (9 December) :—

Doubtless you and others of the Club [the X] do not fully understand the state of mind produced in me, because you are not aware that almost everything said by Huxley [concerning my views] was a misrepresentation more or less extreme, and in some cases an inexcusable misrepresentation. . . . The effect on me has been such that the thoughts and irritations have been going round in my brain day and night as in a mill, without the possibility of stopping them.

12 *December*.—I cannot let things remain in the state in which the controversy in the *Times* left them; and to put them in some measure straight, and rectify to a small extent the mischief done, I am preparing a short article for the *Nineteenth Century*.

With the new year the controversy entered upon a new phase.

To JOHN TYNDALL.

8 *February*, 1890.

I send you a copy of the *Daily Telegraph* [8 February] in which, as you will see, I have had to defend myself against another grave misrepresentation.

One would have thought that after having done me so much mischief and after having professed his regret, Huxley would at least have been careful not to do the like again forthwith, but besides a perfectly gratuitous sneer unmistakably directed against me in the opening of his article in the current number of the *Nineteenth Century*, there comes this mischievous characterization diffused among the quarter of a million readers of the *Daily Telegraph*.

In the *Daily Telegraph* of 23 January, Mr. Robert Buchanan had taken up " the criticism of the socialistic theories of Rousseau by Professor Huxley, in the *Nineteenth Century*." In a second letter (27th) he referred to Spencer as one of those who " are socialists only in the good and philosophical sense, and who are not, like mere communists, enemies of all vested interests whatsoever." In a third communication (3 February) he criticised letters from Professor Huxley of the 29th and 31st respectively. In the former of these Professor Huxley had animadverted on " the political philosophy which Mr. Buchanan idolises, the consistent application of which reasoned savagery to practice would have left the working classes to fight out the struggle for existence among themselves, and bid the State to content itself with keeping the ring." If a man has nothing to offer in exchange for a loaf, " it is not I, but the extreme Individualists, who will say that he may starve. If the State relieves his necessities, it is not I, but they, who say it is exceeding its powers; if private charity succours the poor fellow, it is not I, but they, who reprove the giver for interfering with the survival of the fittest." A keen controversialist like Professor Huxley could not fail to fasten on the sentence in which Mr. Buchanan classed Spencer with socialists in the good and philosophical sense. " I had fondly supposed, until Mr. Robert Buchanan taught me better, that if there was any charge Mr. Spencer would find offensive, it would be that of being declared to be, in any shape or way, a socialist.'' He wondered whether Mr. Buchanan had read *The Man* versus *the State*. '' However this may be, I desire to make clear to your readers what the ' good and philosophical sort of Socialism,' which finds expression in the following passages, is like.'' Professor Huxley then gave quotations from, or references to, passages in *The Man* versus *the State*, pp. 19, 21, 22, 24, 27, 34, 35.[1]

To Robert Buchanan.

5 *February*, 1890.

Thank you for your last letter to the *Daily Telegraph*, received this morning. You have shown yourself extremely chivalrous in taking up the question in this and in the preceding letters.

In the course of our conversation on Sunday I did not to any extent enter upon the questions at issue. . . . It seems to me, however, that candour requires me to say that I cannot entirely endorse the version you give of my political views. Unless understood in a sense different from that which will ordinarily be given to them, I hardly see how the words '' higher Socialism '' are applicable. It is true that I look forward to a future in which the social organization will differ immensely from any we now know, and perhaps from any we now conceive. . . . But I hold that competition and contract must persist to the last and that any equalizations which interfere with their free play will be mischievous. The fact that from the beginning of my political life I have been an opponent of national education, and continue to

---

[1] The corresponding pages in the library edition are 297, 300, 300-1, 303, 306, 315, 316.

be one, will show you that I cannot coincide in your view that it is the duty of society to prepare its individual members for the battle of life. I hold it to be exclusively the duty of parents. . . .

Sanguine of human progress as I used to be in earlier days, I am now more and more persuaded that it cannot take place faster than human nature is itself modified; and the modification is a slow process, to be reached only through many, many generations. When I see the behaviour of these union men in the strikes we have had and are having; when I see their unscrupulous tyranny and utter want of any true conception of liberty, it seems to me unquestionable that any new *régime* constituted in their interests would soon lapse into a despotic organization of a merciless type.

Borrowing as a heading for a letter to the *Daily Telegraph* (8 February) Professor Huxley's phrase " Reasoned Savagery,'' Spencer pointed out that '' for nearly fifty years I have contended that the pains attendant on the struggle for existence may fitly be qualified by the aid which private sympathy prompts.'' '' Everyone will be able to judge whether this opinion is rightly characterised by the phrase ' Reasoned Savagery.' ''

To realise the bitterness of Spencer's feelings it is necessary to be reminded of the sense of injustice that rankled in his breast on reflecting that, notwithstanding the precept and example of a lifetime in denouncing every form of oppression and injustice, he should be charged with upholding brutal individualism and his views should be branded as '' reasoned savagery.'' One must also remember that the ill-health and depression, which in recent years had kept him away from London and more or less in retirement, had induced a state of

34

abnormal sensitiveness to criticism. Moreover, clinging to friendship so tenaciously as he did and entertaining such a high ideal of its obligations, he felt with special keenness an act which, rightly or wrongly, he regarded as unfriendly. Taking into account all the circumstances one can understand the difficulty he had in responding to the efforts of the friends of both to repair the breach. These efforts were after a time given up, and Professor Huxley's name, hitherto so frequently met with, almost disappears from the correspondence for some years. It was not till towards the close of 1893 that cordial relations were re-established.

And yet in the spring of that year the prospect of a resumption of friendly relations was by no means bright. Though alive to " the dangers of open collision with orthodoxy on the one hand and Spencer on the other," Professor Huxley introduced into his Romanes lecture passages which Spencer understood to be directed against him.

To JAMES A. SKILTON.

PEWSEY, 29 *June*, 1893.
I am glad to hear that you think of taking up Huxley's " Evolution and Ethics." . . . Practically his view is a surrender of the general doctrine of evolution in so far as its higher applications are concerned, and is pervaded by the ridiculous assumption that, in its application to the organic world, it is limited to the struggle for existence among individuals under its ferocious aspects, and has nothing to do with the development of social organization, or the modifications of the human mind that take place in the course of that organization. . . . The position he takes, that we have to struggle against or correct the cosmic process, involves the as-

35

sumption that there exists something in us which is not a product of the cosmic process, and is practically a going back to the old theological notions, which put Man and Nature in antithesis. Any rational, comprehensive view of evolution involves that, in the course of social evolution, the human mind is disciplined into that form which itself puts a check upon that part of the cosmic process which consists in the unqualified struggle for existence.[1]

Spencer had made up his mind not to take the matter up himself, but his resolution gave way on reading a review of the lecture in the *Athenæum* for 22 July. The result was a letter on " Evolutionary Ethics " in that Journal for 5 August. Towards the close of the paper he enumerated eight fundamental points of agreement between himself and Professor Huxley. " Obviously, then, it is impossible that Professor Huxley can have meant to place the ethical views he holds in opposition to the ethical views I hold; and it is the more obviously impossible because, for a fortnight before his lecture, Professor Huxley had in his hands the volumes containing the above quotations along with multitudinous passages of kindred meanings." Learning that these words were taken to imply that Professor Huxley had adopted views set forth in the *Ethics* without acknowledgment, he sent a copy of " Evolutionary Ethics " on which he wrote " a few undated lines," signed " H.S." A reply in the third person " quite starled " Spencer, who had no thought of discourtesy

---

[1] With this description of Professor Huxley's views the reader may compare, besides the Romanes lecture itself, the Prolegomena published later (Huxley's *Collected Essays*, vol. ix. Also letter to Mr. Thomas Common in *Life and Letters*, ii., 382).

in the form of his memorandum, and no idea that the closing sentence of " Evolutionary Ethics " could be interpreted to imply a charge of appropriating ideas without acknowledgment. An exchange of conciliatory notes dissipated the stormy clouds and prepared the way for the final reconciliation.

FROM T. H. HUXLEY.

24 *October,* 1893.

I am very sorry to hear that you are ill and I would gladly do anything that might help to alleviate perturbations of either mind or body.

We are old men and ought to be old friends. Our estrangement has always been painful to me. Let there be an end to it. For my part, I am sorry if anything I have said or done has been, or has seemed, unjust.

To T. H. HUXLEY.

26 *October,* 1893.

Your sympathetic letter received this morning has given me great satisfaction. We are both of us approaching our last days, . . . and to whichever of us survived it would have been a sad thought had forty years of friendship ended in a permanent estrangement. Happily by your kind expressions that danger is now finally averted and cordial relations re-established.

(ii.)

When examining Spencer's various utterances on the Land Question in *A Perplexed Philosopher,* Mr. Henry George went out of his way to ascribe the changes of view to unworthy motives, alleging that the recantation of early opinions had been made with a view to curry favour with the upper classes. This attack upon his character Spencer felt very keenly. In a letter to Mr.

37

Skilton of New York, dated 6 January, 1893, he says he would himself decline to take notice of such publication.

My American friends may, however, if they like, take the matter up, and may effectually dispose of its libellous statements. By way of aiding them in doing this, I will put down sundry facts which they may incorporate as they see well.

In the first place, irrespective of numerous utterly false insinuations, there are two direct falsehoods. . . .

The first of them is contained in the Introduction, p. 9, where he says I have placed myself " definitely on the side of those who contend that the treatment of land as private property cannot equitably be interfered with." I have said nothing of the kind. I have continued to maintain that the right of the whole community to the land survives and can never be destroyed; but I have said . . . that the community cannot equitably resume possession of the land without making compensation for all that value given to it by the labour of successive generations. . . . The sole difference between my position in *Social Statics* and my more recent position is this: In *Social Statics* I have . . . tacitly assumed that such compensation, if made, would leave a balance of benefit to the community. Contrariwise, on more carefully considering the matter in recent years, I have reached the conclusion that to make anything like equitable compensation the amount required would be such as to make the transaction a losing one. . . . And . . . I reached the conclusion that the system of public administration, full of the vices of officialism, would involve more evils than the present system of private administration. . . .

The second falsehood is the statement on p. 201 that " the name of Herbert Spencer now appears with those of about all the dukes in the kingdom as the director of an association formed for the purpose of defending private property in land." . . . So far as I know there is no such association at all. The only association which can be referred to is the Liberty and Property Defence League, . . . but I am not a member of that association. . . . If he means the Ratepayers' Defence League, the reply is that this is not an association for defending landed property, but for defending the interests of occupiers, and I joined it as a ratepayer to check the extravagant demands on ratepayers made by the County Council. . . .

As to the alleged cultivation of social relations with the landed classes, it is sufficiently disposed of by the fact that ever since my visit to America I have been so great an invalid as to be prevented from going into society. Not once in the course of the last ten years have I had any social intercourse with those of the classes referred to.

By way of meeting the various counts of Mr. George's indictment respecting motives, I will set down the facts, which prove motives exactly contrary to those he alleges.

The first concern pecuniary advantages. The first line of his motto from Browning is " Just for a handful of silver he left us.'' The facts of my career are these. For the first ten years, from 1850-60, I lost by every book published; the returns not sufficing to anything like repay printing expenses. During a period of nearly ten years subsequently, the returns on my further books were so small as not to meet my necessary expenses, so that I had continually to trench upon my small property, gradually going the way to ruin myself, until at length I notified that I must discontinue altogether: one result of this notification being the American testimonial. When, some little time after, the tide turned and my works began to be remunerative, what was my course? Still living as economically as possible, I devoted the whole surplus of my returns to the payments for compilation and printing of the *Descriptive Sociology,* and this I continued to do for a dozen years, until, year by year deliberately sinking money, I had lost between

£3,000 and £4,000 (over £4,000 if interest on capital sunk be counted). I finally ceased, not only because I could no longer afford to lose at this rate, but because the work was altogether unappreciated. This was not the course of a man who was to be tempted by " a handful of silver! "

The second line of his motto is " Just for a ribbon to stick in his coat." If, as it seems, this quotation is intended to imply my anxiety for honours, no allegation more absolutely at variance with well-known facts could be made. . . . It is said that I seek political honours. Well, if so, I could not have gone about to achieve them in more absurd ways. . . . I have singled out Mr. Gladstone, at that time Prime Minister, as a sample of the unscientific mind; and more recently . . . I have singled out the then Prime Minister, Lord Salisbury, to ridicule his reasoning. So that by way of achieving honours accorded by the State, I have spoken disrespectfully of the two men who had in their hands the distribution of such honours.

To C. Kegan Paul.

10 *January,* 1893.

This morning announces the publication of a book by you entitled *A Perplexed Philosopher* by Mr. Henry George. Have you looked at it? You need not look far: it will suffice if you read the quotation from Browning on the title page.

Probably you know enough about my career to judge what warrant there is for the implied parallel, and whether you think it desirable to identify yourself with the book as its publisher.

12 *January.*—My letter gave no indication of any objection I have to critical argument; even the most trenchant. That, with my antecedents, you should assume that I have any objection to an attack upon my views surprises me.

40

But I spoke of the book as a " laboured calumny," and I thought that you might not like to be instrumental in circulating libellous statements.

To James A. Skilton.

1 *March,* 1893.

You appear to look largely or mainly at the general question, whereas to me the general question is of no importance. The Synthetic Philosophy can take care of itself. . . . Similarly about the Land Question. I have never dreamed of entering into controversy with Mr. Henry George about that or anything else. . . .

The only thing about which I am concerned is the personal question—the vile calumny which the man propagates, and the only question is whether it is worth while to do anything in the way of rebutting this.

He was anxious that the authenticity of the facts communicated to Mr. Skilton should be guaranteed by more than one name. The reply was accordingly prepared by a committee formed from among his New York friends, and published in the *Tribune* (November 12).

To James A. Skilton.

St. Leonards, 25 *November,* 1894.

Thank you for all the trouble you have taken in the George business. There have been in the course of the arrangements sundry dangers which have now been happily avoided, and the final result is as good as I could wish. Whatever Mr. George may say, I do not think he will succeed in neutralizing this effective exposure. . . .

If you feel inclined now to make a flank attack by dealing with Henry George and his doctrines, by all means do so, but if you do, please take care not to bring my name or my views into the matter. I do not wish to be in any way implicated.

41

13 *December.*—A few days ago I decided that by way of setting finally at rest this abominable business in America, it would be well if I published there the pamphlet referred to in the inclosed preface which I drew up for it—a pamphlet not at all in any direct way replying to Mr. George, but indirectly disposing of his allegations. I have, however, since come to the conclusion that this course may be of doubtful policy, since, conclusively disproving all he says as the pamphlet does, it will, nevertheless, furnish him with texts for further diatribes. I send over the preface to you and to your co-signatories to ask an opinion on this point. . . .

From the above you will see that I hesitate a little as to the propriety of giving Mr. George any further opportunities of carrying on the controversy, and for this same reason I hesitate respecting your proposed war with him carried on independently.

24 *December.*—I am again in two minds as to the best course to pursue. It does not matter how conclusive the case may be made against Mr. George, he will still go on arguing and asserting and multiplying side issues about irrelevant matters. The politic course, therefore, is to make one good point and there leave it.

If I am right in the inference that in *Progress and Poverty* he said nothing about my insisting on compensation, that should be the point made.

12 *January,* 1895.—Lies and treacheries are implements of war regarded as quite legitimate in actual war. I saw a while ago in some speech of a trade-unionist, that they regarded their relations with the masters as a state of war, and that their acts, ordinarily regarded as criminal, were legitimate. Doubtless Mr. George and the Land Nationalizers think the same thing and are prepared to abandon all moral restraint in pursuit of their ends. Hence this proceeding of his—congruous with all his other proceedings. Hence, too, similar proceedings

over here. Though I interdicted the republication of the correspondence in the *Daily Chronicle* along with that pamphlet you have, yet they have now issued it separately without asking me. . . .

As to your proposals for a brief treatise on the Land Question at large from me in further explanation, I do not see my way. If I were to say anything more . . . it would be merely in further explanation of the attitude I have taken. . . . As to anything larger, such as you adumbrate—a general [conception] of the relations of men to the soil based on general sociological principles, I have got nothing to say.

The correspondence in the *Daily Chronicle* referred to in the last quoted letter arose out of the leaflet issued with Spencer's assent by the Land Restoration League, giving in parallel columns extracts from *Social Statics* and from " Justice."

The matter might have ended here but for a lecture by Mr. William Lloyd Garrison, junr., delivered in New York on 6th January, 1895.

To William Jay Youmans.

22 January, 1895.

The inclosed report of Mr. Garrison's lecture, which Mr. Skilton has sent me, opens my eyes to the fact that it is needful that the public should be disabused of the notion that I have changed my essential convictions. The whole of Mr. George's vituperation and the whole of this lecture proceed on the assumption that I have repudiated my views on the ownership of land, which I have not, having only changed my view with regard to the financial policy of a change. If this fact is made clear it takes the wind out of Mr. George's sails.

Inclosed I send the draft of a letter in which this is demonstrated, and unless you see strong reason to the

43

contrary, I should be glad if some one—either yourself, or Dr. Janes, or Mr. Skilton—would publish this letter in *The Tribune* or elsewhere; if possible, in several places.

On the advice of Mr. Skilton and Dr. W. J. Youmans the letter was published as a preface to the parallel-column pamphlet on the Land Question.[1]

To JAMES A. SKILTON.

22 *February*, 1895.

Herewith I enclose the postscript for the pamphlet. In pursuance of the resolution which you intimate to me as agreed upon by friends, the pamphlet may now with its preface and postscript be issued without further delay. With its issue I must wash my hands entirely of the whole of the George business.

The correspondence continued in a somewhat desultory fashion into the following year. Into the merits of the controversy it is unnecessary now to enter. It has already lost whatever interest it may have had for the general reader. The foregoing outline of a very lengthy correspondence seemed expedient, however, because it throws into relief two characteristics of Spencer —his morbid sensitiveness to insinuations against the purity of his motives, and the undue weight he attached to charges of intellectual inconsistency. To these two points all his letters in the correspondence are addressed. As for the aspersion on his moral character, it is easy for an outsider to say that he might have treated it with

---

[1] *Mr. Herbert Spencer on the Land Question,* published by D. Appleton & Co., New York, 1895.

silent contempt, but few persons, when their character is attacked, can adopt an attitude of callous indifference.

(iii.)

The earliest notice of Dr. Weismann to be found in the correspondence is in a letter to Mr. Howard Collins (26 February, 1890), in which reference is made to an article in *Nature* (6 February). A few days after this he wrote to *Nature* (6 March) that it would "be as well to recall the belief of one whose judgment was not without weight, and to give some of the evidence on which that belief was founded." "Clearly the first thing to be done by those who deny the inheritance of acquired characters is to show that the evidence Mr. Darwin has furnished . . . is all worthless." To this suggestion Professor Ray Lankester responded in *Nature* (27 March) that biologists had already considered the cases cited by Mr. Darwin. "It is extremely unfortunate that Mr. Spencer has not come across the work in which this is done."

To F. HOWARD COLLINS.

1 *April,* 1890.

I have sent to *Nature* (3 April) . . . a short letter *à propos* of the question of inherited effects of use and disuse, or rather presenting a problem to those who assign "panmixia" as an adequate cause for decline in the size of disused organs.

I have taken the case of the drooping ears of many domesticated animals. . . . The point to insist on will be, first, as I have pointed out, in domestic animals no selection either natural or artificial goes on in such way as to make economy in the nutrition of an organ important for the survival of the individual, and that in fact no individuals survive from economical distribution of nutriment such as would cause decrease in unused organs. Then, second, beyond that, the point to be insisted upon is that these muscles are of such extremely small size that no economy in the nutrition of them could affect the fate even of animals subject to the struggle for existence and profiting by economical distribution of nutriment.

With the view of emphasising this last point, I should very much like to have it ascertained and stated what are the weights of the muscles which move the ears in a cow.

Against others than biologists he had to defend his position. In an address as Lord Rector of Glasgow University in November, 1891, Mr. A. J. Balfour referred to the theory of the inheritance of acquired characters applied by Spencer " so persistently in every department of his theory of man, that were it to be upset, it is scarcely too much to say that his Ethics, his Psychology, and his Anthropology would all tumble to the ground with it." The expediency of replying to this and other points in the address and the form the reply should take were discussed with Mr. Collins.

To F. HOWARD COLLINS.

30 *November,* 1891.

I have sent Mr. Balfour a copy of *Factors of Organic Evolution.* Suppose you send him a copy of your pamphlet on the Jaw as bearing on the question of inheritance of acquired characters.

6 *December.*—Do not in your specification of points to be taken up *versus* Balfour do more than just give me the *heads* of them so far as to show your lines of argument.

46

7 *December.*—I hesitate about your article on Mr. Balfour. Various of the points are good, though you have omitted the two which I should myself have taken up. But it is undesirable to have it done unless it is done in an almost unanswerable way, and I feel that a good deal of critical oversight from me would be needful. This would entail more labour than I can afford. . . . Moreover, the thing would be almost certain to entail controversy—probably Mr. Lilly would " go for " you —and eventually I might be drawn into the matter. . . . The only safe way that occurs to me is that of setting down a number of " Questions for Mr. Balfour," which might be the title.

12 *December.*—The temptation to do good has to be resisted sometimes as well as the temptation to do evil; and I now illustrate this truth in having resisted the temptation to reply to Mr. Balfour. It is a strong temptation, and I should greatly enjoy a little slashing polemic after two years of continuous exposition.

22 *January,* 1892.—Recently a member of the Athenæum named to me certain investigations, made by a medical man, I think, showing that colour-blindness is more frequent among Quakers than among other people; and thinking over the matter since, this recalled a vague recollection which I have that somebody—I think at Darlington—had found that a bad ear for music was more common among Quakers than among others. Now if these two things can be proved, they alone may serve to establish the hereditary transmission of effects of disuse. Here is a direction in which you may work.

Mr. Collins's pamphlet on " The Jaw as bearing on the question of Acquired Characters," mentioned above, had been prepared at Spencer's instigation. Before its issue a brief abstract was sent to *Nature,* which took no notice of it; thus furnishing occasion for insinuations of bias, which were repudiated when the pamphlet was reviewed later (6 August, 1891). In October, 1892, Spencer again expressed his dissatisfaction with the conduct of *Nature,* adding: " I shall not let the matter drop; and if this burking of evidence is persisted in, I will expose the matter be the cost what it may."

To J. Norman Lockyer.

19 *November,* 1892.

I presume you have not read Mr. Collins's letter on " Use and Heredity " enclosed, and that it has been declined by your referee rather than by yourself. It is an important letter giving the results of careful inquiries, and the question on which it bears is the most momentous with which science is at present concerned, for it bears on our fundamental conceptions of human nature, of human progress, and of legislation.

For some time past it has been manifest that the conducting of *Nature* has been such as to favour those who take one side of the controversy on this question. . . .

Curiously enough, I am about to commence on Monday a letter setting forth a new kind of evidence bearing, as I think, in a conclusive way upon the matter, and I was of course intending to send this letter to *Nature.* As things stand, however, it seems scarcely worth while to do this, and I may probably have to diffuse it among men of science in a separate form.

In a subsequent letter (23 December) he examined in detail the reasons assigned for rejecting Mr. Collins's letter, the principal one being the insufficiency of the data brought forward respecting the variation in the size of jaws in certain races consequent on a variation of function. The evidence was, in his opinion, sufficiently cogent to justify acceptance. Meanwhile he had taken steps to deal with the general question.

To the Editor of the *Contemporary Review*.

21 *November*, 1892.

I have in contemplation an article, the object of which will be to raise, for more definite consideration, certain aspects of the doctrine of Natural Selection: the purpose being to show that Natural Selection *taken alone* is utterly inadequate to account for the facts of organic evolution. Two out of the three reasons I have already indicated, but I propose now to set them forth more fully and as a distinct challenge to those who think that Natural Selection alone suffices; requiring of them to deal with these insurmountable difficulties, as I consider them to be. The third reason is an entirely new one, recently arrived at.

"The Inadequacy of Natural Selection," which appeared in the *Contemporary Review*, in February and March, 1893, was the occasion for the first interchange of letters between him and the late Duke of Argyll, who addressed him as an acquaintance on the strength of their having once met at, he thought, "one of Monckton Milnes' breakfasts."

To the Duke of Argyll.

8 *March*, 1893.

I am much obliged by your kindly expressed letter of the 4th, and am gratified to receive indication of your partial if not entire agreement.

I have an agreeable remembrance of the incident to which you refer, though my impression as to time and place is not the same. The occasion, I believe, was a dinner at the house of Mr. Gladstone, when he resided

49

in Harley Street. My recollection includes a brief interchange of remarks respecting a geological formation on the shores of Loch Aline, where I frequently visited friends owning the Ardtornish estate.

. . . The essay in the *Contemporary,* with sundry postscripts, I intend to republish next month for broadcast distribution throughout England, Europe and America. May I, in one of the postscripts, express my indebtedness to you for drawing my attention to the case of the negroes?. . .[1]

One of the postscripts to which I have referred will be devoted to dealing with the points on which your letter comments, namely, the misapprehension current among biologists concerning the nature of the belief in natural selection, with the view of showing that they are proposing to overturn, by a fallacious inference from an inference, certain results of direct observation.

I quite admit the multitudinous difficulties which stand in the way of the doctrine of evolution as interpreted solely by the two factors named, but I hesitate to allege another factor, knowing how often it has happened that problems which appear insoluble are readily solved when the method is disclosed.

The controversy was also the means of renewing an acquaintanceship of very old standing. Seeking '' a piece of information '' for use in the Weismann controversy, he wrote to Dr. David Sharp, of the University Museum of Zoology, Cambridge, assuming him to be the David Sharp with whose father he had lived at 13, Loudoun Road, St. John's Wood, in 1857-58. '' Some day when in London, if you would call upon me, . . . I should be glad to renew old memories.''[2]

---

[1] See pamphlet, p. 60. The Duke's name was omitted, he says, "lest some ill-natured people should regard me as a snob."

[2] *Autobiography,* ii., 31.

Spencer's article set the ball rolling. Dr. Chalmers Mitchell pointed out in *Nature* (15 February, 1893) that " in the matter of Panmixia, Mr. Herbert Spencer has misunderstood Weismann completely. Panmixia does *not* imply selection of smaller varieties, but the cessation of the elimination of smaller or more imperfect varieties." In the *Contemporary Review* for April Mr. Romanes noted that Spencer did not see the difference between the new doctrine of Panmixia, or cessation of Selection, and the old doctrine of Reversal of Selection; both of which are causes of degeneration. Correspondence with Mr. Romanes followed during the next few months, " but without getting any ' forerder,' " as Mr. Romanes remarked in a letter to Mr. Thistleton Dyer in July.[1]

Meanwhile he was busy with another article—" Professor Weismann's Theories "—published in the *Contemporary* for May, and circulated as a postscript to the previous articles. " It is a keen piece of controversy, but I wish you were well out of it," was Professor Tyndall's comment. Mr. George Henslow expressed cordial agreement; sending also a copy of " two chapters in a work on which I am engaged in which I endeavour to prove that the peculiarities of plants residing in deserts, water, Alpine regions, &c., are in all cases due to the response of the plants themselves to their environments respectively, without the aid of Natural Selection as far as structure is concerned." Another correspondent—Sir Edward Fry—had arrived at the opinion that the various ways in which mosses are reproduced furnished a strong argument against Pro-

---

[1] *Life of G. J. Romanes,* p. 307.

fessor Weismann. A copy of his work on *British Mosses* was, therefore, sent to Spencer.

To Sir Edward Fry.

7 June, 1893.

I am much obliged to you for your note and the accompanying volume. The facts it contains would have been of great use to me in writing the late articles in the *Contemporary,* had I known them. To me it seems that of themselves they suffice to dispose of Weismann's hypothesis, the wide acceptance of which I think discreditable to the biological world.

The hypothesis of a " germ-plasm," as distinguished from the general protoplasm, seems to me a pure fiction, utterly superfluous, and utterly discountenanced by the facts; and the phenomena presented by the mosses are among those showing in the clearest way that there is but one plasm capable of assuming the form of the organism to which it belongs when placed in fit conditions: one of the fit conditions being absence of any considerable tissue-differentiation.

On the side of Professor Weismann, Mr. Romanes again came forward (*Contemporary* for July), the proof being sent to Spencer, who wrote a note to be printed with the article. Professor Marcus Hartog, in the same number, wrote against Weismannism, also criticising Mr. Wallace. As to the views of the latter, Spencer had already been in communication with Professor Hartog.

To Marcus Hartog.

5 May, 1893.

Have you looked at Mr. Wallace's article in the *Fortnightly?* I . . . am astonished at the nonsense he is writing. He seems to be incapable of understanding the point at issue. On page 660 especially, he actually concedes the whole matter, apparently not perceiving that he does so. This ought at any rate to be effectually pointed out, since committing suicide as he thus does, there is one antagonist less to deal with.

Professor Weismann himself now intervened in an article entitled " The All-Sufficiency of Natural Selection," the first part of which—replying to Spencer—appeared in the *Contemporary Review* in September, and the second in October. Professor Hartog proposed to reply to Weismann's Part I. in case Spencer did not.

To MARCUS HARTOG.

BRIGHTON, 22 *September,* 1893.
Thanks for your proposal to take up Weismann in case I do not. I have, however, decided to respond to him myself, and am even now engaged in writing an answer [1]. . . .
It will, I think, be very well, however, if you will keep the matter in mind and be prepared with a paper setting forth the argument which you briefly indicate. . . .
P.S.—If you write such a letter, pray do not admit that Weismann has shown that the specialisations of social insects can be interpreted only as due to natural selection. I am about to contend that they can be otherwise interpreted.

Another contribution from Spencer's pen appeared in the *Contemporary* for October, 1894, under the heading " Weismannism Once More."

FROM DAVID SHARP.

28 *October,* 1894.
Thank you very much for the separate copy of " Weismannism Once More "; containing the postscript

---

[1] *Contemporary Review* for December, 1893.

on last page about Hertwig, which I had not seen before, and which I think very good and interesting.

The view that evolutionists will ultimately take as to the essential nature of reproduction is one exactly the antithesis of Weismann's, viz., that the best form of germ is that which accurately carries the processes of the parents, it being understood that the processes of the parents form part of a consensus with the processes of previous parents. This last qualification is very important, and explains why I have long felt it to be impossible to expect any considerable inheritance of mutilations.

I hope you need not now trouble yourself more about Weismann. I feel no doubt that his theory will before long pass into discredit. It had this of value that it endeavoured to substitute a genuine conception of that awful X we call heredity.

In my opinion what is most wanted to secure the symmetry and add to the permanent value of your work is not the upsetting of Weismann, but that chapter on the relations of the inorganic and organic which in your original prospectus you pointed out ought to be written.

Professor Burdon Sanderson deprecated " the acceptance by outsiders of the scheme of doctrine of Professor Weismann as a safe basis for speculation, and still more, the way in which it is now dogmatically taught to students of what is called Elementary Biology."

To J. S. BURDON SANDERSON.

ST. LEONARDS, 10 *November*, 1894.

I was greatly pleased to have your sympathetic letter concerning the Weismann business. Coming from one whose judgment has so high a value as yours the general agreement implied was a source of much satisfaction to me.

I have been alike astonished and exasperated at the manner in which biologists at large have received Weismann's theory. Considering that it is so entirely speculative and cannot assign, so far as I know, a single fact which serves for proof, it is amazing that men who, perhaps more than most men of science, rely upon facts, should have so widely accepted it.

Of Sir Edward Fry's letter in *Nature* (1 November, 1894), discussing the meaning of the word " acquired " as used in the Weismann controversy, Spencer writes:—

To Sir Edward Fry.

3 *November,* 1894.
I am glad you have taken up the matter and have brought your long-exercised judicial faculty to bear upon the definitions of the words used, and have brought to light the confusion of thought in which the matter is at present involved.

Until the introduction of the phrase " acquired characters " within these few years, I had myself always used the expression " functionally-produced modifications," and all through *The Principles of Psychology,* published in pre-Darwinian days, the phenomena of evolution are ascribed (far too exclusively, as I now admit) to the inheritance of functionally-produced modifications. This phrase is, I think, the better one, as excluding various misapprehensions, and I regret now that I ever, for brevity's sake, adopted the recent phrase.

The controversy was now practically ended as far as Spencer was concerned. Professor Weismann's article " Heredity Once More " in the *Contemporary Review* for September, 1895, called forth a letter from Spencer under the same title [1] in which he agreed with Professor Weismann that further controversy would be futile—" especially so if new hypotheses are to be perpetually introduced to make good the shortcomings of the old. I willingly yield, therefore, to his suggestion to ask no more questions; and I do this the more willingly, because I have failed to get any answer to the crucial question which I asked at the outset." [2]

It is not for a layman to express an opinion on a question that divides biologists into distinct schools, more especially when he takes into account the weighty names on each side of the controversy. At the same time, bearing in mind how frequently the charge of *a priori* reasoning has been brought against Spencer, one cannot help remarking on the hypothetical nature of Professor Weismann's premises and the *a priori* character of his arguments. The demands he makes on one's credulity are, to say the least, not less numerous or less astounding than those made by the opposite school. Professor Marcus Hartog's description of Professor Weismann's work on Amphimixis, may be applied to the theory as a whole. It is " a magnified castle built by the *a priori* method on a foundation of ' facts ' carefully selected, and for the most part ill-known, misinterpreted, or incomplete." One's confidence in Professor Weismann's doctrine is apt to be shaken by the

---

[1] See *Contemporary Review*, October, 1895.

[2] Spencer's articles were afterwards reprinted in the new edition of the *Principles of Biology*, i., pp. 602-691, Appendix B. In Appendix C (pp. 692-695) a summary is given of the evidence in favour of "The Inheritance of functionally-wrought Modifications." His last public utterance on the subject is to be found in a short paper on "Some Light on Use-Inheritance," contained in *Facts and Comments* (pp. 128-134), published in 1902.

concessions he has to make: such, for example, as the admission that the germ-cells do not lead " a charmed life " uninfluenced by the body-cells, and the admission that the body-cells may carry with them some germ-plasm. " The New Biology " may, in course of time, help us to adjust the claims of the rival theories.

CHAPTER XXIII

COMPLETING THE SYNTHETIC PHILOSOPHY

(*June*, 1893—*November*, 1896)

NEVER had a change from London been more welcome than in 1893. His domestic troubles had utterly unhinged him. His feelings found expression in a letter to Miss Youmans from Pewsey. " My relations with the Misses —— will hereafter, I fear, be not altogether pleasant. The fact that, after all my kindnesses to them, their return is to calumniate me to their friends and to some of my friends can hardly be forgotten, and I don't know exactly how we shall get on with that fact in my consciousness." To put the evil day off he went to Brighton for September. There was no lack of friends ever ready to extend hospitality; but as he said in reply to an invitation from Lord Dysart: " I cannot keep well for long even when I am master of my own circumstances, and I am sure to go wrong in health when I attempt to conform my daily *régime* to the routine of any other house than my own."

Presentation copies of books afforded opportunities of enforcing one or other of his favourite doctrines.

To HORACE SEAL.

11 *July*, 1893.

I am much obliged by the copy of your little book on *The Nature of State Interference.*

58

Will you excuse me if I say that you have I think, in the first place, identified two things which are not at all to be identified—social co-operation and State-interference; and that you have in the second place not distinguished between the purposes for which State-interference is peremptorily demanded and those for which it is not demanded. Your illustrations of the advantages derived from what you rightly consider analogous to State-interference in the animal kingdom are cases in which the organism has to operate on the environment, and for this purpose unquestionably State-interference —that is to say, centralization of the powers of the aggregate—is essential; but it is not called for, nor advantageous, for carrying on the processes of internal sustentation. . . . While societies, as chiefly in the past and partly in the present, carry on predatory activities upon other societies, subordination of the individual to the State is requisite, and is and must be the more extreme in proportion as the predatory activities are dominant; but in proportion as societies become peaceful, and the lives they carry on become lives of internal activities only, the need decreases, and there remains only the need for that subordination of the individual to the State which is requisite for maintaining orderly or non-aggressive cooperation. Your tacit assumption that Individualism means the solitary life of the individual is an entire misapprehension. It may and does go along with an elaborate form of mutual dependence.

To Mrs. Arthur Stannard.

6 *October,* 1893.

I thank you for the copy of your novel, *The Soul of a Bishop.* . . .

I judge of the purpose of the book from the last few paragraphs. You will scarcely expect me to coincide with your view.

The current creed represents the power which is manifested to us in the universe as having created myriads of men of whom, according to the Christian theory, immensely the greater number must be condemned to eternal torment. If one man were to condemn another man to eternal torment, even for the most grievous offence, and calmly looked on at his sufferings, I should regard him with horror. I do not understand why my feeling must be changed when in place of a man a God is conceived, and in place of a single sufferer myriads of sufferers—rather would it be intensified.

Popular nostrums for the cure of social disorders he invariably tested by appeal to experience and by reference to underlying principles. There was no lack of sympathy with the unhappy lot of certain sections of society; though his merciless exposure of visionary, sentimental remedies often caused him to be considered unsympathetic. He felt bound to give expression to his deep-rooted conviction that many of the proposed measures of relief were worthless or at best mere palliatives, and that some of them would intensify rather than diminish the mischief they were intended to remove. Again and again did he urge the Hon. Auberon Herbert to direct his energies to the exposure of the fallacious reasonings and useless remedies everywhere met with in connexion with social and political matters.

To the Hon. Auberon Herbert.

7 November, 1893.

You might write an article on " Experience does not make Fools wise." For this you may take as text the demand for a " living wage," as though that had not been tried and abandoned centuries ago. And again, under the same head the proposal to provide work for the unemployed, as though that had not been tried in workhouses from Elizabeth's time downwards and been a miserable failure.

January, 1894.—At present nobody is content with the natural rewards of his own efforts, but everybody wants to be better off at somebody else's expense. This is an ethical crime and will bring on the society throughout which it prevails the punishment of criminality.

To MONCURE D. CONWAY.

12 *December,* 1893.

I have just been reading in the *Open Court* your first article on Liberty, and have read it with great satisfaction. . . . As you rightly point out, people do not at all understand the principles of liberty.

But here there is, I think, a shortcoming in your conception. They have no *true idea of liberty* because they have no true *sentiment of liberty.* No theory is of much service in the matter without a character responding to the theory—without a feeling which prompts the assertion of individual freedom and is indignant against aggressions upon that freedom, whether against self or others. Men care nothing about a principle, even if they understand it, unless they have emotions responding to it. When adequately strong the appropriate emotion prompts resistance to interference with individual action, whether by an individual tyrant or by a tyrant majority; but at present, in the absence of the proper emotion, there exists almost everywhere the miserable superstition that the majority has a right to dictate to the individual about everything whatever. . . . To dissipate the superstition that the majority has unlimited powers is of more importance than anything else in the field of politics.

His hopes of completing his work were about this time by no means bright—in fact he told a friend that its completion was scarcely probable. In such a frame of mind there could be but one answer to Mr. Romanes's enquiry whether he would give next year's Romanes Lecture. "If I were to attempt it I should probably die on the platform." The same was his feeling when invited by the members of the Oxford University Junior Scientific Club to deliver the next "Robert Boyle" lecture. His doubts as to the probability of finishing his work were strengthened by the shock he received on hearing of the death of Professor Tyndall. He himself was to winter at St. Leonards and had hoped to persuade the Tyndalls to come there.

To Mrs. Tyndall.

6 *December*, 1893.

You will scarcely need to be told how shocked I was when yesterday morning there came the sad news of Dr. Tyndall's death. . . .

The consciousness that he had passed so weary and suffering a life for a long time past must be in some sort a set off to the grief coming upon you, and that the ending has been so sudden and painless is a further set off.

In respect of his last hours he was in fact to be envied. Had I finished my task I should be very willing to promptly pass away in the same quiet manner.

But I well know that in these cases words of consolation are of no avail and only lapse of time can bring mitigation.

A volume by Mr. Andrew Lang, dealing amongst other things with the Ghost Theory, had been announced.

JOHN TYNDALL.

COMPLETING THE SYNTHETIC PHILOSOPHY

To Andrew Lang.

21 *February*, 1894.

In their original forms Tylor's view and mine are distinctly antithetical. With him animism is original and the ghost-theory derived. . . . Tylor has insensibly abandoned his original view. It may, however, I believe, be shown that by more than one there had previously been suggested the belief that the Ghost-Theory is the root of religious ideas.

26 *February.*—By way of criticism upon your belief, or half-belief, let me suggest to you that the great difficulty is in getting true evidence. People are so careless in their observations and so careless in their statements, and so careless in their repetitions! . . .

I continually meet with paragraphs about myself, many absurd and many utterly baseless. An American interviewer described me as always wearing white gaiters. I never wore any in my life. It was said that I invariably carry an umbrella, and a bulky one. For many years past I have not walked at all, and when I did walk I never carried an umbrella unless it was raining or obviously certain to rain. It is said that I take my meals alone and dislike dining with others. Absolutely the reverse is the fact. I dislike to take a meal alone. I was asked by a lady whether it was true that I lived chiefly on bread and coffee; a statement absolutely baseless. I was asked whether I changed my occupation every ten minutes—a statement which had a certain slight basis, but an extremely small one. I saw a paragraph stating that on one occasion I could not manage my sister's children. The only sister I ever had died when two years old. . . . And so on, and so on, almost without end. . . .

Now with such multitudinous recklessnesses of statement as these, and even mistakes of identity, how is it possible to put any confidence in testimonies with regard to so-called supernatural occurrences? . . .

Most people cannot state truly what they see, and most people cannot re-state truly what they have been told. Hence I hold it far more likely that in all these cases the testimony is bad than that the alleged phenomenon is true.

P.S.—Then there is the element of coincidence—an all-important element. Out of the tens of thousands of incidents occurring to individuals and the myriads occurring to the members of a community it is certain that some should have a strange congruity. These congruities are more frequent than we suppose. I can give you from my own life several most remarkable ones.

28 *February.*—A question of statistics, yes. A dreams he meets B; does not do so, and thinks nothing about it. Ten thousand such cases occur nightly. After a million cases have occurred some A does meet some B; thinks it supernatural and talks about it. Thus the non-coincidences leave no marks; the coincidences survive.

To JOHN FISKE.

27 *March,* 1894.

Thanks for the sympathetic expressions of your dedication, [of the *Memoir of E. L. Youmans*] which took me by surprise. I had thought nothing about a dedication, but, if I had, I would have suggested that the sister should have been the honoured person, since her great devotion to him through so many years gave her a high claim. [The book] will doubtless do good service in bringing that posthumous honour to Youmans which he so amply deserves. So self-sacrificing a servant of humanity is rarely met with.

The " disasters and perplexities of things " had during the spring induced a condition of great depression. His friends and acquaintances were " disappearing at

the rate of twenty a year." He was unhappy in his
home life. His despondency was increased by " the
atrocious weather " he experienced in Wiltshire. His
intention had been that this, his sixth visit to Pewsey,
should last till the end of September, but by the end of
June he was tired of it. The patience of his host and
hostess was also showing symptoms of giving way, owing to his fastidiousness. He returned to town in the
second week of July, and on the recommendation of Dr.
Buzzard went to Cliftonville, near Margate, for August
and part of September.

To G. J. HOLYOAKE.

MARGATE, 10 *September*, 1894.
Profoundly averse as I am to State-socialism and
State-meddling, I feel bound to aid all efforts to en-
courage the only type of industrial organization which
holds out any hope of better things. I am not very sanguine of the results, for it seems to me that only a small
proportion of men are good enough for industrial relations of a high type. But be this as it may, everything
should be done to facilitate the experiment, and I therefore send you a subscription of two guineas.

17 *September.*—I dislike to be *affiché,* as the French
say, and I have of late years suffered much from being
thus placarded.
A while ago I attended what I supposed to be a private meeting in the interests of the Society for the Prevention of Cruelty to Children, and a few words which
I was induced to say, were, to my great dismay, reported in the next day's papers, so that I had to explain
that my remarks were made without much consideration.[1]

---

[1] See vol. i., chap. xx., p. 405.

At the instigation of some Jewish periodical I expressed my detestation of the persecutions in Russia, thoughtlessly supposing that my letter would have no further circulation. But it got quoted in certain papers, not only here but on the Continent, and even in Russia, where, as Mr. Caine reported, it produced a howl—a result which I had never intended.

Last year I was led to send a contribution to the Anti-Gambling League, feeling compelled to do so because of the strong condemnation of gambling I had uttered in *The Study of Sociology,* and though I marked my accompanying note " private," its substance, or what professed erroneously to be its substance, was published in the evening papers.[1]

Then just recently, as you must have seen, my protest against the misrepresentation of my views about land-ownership has entangled me in a controversy in the *Daily Chronicle.*[2]

. . . These various occurrences are liable to produce the impression that I want to pose as a philanthropist or as an aider in philanthropic undertakings. I shrink from any such interpretation.

You must therefore abide by my endorsement " private," and keep my note unpublished; and you must please also not signalise the fact that I have contributed to the fund.

His German translator, Dr. Vetter, in whose intelligence and judgment Spencer had aways placed the utmost reliance, had died early in 1893. Dr. Vetter's place was taken in the following year by Professor Victor Carus. One of his French translators, M. Auguste Burdeau, was also removed by death. This meant the loss of a friend for whose character and ability Spencer had a genuine regard.

---

[1] *Supra,* chap. xxi., p. 23.   [2] *Supra,* chap. xxii., p. 41.

To Madame Burdeau.

21 *December,* 1894.

There are condolences as a matter of form and there are condolences as expressions of real feeling. Those which I now offer you belong to the latter class. For these many years past I have admired M. Burdeau. . . . At the time when he was preparing his version of my Essays I was struck by his conscientious care to ensure accuracy. . . . The traits of character then disclosed on small occasions have since been disclosed on large occasions, and joined with his intelligence and wide culture made him so valuable a servant of the State. I regret in common with his countrymen that his character and capacity, through which still greater things might have been expected, should have been prematurely lost to France.

He had never got over his disappointment at the futile result of the " Record of Legislation " he and Mr. Donisthorpe had planned and begun in 1892. Circumstances at the end of 1894 seemed favourable for another attempt being made to rouse public interest.

To Wordsworth Donisthorpe.

11 *November,* 1894.

You have no doubt seen in the papers notices of Mr. Ilbert's scheme for a comparative record of Laws of the English speaking peoples. This is so nearly allied to the scheme of a record of English laws from the beginning that I think it is desirable to make public the prior movement. . . . I think of writing a letter to the *Times* describing what you and I had done, and sending with it a sample of the impressions taken of the tables as drawn up, by way of showing what had been accomplished. . . . I mean to embody in it some sarcastic criticisms upon the wealthy classes as to their

67

utter lack of all initiative and lack of all conception of any but the most commonplace philanthropic undertakings.

18 *November.*—You are quite welcome to mention the fact you refer to, namely, that a long time ago I enunciated the doctrine that the State should administer civil justice gratuitously. There is a passage in " Justice " setting forth this doctrine and defending it.

23 *November.*—If the State became responsible for the administration of civil justice in the manner implied in the passage from the *Principles of Ethics,* I take it that an entire change of method would be a concomitant. The State would now not stand in the position of umpire, but would become an active investigator. On complaint being made to the local authority that some aggression had been committed or some non-fulfilment of an agreement, the first step might be that of sending an appointed functionary—an officer of first instance—to interview jointly the two disputants, and hear from them their respective statements, and explain to them the law affecting the matter. In nine cases out of ten the presence or absence of a wrong is clear enough, and the opinion of this official on the matter would suffice to effect a settlement. In cases where one of the disputants did not yield, or in cases where the official himself was in doubt, there would then be a reference to a higher legal authority, before whom, with the aid of this officer of first instance, the case would be set forth and who would himself cross-examine the parties in respect of the transaction. If, after his decision, there was still resistance on the part of one, any further appeal might be at the cost, or if not the whole cost then the part cost, of the persisting suitor: the distinction made being that where there was an evident breach of an obvious law the cost should be borne by the recalcitrant person, but not so where the interpretation of the law in the

particular case might fairly be considered a matter of doubt.

I should add that along with any such change of administration it is implied that there should be such change in the law itself as to make it comprehensible and definite. A clearly and rationally organised body of law, comprehensible by the ordinary citizen, would itself exclude the greater proportion of aggressions, and when breaches of laws, clearly understood, were in some such way as that described promptly dealt with, without cost to the injured person, there would be very few such breaches.

25 *November*.—Please say nothing about my views on the administration of civil justice.

13 *January*, 1895.—Thanks for the copy of your new volume [a second series of individualist essays]. . . . I regret that you have used the word " anarchist " or " philosophical anarchist." It has at present, and quite naturally, so bad an odour that use of it raises a preliminary prejudice against any conclusions which appear to be congruous with anarchist doctrines. You cannot get people to distinguish. Moreover, the word seems to me broader than is appropriate to your meaning, since you recognise the need for *some* government.

I wish you would deal with Mr. Sidney Webb. I see by this week's *Spectator*, which partly reprobates and partly commends him, that he has in the *Contemporary* been setting forth the beneficial achievements of the County Council, which you and I regard as mischievous rather than beneficial. If you could contribute to the *Contemporary* an article showing the socialistic character of these achievements, and pointing out that the *Spectator* and others who approve are simply furthering the socialism which they condemn in the abstract, you would do good service.

A year before this, on the occasion of the bomb outrage by Vaillant in Paris, he thanked M. Jean Schmidt for an article in the *Figaro* representing his views as being '' of the absolutely opposite kind '' to anarchic.

To HENRY CHARLTON BASTIAN.

MARGATE, 17 *August*, 1894.

There has been for some time a conspiracy afoot among retail booksellers and publishers, which is intended to have the effect of abolishing the present system of making discounts of 2d. and 3d. in the shilling. . . .

A generation ago I was one of those who took part in the agitation which abolished the then existing system of retailer's discounts of 33 per cent., which were maintained by allowing no retailer to make an abatement and regarding as black sheep those who did, and preventing them from getting books if possible.

This system they are now quietly endeavouring to re-establish. I want to get full particulars of the proceedings before taking action.

He wished Dr. Bastian to ascertain from one of the large retail booksellers how the new system of marking books as '' net '' affected discount booksellers. '' Do not mention my name. If I take public action in the matter it will be anonymously, for I do not want to set the trade against me.'' A communication in the form of a letter '' From a Correspondent '' appeared on 24 October. In this letter he gave an account of the negociations in 1852 which ended in abolishing the coercive regulation according to which a retail bookseller who sold books at lower rates of profit than those prescribed was prevented from obtaining supplies of books.

All know what has since happened, or rather all know what have been the usages for the last generation, though they may not know how they arose. The practice of allowing a discount of 2d. in the 1s. from the advertised price of a book was quickly established, and after a time the discount was by many, and eventually by most, retailers increased to 3d. in the 1s., or 25 per cent. That benefit has resulted cannot well be questioned. . . . Increased sales consequent on lower prices have thus made possible much of the best literature which would else have been impossible. These advantages are now being furtively destroyed. Some three years ago, in certain advertisements of books, the word " net " was inserted after the price, implying that no discount would be allowed. . . . Already coercive measures, like those which a generation ago maintained this system, are growing up. Booksellers who have allowed small discounts from " net " prices have received warnings that, if they do so again, supplies of books will be denied to them. . . . Doubtless we shall hear a defence of these resuscitated regulations. Some will say that retailers should be properly paid for their work, and that underselling by one another does them great mischief. Others will say that publishers benefit by giving retailers a sufficient stimulus to push their books. The authors, too, will be said to gain by the increased sales resulting. It will even possibly be urged that the public are benefited by having books brought under their notice better than they would otherwise be. To these and other pleas there is a brief, but sufficient, reply. They were urged a generation ago, and a generation ago they were examined and rejected.[1]

Professor Henry Drummond had for years acknowledged himself as an admiring student of Spencer's writings. It was with no little surprise, therefore, said

---

[1] *Various Fragments*, pp. 171-196.

Professor Drummond's biographer, that his friends read Mrs. Lynn Linton's article in the *Fortnightly Review* for September, 1894, in which she "made a furious onslaught on what she alleged to be Drummond's ' pseudo-science and plagiarisms,' overlooking, as her critics pointed out, his acknowledgments of indebtedness to Herbert Spencer and other writers on the very points with reference to which she made her serious charges." The prime mover of Mrs. Lynn Linton's article was Spencer himself.[1]

To Mrs. Lynn Linton.

6 *June*, 1894.

Professor Drummond . . . in his recently published work, *The Ascent of Man*, with the airs of a discoverer and with a tone of supreme authority sets out to instruct me and other evolutionists respecting the factor of social evolution which we have ignored—altruism.

. . . I do not, of course, like to undertake it [a reply] myself, but I should be very glad if somebody would undertake it for me, and on looking round for a proxy I thought of you. With your vigorous style and picturesque way of presenting things, you would do it in an interesting and effective way, at the same time that you would be able to illustrate and enforce the doctrine itself.

3 *September*.—When I returned you the MS. I thought your article vigorous and effective, and now that I have read it in print I see that it is still more vigorous and effective. . . .

The fact that the *Standard* devotes an article to you is sufficiently significant, and I join in the applause given by the writer to your denunciation, not of Pro-

---

[1] *Life of Mrs. Lynn Linton*, pp. 310-12.

fessor Drummond only, but of the public taste which swallows with greediness these semi-scientific sentimentalities.

He was not so successful in inducing any of his scientific friends to reply to Lord Salisbury's address as President of the British Association at Oxford.

To ALFRED R. WALLACE.

10 *August*, 1894.

If we differ on some points we agree on many, and one of the points on which we doubtless agree is the absurdity of Lord Salisbury's representation of the process of Natural Selection, based upon the improbability of two varying individuals meeting. His nonsensical representation of the theory ought to be exposed, for it will mislead very many people. I see it is adopted by the *Pall Mall*.

I have been myself strongly prompted to take the matter up, but it is evidently your business to do that. Pray write a letter to the *Times* explaining that selection, or survival of the fittest, does not necessarily take place in the way he describes. You might set out by showing that whereas he begins by comparing himself to a volunteer colonel reviewing a regiment of regulars he very quickly changes his attitude and becomes a colonel of regulars reviewing volunteers, making fun of their bunglings. He deserves a severe castigation. There are other points on which his views should be rectified, but this is the essential point.

To T. H. HUXLEY.

LONDON, 1 *October*, 1894.

Is nobody going to give a dressing to Lord Salisbury? Sometime ago I wrote to Wallace wanting him to take up in the *Times* the question of Natural Selection in respect of which the argument used is so absurd, but Wallace pleaded that he was busy with other things. Your mouth is, I suppose, closed by your position as seconder of the vote of thanks at the Association meeting.

The theologically-minded have been hurrahing and throwing up their caps, and it is, I think, needful that they should be sobered a little by being shown the fallacy, and indeed the folly, of his lordship's criticisms. Old and feeble as I am I feel strongly prompted to do it—the more so as there are various things of importance to be said incidentally.

FROM T. H. HUXLEY.

3 *October,* 1894.

I am writing something for the half jubilee of *Nature* in November next—in which I think I shall rub in Lord Salisbury's surrender in essentials a little more strongly than I could do at Oxford; but, as to his criticisms of Natural Selection and so on, I really doubt if they are worth powder and shot.

But if you think otherwise go ahead by all means— I earned the prize of virtue at Oxford, though I shall not get it. You may imagine how tempting it was to me to tear the thing to pieces. But that was hardly the line for a seconder, and I restrained myself to such damage as I could do, by warmly praising all the concessions which that dexterous debater had left in shadow.[1]

Having failed to get any one to write, Spencer would probably have allowed the matter to rest, but for the circumstance that a translation of the address had been honoured by being presented to the French Academy. Hence his article on " Lord Salisbury on Evolution." This was generally regarded in France as victorious on

---

[1] *Life of Professor Huxley,* ii., 400-407.

all points, so M. Léon Say told Dr. Cazelles when they met at the funeral of M. Floquet. Thanks to the interposition of M. du Mesnil and M. Milne Edwards, it was laid on the table of the Académie des Sciences by Professor Perrier.

To Mrs. Tyndall.

London, 23 October, 1894.

I am about to make arrangements for going again to St. Leonards, . . . I want you to do me the great favour of coming to stay with me there as long as you can. I am thinking of asking as one to visit me Miss Cross, sister of Mr. John Cross who married George Eliot—a very amiable woman and intelligent, who wrote one charming story and ought to write others. Then, as another guest, I shall probably have Miss Gingell, a Gloucestershire lady, who compiled a volume of aphorisms from my writings, when unknown to me. Another I may probably ask is Miss Edith Hughes, daughter of an enthusiastic adherent of mine in Birmingham. . . . Last winter one of the two ladies who formed the circle was Miss Charlotte Shickle . . . who did the housekeeping for me. She is a good soul—good in a very unusual degree, I never met any one who, when a kind thing was to be done, rushed at it in the same way.

Soon after settling at St. Leonards he gave formal notice determining the agreement between the Misses —— and himself; the reason assigned being the heavy expense entailed by being so much away from London. But as his plans were not yet matured he thought it might be convenient for both parties if the actual termination were postponed, subject to a month's notice. " The remembrance of times spent with you and your sisters during 1889, '90, '91, and '92 will always be pleasant to me." His plans were certainly not matured at the date of giving notice; for it was not till 1897 that the Avenue Road establishment was broken up.

To Count Goblet d'Alviella.

7 *January*, 1895.

Thanks for your letter and for the accompanying little volume *Vie et Œuvre de Emile de Laveleye*. . . . You comment upon the conflict between the opinions of M. de Laveleye and my own. The fact was, M. de Laveleye never knew what my views were. He, in common with many others, laid hold of some one portion and formed his conclusions from it without due recognition of correlative portions. Because I hold that the struggle for existence and the survival of the fittest should be allowed to go on in Society, subject to those restraints which are involved by preventing each man from interfering with the sphere of action of another, and should not be mitigated by governmental agency, he, along with many others, ran away with the notion that [my belief was that] they should not be mitigated at all. . . . I regard voluntary beneficence as adequate to achieve all those mitigations that are proper and needful. M. de Laveleye did not see that that which he agreed with me in denouncing and fearing—the universal supremacy of the State—is the outcome of that policy of benevolent interference which it appears he advocated.

To J. A. Skilton.

10 *January*, 1895.

If, as it would seem, you think that I have got a scheme for the future of society in my head you are altogether mistaken. Your conception of applied sociology—a bringing to bear of evolutionary principles on social organisation with a view to its improvement—is one which I do not entertain. The sole thing about which I feel confident is that no higher types of social organisation can grow until international antagonisms and, consequently, wars cease. . . . You have faith in teaching, which I have not—you believe men are going to be changed in their conduct by being shown what line of conduct is rational. I believe no such thing. Men are not rational beings, as commonly supposed. A man is a bundle of instincts, feelings, sentiments, which severally seek their gratification, and those which are in power get hold of the reason and use it to their own ends, and exclude all other sentiments and feelings from power. . . . There is no hope for the future save in the slow modification of human nature under social discipline. Not teaching, but action is the requisite cause. To have to lead generation after generation a life that is honest and sympathetic is the one indispensable thing. No adequate change of character can be produced in a year, or in a generation, or in a century. All which teaching can do—all which may, perhaps, be done by a wider diffusion of principles of sociology, is the checking of retrograde action. The analogy supplied by an individual life yields the true conception. You cannot in any considerable degree change the course of individual growth and organisation—in any considerable degree antedate the stages of development. But you can, in considerable degree, by knowledge put a check upon those courses of conduct which lead to pathological states and accompanying degradations.

Any one who wishes to aid social advance should devote all his energies to showing, that no fundamental and permanent progress in social life can be made while warlike activities and the social organisation appropriate to them continue.

2 *February.*—A true theory of social progress is not a *cause* of movement but is simply oil to the movement —serves simply to remove friction. The force producing the movement is the aggregate of men's instincts and sentiments, and these are not to be changed by a theory.

77

You think that I have got some message and that utterance of it might stave off impending evils. I have but one message—Be honest: regard the equitable claims of others while maintaining your own. The disregard of all save personal interests is the underlying cause of your present state and of impending disasters. As I said years ago à *propos* of American affairs, a fatal trait in your society is the admiration of " smart " men, and I believe I said or implied that a people among whom there is admiration for " smart " men will come to grief. If you think that a healthier ideal can be established in American society by teaching, I entirely disagree. Under your present condition men could not be got to listen. Even if they listened, they would not be convinced. And even if they were convinced, their conduct would not be appreciably affected. When men are under the influence of pronounced feelings no amount of reason changes their behaviour.

To J. W. CROSS.

18 *January*, 1895.

While she was with me your sister named the opinion you had expressed that a crash is impending in the United States—a financial crash, I gathered from her statement. I too am expecting a crash, but have been rather contemplating a social than a financial crash. Probably either will be a factor in producing the other. That a dreadful catastrophe is coming I do not feel the slightest doubt. The Americans are now beginning to reap the far-reaching and widely-diffused consequences of their admiration for smart prigs, and the general mercantile laxity.

To MRS. TYNDALL.

31 *May*, 1895.

Fundamentally regarded, the condition of things is this. Men within these few generations have become emancipated from the restraints which a strong social organisation had over them. They are rapidly proving themselves unfit for the condition of liberty, and they are busy unconsciously organising for themselves a tyranny which will put them under as strong a restraint as, or a stronger restraint than, before.

22 *June.*—We are coming to a maladministration of justice like that in Ireland.

Having been informed that the Italian socialist, Professor Ferri, had adduced his authority in support of socialism, he wrote (June 12, 1895) an indignant protest, which was published in *La Riforma.* In a letter (19 June) to the editor of *La Riforma,* Signor Ferri pointed out that Spencer was under a misapprehension.

No socialist has ever dreamt to include among the supporters of Socialism the greatest living philosopher. . . . But it is necessary to distinguish between the personal opinions of H. Spencer and the logical outcome of the positive theory of universal evolution, which he has developed better than any other writer, without however obtaining an official patent against the unrestricted expansion which is daily given to that theory by the work of other thinkers. In the preface to my book I stated that Spencer and Darwin had stopped midway, and consequently without reaching the logical consequences of their doctrine.

A copy of his article on " Mr. Balfour's Dialectics," published in the June number of the *Fortnightly Review,* was put aside with a view to its appearance in a permanent form in the next edition of the essays. But in a note written on this copy in November, 1897, he says that " in consequence of Mr. Balfour's noble behaviour in actively aiding the portrait presentation scheme, I have decided that I cannot with good taste republish it."

The Order " Pour le Mérite " was offered him, but declined in a communication to the German Ambassador (1 June, 1895).

Mr. Herbert Spencer presents his compliments to His Excellency the German Ambassador, and begs to acknowledge the receipt of his letter of May 31, notifying the fact that the German Emperor has conferred on Mr. Spencer the Royal Order " Pour le Mérite " for arts and sciences. Naturally the fact cannot but be a source of satisfaction to him.

On various occasions during the last five and twenty years Mr. Spencer has declined the honours that have been conferred on him; and to accept the honour now conferred would not only be inconsistent with his convictions, but would imply a slight upon the learned bodies whose honours he has on past occasions declined. Though the fountain of honour is not in this case of the same nature as in previous cases, yet the reasons which prompted his course remain the same. What those reasons are may be seen from certain passages in a letter addressed to the French Academy in May, 1883, after Mr. Spencer had been elected a Foreign Associate of that body. . . .[1]

Mr. Spencer, without undervaluing the distinction of inclusion in the Royal Order " Pour le Mérite," feels compelled to pursue the course he has hitherto pursued and, therefore, to decline the accorded honour.

About a week later he was informed by Professor Theodor Gomperz of Vienna that the Imperial Vienna

---

[1] See vol. i., chap. xvii., p. 310.

Academy had elected him a foreign honorary member. Having seen in the papers that Spencer had been declining as a matter of principle all honours, Professor Gomperz, who had taken the initiative in the election, hoped that the rumour was untrue.

But if it should be true (he wrote), I must request you, kindly to write a line as soon as you find time for it. For our act of election is only *a preliminary;* the nomination belongs to the prerogative of His Majesty the Emperor. And if you should be firmly resolved to refuse such a nomination, our election would (I suppose) not be submitted for sanction to His Majesty. You would then be spared the unwelcome necessity of meeting an act of respectful sympathy by a flat refusal, and we would be spared the still more unpleasant necessity of exposing our sovereign to such a refusal.

Spencer was sorry to be unable to contradict the rumour as to his attitude towards honours, the reasons given being those with which the reader is now familiar. A similar course was followed when he was offered the membership of the Royal Lombardian Institute of Sciences and Letters, and the degree of Doctor of the University of Buda Pesth.

FROM MRS. TYNDALL.

5 *June*, 1895.

Talking of your early life reminds me that I met yesterday a Miss ——, who mentioned that she had heard her father tell of a time in your engineering days when you were in the habit of eating tallow candles, the inference being drawn that your brain thereby became specially nourished. How such a ridiculous story came to be invented I do not know.

To Mrs. Tyndall.

6 *June,* 1895.

Thank you very much for the amazing story you send me. I could fill a small volume with absurd stories about myself, of some of which I can trace the origin, but others without any imaginable origin. This most absurd one which you send is one of the last class. It is the more remarkable as coming from one who might reasonably be supposed to know.

In place of Pewsey the summer resort for 1895 was Westerham, Kent, whither he went about the middle of June. He had not been there many days when a severe blow fell upon him by the death of Professor Huxley.

To Mrs. Huxley.

Westerham, 2 *July,* 1895.

If recovery had become hopeless, longer continuance of life under such suffering as has of late been borne was scarcely to be desired, and this thought may be entertained as in part a consolation in your bereavement. A further consolation, and one which will be of long duration, is derivable from the contemplation of his life as having been model—exemplary in the capacities of husband, father, citizen and teacher.

The death of Lord Pembroke, whose character and aims he estimated very highly, removed one more from the ever narrowing circle of his friends and acquaintances. Hitherto Lady Pembroke's correspondence with Spencer had for the most part related to political or scientific questions of general interest; but after Lord Pembroke's death her letters took an entirely new turn: the nature of life and mind, the unimportance of matter, telepathy, a future existence, being among the subjects dilated upon. Occasionally, in discussing these subjects, she felt she was getting beyond her depth, as when she said: " I trust I am not writing presumptuous nonsense to the greatest philosopher of the day."

To THE COUNTESS OF PEMBROKE.

26 *June,* 1895.

On the great questions you raise I should like to comment at some length had I the energy to spare. The hope that continually groping, though in the dark, may eventually discover the clue, is one I can scarcely entertain, for the reason that human intelligence appears to me incapable of framing any conception of the required kind. . . . It seems to me that our best course is to submit to the limitations imposed by the nature of our minds, and to live as contentedly as we may in ignorance of that which lies behind things as we know them. My own feeling respecting the ultimate mystery is such that of late years I cannot even try to think of infinite space without some feeling of terror, so that I habitually shun the thought.

5 *July.*—The general question is too wide for discussion in a letter, but I may suggest the consideration of a fact which perhaps will throw doubt upon your assumption that life is a *thing* instead of being a process. It is well known among naturalists that certain minute forms of aquatic life, as, for example, the Rotifers, may be dried up until they resemble particles of dust, and that, though then dead in so far as absence of all vital manifestations is concerned, they, when duly supplied again with water, perhaps after years, absorb it, and recommence their lives. If we understand life to be a process this is comprehensible, but if we understand life to be a thing it is not comprehensible.

However, without pushing the argument further I may end up by saying that the whole thing is at bottom an insoluble mystery, and I quite understand your attitude in entertaining what Tennyson calls the " Larger hope.''

5 *November*.—Respecting your question concerning " conjectures,'' I have ceased to form any, since the more the mystery of things is thought about the more mysterious it becomes. As I said at the close of an essay written many years ago, " the Ultimate Power is no more representable in terms of human consciousness than human consciousness is representable in terms of a plant's functions.'' And, of course, what is here said respecting the Ultimate Power holds equally respecting the Ultimate Process.

The simple fact, that the endeavour to answer the question whether space is infinite or not infinite leads us to alternative impossibilities of thought, suffices to show that no conjectures we can frame with regard to the reality of things can have any approach to the truth.

19 *January*, 1896.—I remember hearing Professor Owen say that it is given only to the man of science to know what a fact is, and my own experience endorses the saying. The mass of mankind are so uncritical that they do not distinguish between valid and invalid evidences. When in past years I looked into alleged non-natural phenomena I found the ideas of what constitutes proof so loose that I ceased to pay any attention to the matter. . . .

A special combination of qualities is required for an examiner in such cases: he must have both scientific knowledge and definite ideas of causation, and also a knowledge of human nature and a quick perception of human motives and conduct. Most are deficient in one or other qualification. Being myself deficient in the last, I would not trust my own conclusions were I to take part in a séance or in kindred testing of alleged abnormal manifestations. I am so wanting in quick observation of people's doings, feelings, intentions, etc.,

84

that I should be easily deluded. But my own experience is that remarkable coincidences occur with such comparative frequency as to be quite capable of accounting for the occasional instances of things apparently supernatural. I have myself sometimes had promptings to believe in a supernatural agency, caused by the repeated experiences of coincidences in various ways injurious. . . . And simple induction would I think almost have led me to believe in supernatural agency were it not that with me the conviction of natural causation is so strong that it is impossible to think away from it.

But I should have been more apt to accept a supernatural explanation had it not been for the many experiences I have had of meaningless coincidences, showing how frequent and how astonishing they are. . . . If meaningless coincidences are thus frequent, there must occasionally occur coincidences that have meaning—coincidences of which the elements are related in some significant way, and when they do occur they attract attention from their resemblance and suggest a supernatural cause. It is this consideration which has joined in making me reject the supernatural interpretation above referred to.

21 *January.*—If I find myself obliged to hold that there are supernatural manifestations and a supernatural interference with the order of things, then my personal experience would force me to the conclusion that the power underlying things is diabolical.

Were I well enough, . . . I should be pleased were you to honour me with a call on your way to Eastbourne, but unhappily listening tries me nearly as much as talking. . . . I may however be considerably better by the time referred to and in that case should gladly listen to the experiences you name.

This closes the correspondence so far as regards the supreme question discussed, with exception of a letter from Lady Pembroke in May, in which she says (probably with reference to the visit above referred to): "After our last conversation I think you will believe that I have fallen away from the school of precise thinking."

While these lines are being written, the death of Lady Pembroke on August 31, 1906, is announced. Another of Spencer's friends—the Dowager Countess of Portsmouth—died on the same day. Lady Portsmouth had for years been unwearied in her kindnesses and unwavering in her admiration of his character. When sending him a copy of the reprinted essays, etc., of her brother, the late Earl of Carnarvon, she wrote: "It is possible you differed on some subjects. It is possible you agreed on many. It is quite certain that you stood together in a noble love of justice and truth."

In July, 1895, a proposal that he should sit for his portrait to Mr. McLure Hamilton was declined for the reasons given some seven years before when he was asked to sit to Millais.[1] Later in the year, in connexion with Mr. Watts' gift to the National Portrait Gallery, a suggestion was made by Mr. Collins in the *Times* (December 11) to have a portrait painted by Watts and added to the national collection.

To F. Howard Collins.

12 *December*, 1895.

I was startled by your letter in yesterday's *Times*. . . . It is vigorously written, and its point artistically brought out. It will greatly astonish most people by the claim it makes, which, I doubt not, they will think absurd.

---

[1] See vol. i., chap. xix., p. 378.

I fear, however, that in respect of the result desired it is unlikely to succeed. Probably this gift made by Mr. Watts, if it does not mark the end of his career as an artist, marks the end of his career as a portrait-painter, and I should think that at his age he will probably object to undertake anything more.

A notice was also sent by Spencer to the *Times* (December 14) to the effect that the letter " was written and published entirely without his knowledge, and that he must not in any way be held responsible for the suggestion contained in it." On the 17th he informed Mr. Collins: " Please take no further step in the matter of the portrait. I am no admirer of Watts and should have no desire to sit to him, even if he assented. As to any other plan that may be proposed, I know of none to which I should not raise objection." Mr. Watts was far from assenting. In a letter to Mr. Collins he expressed his feeling that any attempt he might make would be likely to end in failure.

A request from Mr. A. Mordan, of Reigate, that he would sit to Mr. Wells for a portrait to be presented to the National Portrait Gallery was also declined.

While at Westerham he sent a letter to *Nature* on " The Nomenclature of Colours," quoting a passage from the unpublished *Autobiography* (i. 355).

To F. Howard Collins.

4 *September,* 1895.

My objection to your proposed chart of colours is that, in the first place, it does not make the composition of each colour obvious, which is a primary desideratum, and in the second place, that it does not give in juxtaposition with each colour its assigned name. Hence the memory is not in either way aided to the same extent, and further there is no such advantage as that given by the method of " boxing the compass " of colours, namely, that the mode of naming each colour and its relative position can be easily recalled when it has been forgotten, since the *method* of naming is easily recovered.

Reference to the above led him to bring to light a " Classification of Artistic Characters of Paintings," which he had drawn up probably during or about the time of his visit to Italy in 1868, and of which he says: " These were drawn up at a time when I hoped I should one day deal with Æsthetic Progress, and my intention was to go through Home and Foreign Picture Galleries to classify pictures in respect of these traits." The classification embraced four heads:—Subject, Form, Colour, Shade.[1]

His loyalty to the memory of Dr. Youmans was shown by his letter to the *Times* in September, pointing out how unceasing had been his friend's efforts in the United States to uphold the interests of authors. The strength of this feeling was shown some two months later when invited by the London editor of *McClure's Magazine* to contribute to that journal.

---

[1]

R—religious	C.P.—colour primary
RW—religious worship	C.Pu—colour pure
M—mythology	C.St—colour strong
L—loyal	C.S.—colour secondary
P—political	C.T—colour tertiary
	C.M—colour mixed
	C.Im—colour impure
S—symmetrical	N.S—no shade
US—unsymmetrical	H.S—half shade
A.S—attitudes symmetrical	F.S—full shade
A.US—attitudes unsymmetrical	S.S—strong shade
A.A—attitudes alike	S.U—shading uniform
A.D—attitudes distorted	S.C—shading contrasted

I have, in virtue mainly of my indebtedness to my old friend for all he did on my behalf in the United States, felt bound to make the *Popular Science Monthly* my sole medium for publication of articles in the United States, and the obligation, which was peremptory during his life, remains strong after his death, since his brother occupies his place and has continued his good offices on my behalf.

Copyright between the mother country and Canada had, about this time, assumed an acute form, in consequence of the Dominion Parliament requiring that to secure copyright a book must have been printed in Canada. Professor Goldwin Smith contended for the excision of this clause. In favour of its retention Sir Charles Tupper quoted a document signed many years before by fifty British Authors, of whom Spencer was one. Thereupon Spencer wrote to the *Times* (22 October) explaining the general purport of that memorial (which he had himself drawn up), pointing out that the inferences Sir Charles Tupper had drawn from it were not warrantable, and quoting Professor Goldwin Smith's opinion that the clause requiring a book to be printed in Canada must be " excised." This word " excised " appeared in the cablegram to Canada as " exercised." Professor Goldwin Smith naturally protested against this inversion of his meaning, which to Spencer looked like a deliberate falsification in Canadian interests. By way of counteracting any such purpose, assuming it to exist, he wrote to the Colonial Secretary. While not doubting that the Canadians had a keen eye to their own interests, Mr. Chamberlain did not think they differed from other people. Mr. Hall Caine had, he hoped, helped to make an arrangement possible which would be satisfactory to English authors.

Once more, and for the last time, he had to defend his independence of Comte.

To Lester F. Ward.

19 *September,* 1895.

I have just received a copy of your essay on " The Place of Sociology among the Sciences," and on glancing through it am startled by some of its statements.

(1) You have not, I presume, read my essay on " The Genesis of Science," otherwise you would scarcely say that Comte's classification represents the genetic or serial order of the sciences. . . .

(2) But I am much more amazed by your statement respecting Comte's system that " Spencer himself, notwithstanding all his efforts to overthrow it, actually adopted it in the arrangement of the sciences in his Synthetic Philosophy." Now in the first place, if you will look at my essay on " The Genesis of Science," you will see that the first two great groups of sciences—the Abstract, containing logic and mathematics, the Abstract-Concrete, containing mechanics, physics, and chemistry—have no place whatever in the Synthetic Philosophy. . . .

Setting aside the fact that, as I have pointed out, the sciences which deal with the forms of phenomena and those which deal with their factors make no appearance whatever in the order of sciences forming the Synthetic Philosophy, there is the fact that even if the sciences as involved in the Synthetic Philosophy are compared with the system of Comte, they are shown to be wholly incongruous with it. If you will turn to the original preface of *First Principles,* in which an outline of the Synthetic Philosophy is set forth, you will see there, between the programme of *First Principles* and the programme of the *Biology* a note in italics pointing out

90

that in logical order there should come an application of First Principles to inorganic nature, and that the part of it dealing with inorganic nature is omitted simply because the scheme, even as it stood, was too extensive. Two volumes were thus omitted—a volume on astronomy and a volume on geology. Had it been possible to write these, in addition to those undertaken, the series would have run—astronomy, *geology*, biology, *psychology*, sociology, ethics. Now in this series those marked in italics do not appear in the Comtian classification at all.

(3) But now, in the third place, I draw your attention to Table III. in my " Classification of the Sciences." There you will see that the order of the works already existing in the Synthetic Philosophy, and still better the order in which they would have stood had the thing been complete, corresponds exactly with the order shown in that table, and is an order which evolves necessarily from the mode of organisation there insisted upon, and corresponds also to the order of appearance in time, if you set out with nebular condensation and end with social phenomena. The order of the Synthetic Philosophy does *not* correspond with that of Comte, and it *does* correspond with the order shown in my own " Classification of the Sciences."

On the appearance in the *Review of Reviews* for November of Mr. Grant Allen's " Character Sketch," Spencer was again impressed with the weight of his obligations to that singularly able and generous champion.

TO GRANT ALLEN.

18 *November*, 1895.

You have, as always before, proved yourself a most outspoken and efficient advocate—perhaps, in a sense,

almost too efficient, since in some minds the large claims
you make on my behalf may cause some reactive feeling.
I say this partly because, even in myself, the reading
of your exposition last night at the Athenæum oddly
enough seemed to produce a kind of vague scepticism,
as though it could hardly all be true. So you may judge
how largely you have made me loom in the eyes of the
general reader.

It strikes me that in one respect you have been crediting me at your own cost, for in the passage concerning
the relation between growth and reproduction I recognise
less of my own views than of the views you lately set
forth, in which there was very truly expressed the truth
that the ultimate mystery centres more in the ability
of the individual organism to perpetually reproduce its
own structure than in its ability to reproduce like structures.

The earliest of all his friends—Mr. George Holme—
passed away in the beginning of 1896.

To CHARLES HOLME.

8 *February,* 1896.

The last days of a long life when it has passed into
decrepitude with all its miseries are not to be desired,
and when there has been reached that limit after which
nothing can be done and little save pain can be experienced, the cessation of life is scarcely to be regretted.
You and your mother and sisters have this thought as
a set-off against the feeling which must result from the
breaking of the last link with your father.

You have, too, the permanent consolation of remembering that he led what may be characterised as a model
life. . . . With energy and great natural intelligence
he joined, in a degree far beyond that which is usual,
the root of all high character—sympathy. . . . It was

to the existence in him of this predominant sympathy that I owe my life.

To HECTOR MACPHERSON.

20 *February,* 1896.

On returning from Brighton last night, after an absence of three months, I found your little book on Carlyle. . . . I see that it is written in a manner which might well be imitated by biographers—not with unqualified eulogy, but with qualified eulogy. It is curious that to one sympathising with me as you do should have fallen the task of writing the life of one so utterly antagonistic—so antagonistic that on one occasion I saw that he called me an '' immeasurable ass.''

28 *February.*—I have read the greater part of your little book on Carlyle with interest. It is a very good combination of narrative, exposition, characterisation, and criticism, and this union of elements gives in brief space a definite idea of the man.

You have been quite fair to him—more than fair, I think. You have not brought into prominence his less amiable traits. His extreme arrogance should, I think, have been more distinctly indicated, and also the fact that his sympathy with despotic modes of dealing with men was the outcome of his own despotic nature.

20 *March.*—Thank you for your proposal [to write a book on Spencer]. I should of course very well like to see such a book written, and have no doubt that you would do it well.

I think, however, that in inferring from the success of your little book on Carlyle that a book of the kind you name would succeed, you are over sanguine. Biography and philosophy in respect of popular appreciation stand at the opposite poles. To the average mind the one yields much pleasure with no effort, the other yields no pleasure with much effort.

Spencer's dissatisfaction with the decimal system was of long standing.[1] But occasion did not arise for taking the question up till January, 1895, when he wrote a long letter to Lord Kelvin, who had made a public pronouncement in favour of the metric system. After an interval of a little over a year he wrote four letters against the metric system, which appeared in the *Times* (4, 7, 9, 25 April, 1896) and were afterwards sent in pamphlet form to members of the British House of Commons and of the United States Congress.

FROM MISS YOUMANS.

MOUNT VERNON, 20 *February*, 1896.

You are nearing the end of your peerless labour. What superhuman courage and persistence you have shown! You ought to be very proud of yourself. If Edward could only be here in this hour of fulfilment! . . . How well I recall his tender solicitude about you, when in 1865 there was fear that you would not be able to go on with your undertaking. To some question of mine as to how you would bear it he answered " I think it would kill him." But no one except your parents could have been more interested in your success than Edward was. And sad to say, at his death your prospects in this regard were at the worst.

I send you some newspaper slips about the movement here toward arbitration. . . . May I publish what you wrote to Edward when you were trying to start the Anti-Aggression League?

The reply must have been in the affirmative, for in the New York *Evening Post* of 26 March, the correspondence was published, along with a brief sketch of the

---

[1] *Autobiography*, i., p. 248, and Appendix E., p. 621.

origin and work of the Anti-Aggression League, and concluding with Spencer's letter read at the meeting in favour of Anglo-American Arbitration, held in the Queen's Hall, 3 March, 1896.[1]

At length the end of the long path he had marked out for himself to travel was reached.[2] The occasion is thus described by his Secretary, Mr. Troughton:—

Mr. Spencer was seventy-six years of age when he dictated to me the last words of "Industrial Institutions," with the completion of which the *Synthetic Philosophy* was finished—to be precise it was on the 13 August, 1896. Rising slowly from his seat in the study at 64, Avenue Road, his face beaming with joy, he extended his hand across the table, and we shook hands on the auspicious event. "I have finished the task I have lived for" was all he said, and then resumed his seat. The elation was only momentary and his features quickly resumed their customary composure.

---

[1] *Times, Daily Chronicle*, etc., of 4 March, 1896. Also *Various Fragments*, p. 140.
[2] See vol. i., chap. ix., p. 130.

CHAPTER XXIV

CONGRATULATIONS

(*November*, 1896—*January*, 1901)

THE publication of the concluding volume of the *Synthetic Philosophy* was the signal for an outburst of sympathetic appreciation such as falls to the lot of few men. Not from his own country alone, but from many lands; not from adherents only, but from those who did not accept the doctrine of evolution, came expressions of the highest admiration. It was not to his transcendent intellectual power merely that homage was paid. To his moral character—to the high and indomitable purpose that had sustained him throughout these years, enabling him, in face of difficulties that seemed almost insurmountable, ever to keep sight of the goal—to this was offered a tribute as unstinted in its cordiality as it was catholic in its source. Generous testimony was borne to the value of his contribution to the treasure house of thought, but even more generous was the meed of praise called forth by what he had done to purify the aims and strengthen the moral fibre of mankind.

Gratified though he was by these tributes of esteem, he shrank from anything that might have the appearance of a bid for notoriety. He would not allow himself to be interviewed. To the editor of one of the London papers he wrote: " I am at present quite sufficiently *affiché,* and to take any steps which would have the

96

appearance of intentionally making myself more conspicuous would be repugnant to me. Especially, talk concerning myself and my work, which I should hesitate at all times to enter upon, would at the present time be undesirable.'' Again, when Mr. Balfour and Mr. Morley visited him together early in December, though he made no attempt to conceal the pleasure the visit had given him, he requested the members of his household not to speak about it, because he did not wish it to get into the papers.

Not disheartened by the failure of his suggestion some months before to get a portrait of Spencer for the National Gallery, Mr. Collins renewed it in a letter to the *Times* of 17 November, with the result that a committee was at once formed consisting of Sir Joseph D. Hooker (Chairman), the Duke of Argyll, Mr. Arthur James Balfour, Dr. Charlton Bastian, Mr. Leonard Courtney, Mr. Francis Galton, Professor Ray Lankester, Mr. John Morley, Sir Frederick Pollock, Mr. Leslie Stephen, Professor James Sully, and Mr. Howard Collins (Secretary).

TO F. HOWARD COLLINS.

2 December, 1896.

Hitherto I have said nothing concerning the proposal made in the *Times,* chiefly because I believed that there would be but little response. But Mr. Hughes tells me that you are cooperating with Professor Sully in getting together a committee, but does not say to what end. Professor Sully was, as I understood ten days ago, taking steps with a view to a congratulatory address, and I am now in doubt whether the efforts you are kindly making in conjunction with him are in pursuance of that end or in pursuance of the end you suggested. If this last is the purpose, I ought I think to let you know what happened when a kindred proposal was made some eight years ago. . . .[1]

My delay in writing, consequent on the impression I have named, may I fear have resulted in the taking of bootless trouble, but I hope otherwise.

Without waiting till his scruples had been completely overcome, the Committee drew up and obtained signatures to a letter of congratulation, which was presented in little over a month after the day on which his concluding volume appeared.

FROM SIR JOSEPH DALTON HOOKER.

16 *December,* 1896.

I am deputed to transmit to you the enclosed, and obey with unqualified satisfaction.

TO HERBERT SPENCER, ESQ.

LONDON, 16 *December,* 1896.

DEAR SIR:

We, the undersigned, offer you our cordial congratulations upon the completion of your " System of Synthetic Philosophy."

Not all of us agreeing in equal measure with its conclusions, we are all at one in our estimate of the great intellectual powers it exhibits and of the immense effect it has produced in the history of thought; nor are we less impressed by the high moral qualities which have enabled you to concentrate those powers for so many years upon a purpose worthy of them, and, in spite of all obstacles, to carry out so vast a design.

To the many who, like us, have learned to honour the man while profiting by his writings, it would be a satis-

---

[1] See vol. i., chap. xix., p. 378.

faction to possess an authentic personal likeness of the author. It has therefore occurred to us that the occasion might be appropriately marked by requesting you to permit us to employ some eminent artist to take your portrait with a view to its being deposited in one of our national collections for the benefit of ourselves and of those who come after us.

We hope that your health may be benefited by the leisure which you have earned so well, and that you may long continue to enjoy the consciousness of having completed your work.

W. DE W. ABNEY, R.E., C.B., D.C.L., F.R.S., President of the Physical Society.

ROBERT ADAMSON, M.A., LL.D., Professor of Logic, Glasgow University.

GRANT ALLEN, B.A.

ALEXANDER BAIN, M.A., LL.D., Emeritus Professor of Logic, Aberdeen University.

SIR GEORGE S. BADEN-POWELL, K.C.M.G., M.A., M.P.

RIGHT HON. ARTHUR JAMES BALFOUR, P.C., LL.D., F.R.S., M.P.

SIR ROBERT STAWELL BALL, LL.D., F.R.S., Lowndean Professor of Astronomy, Cambridge University.

H. CHARLTON BASTIAN, M.A., M.D., F.R.S., Professor of Medicine, University College, London.

FRANK E. BEDDARD, M.A., F.R.S., Prosector to the Zoological Society.

JOHN BEDDOE, M.D., F.R.S.

SIR WALTER BESANT, M.A.

E. W. BRABROOK, President, Anthropological Institute.

BERNARD BOSANQUET, M.A.

C. V. BOYS, F.R.S., Assistant Professor of Physics, R.C.S.

T. LAUDER BRUNTON, M.D., D.SC., F.R.S.

EDWARD CLODD.

F. HOWARD COLLINS.

SIR J. CRICHTON-BROWNE, M.D., LL.D., F.R.S.

W. H. DALLINGER, LL.D., D.SC., F.R.S.

FRANCIS DARWIN, M.A., M.B., F.R.S.

GEORGE H. DARWIN, M.A., LL.D., F.R.S., Plumian Professor of Astronomy and Experimental Physics, Cambridge University.

W. E. DARWIN, F.G.S.

JAMES DONALDSON, M.A., LL.D., Principal, St. Andrews University.

RIGHT HON. SIR M. E. GRANT-DUFF, P.C., G.C.S.I., F.R.S.

EARL OF DYSART.

SIR JOHN EVANS, K.C.B., D.C.L., LL.D., D.SC., Treasurer of the Royal Society.

SIR JOSHUA FITCH, LL.D.

MICHAEL FOSTER, M.A., M.D., LL.D., D.C.L., Sec. R.S., Professor of Physiology, Cambridge University.

EDWARD FRANKLAND, M.D., D.C.L., LL.D., F.R.S.

RIGHT HON. SIR EDWARD FRY, P.C., LL.D., D.C.L., F.R.S.

SIR DOUGLAS GALTON, K.C.B., D.C.L., LL.D., F.R.S.

FRANCIS GALTON, M.A., D.C.L., D.SC., F.R.S.

RICHARD GARNETT, LL.D.

SIR GEORGE GROVE, C.B., D.C.L., LL.D.

ALBERT C. L. G. GÜNTHER, M.A., M.D., F.R.S., President of the Linnæan Society.

FREDERIC HARRISON, M.A.

JAMES EDMUND HARTING.

RIGHT HON. LORD HOBHOUSE, P.C.

HENRY HOBHOUSE, M.A., M.P.

SHADWORTH HODGSON, late President of the Aristotelian Society.

SIR JOSEPH DALTON HOOKER, K.C.S.I., C.B., M.D., D.C.L., LL.D., F.R.S.

WILLIAM HUGGINS, D.C.L., LL.D., F.R.S.

J. HUGHLINGS JACKSON, M.D., LL.D., F.R.S.

WILLIAM KNIGHT, LL.D., Professor of Moral Philosophy, St. Andrews University.

ANDREW LANG.

CONGRATULATIONS

E. Ray Lankester, M.A., LL.D., F.R.S., Linacre Professor of Anatomy, Oxford University.

Sir Trevor Lawrence, President of the Royal Horticultural Society.

W. E. H. Lecky, M.A., LL.D., D.C.L., M.P.

J. Norman Lockyer, C.B., F.R.S., Professor of Astronomical Physics, R.C.S.

Right Hon. Sir John Lubbock, P.C., D.C.L., LL.D., F.R.S., M.P.

Vernon Lushington, Q.C.

P. A. MacMahon, R.A., F.R.S., late President of the Mathematical Society.

James Martineau, D.D., LL.D., D.C.L.

David Masson, M.A., LL.D., Emeritus Professor of Rhetoric, Edinburgh University.

Raphael Meldola, F.R.S., President of the Entomological Society.

C. Lloyd Morgan, Principal, University College, Bristol.

Right Hon. John Morley, P.C., M.A., LL.D., F.R.S., M.P.

C. Hubert H. Parry, Principal, Royal College of Music.

General Pitt-Rivers, D.C.L., F.R.S.

Edward B. Poulton, M.A., F.R.S., Professor of Zoology, Oxford University.

Sir William O. Priestley, M.D., LL.D., M.P.

Lord Reay, G.C.S.I., G.C.I.E.

Right Hon. Lord Rayleigh, M.A., D.C.L., LL.D., F.R.S., Professor of Natural Philosophy, Royal Institution.

David G. Ritchie, M.A., Professor of Logic, St. Andrews University.

Sir Henry E. Roscoe, LL.D., D.C.L., F.R.S.

J. S. Burdon Sanderson, LL.D., D.C.L., F.R.S., Regius Professor of Medicine, Oxford University.

George H. Savage, M.D., F.R.C.P.

E. A. Schäfer, F.R.S., Professor of Physiology, University College, London.

D. H. Scott, M.A., Ph.D., F.R.S., Honorary Keeper,
Jodrell Laboratory, Kew.

Henry Sidgwick, M.A., Litt.D., D.C.L., Professor of
Moral Philosophy, Cambridge University.

W. R. Sorley, M.A., Professor of Moral Philosophy,
Aberdeen University.

Leslie Stephen, M.A., Litt.D., LL.D.

G. F. Stout, M.A.

James Sully, M.A., LL.D.

W. T. Thiselton-Dyer, C.M.G., C.I.E., M.A., F.R.S.

John Venn, D.Sc., F.R.S.

Sydney Howard Vines, M.A., D.Sc., F.R.S., Professor
of Botany, Oxford University.

Sir Willoughby Wade, M.D., F.R.C.P.

Alfred Russel Wallace, D.C.L., F.R.S.

Beatrice Webb.

Lady Victoria Welby.

Samuel Wilks, M.D., LL.D., F.R.S., President of the
College of Physicians.

———

HAWARDEN, *November* 30, 1896.

My dear Sir,—It has long been my rule to decline
joining in groups of signatures, nor do I think myself
entitled to bear a prominent part in the present case.
But I beg that you will, if you think proper, set me down
as an approver of the request to Mr. Spencer, whose
signal abilities and, rarer still, whose manful and self-
denying character, are so justly objects of admiration.

I remain your very faithful,

F. Howard Collins, Esq.   W. E. Gladstone.

No time was lost before replying to these cordial congratulations.

2, Lewes Crescent, Brighton,
19 *December,* 1896.

My dear Hooker,—If, as may fitly be said, the value
of congratulations increases in a geometrical progression

102

with the eminence of those offering them, I may, indeed, be extremely gratified by the accumulation coming from men standing so high in various spheres. And an accompanying pleasure necessarily results from the good wishes expressed for my health and happiness during my remaining days.

The further honour offered has caused in me some mental conflict. Eight years ago, to the inquiry whether I would sit for a subscription portrait to be painted by Millais, I replied negatively, assigning the reasons that the raising of funds to pay the costs of conferring marks of approbation had grown into an abuse; that the moral coercion under which contributions were in many cases obtained was repugnant to me; and that I objected to have my known and unknown friends asked to tax themselves to the required extent. These reasons survived, and, swayed by them, I recently sent a copy of the letter in which they had been stated to the gentleman with whom the proposal now made originated, thinking thereby to prevent further trouble. I was unaware to how large an extent the proposal had been adopted and how distinguished were the numerous gentlemen who had given it their support. I now find myself obliged either inconsistently to waive my objection or else rudely to slight the cordially-expressed feelings and wishes of so many whose positions and achievements command my great respect. Between the alternatives there seems to be practically no choice. I am compelled to yield to the request made in so sympathetic a manner by signatories so eminent, and at the same time must express to them through you my full sense of the honour done me.

I am, my dear Hooker, sincerely yours,
HERBERT SPENCER.

The consent to sit for his portrait, thus reluctantly obtained at the moment when he was impressed with a sense of the kindness of those who proposed to honour him in so conspicuous a manner, was followed by mis-givings after a few days reflection. His scruples again came to the surface on being asked: " Have you thought over the question of the artist ? "

To Sir Joseph Dalton Hooker.

30 *December,* 1896.

Your question is simple, but the answer is not so simple.

Some three months ago, before his departure for America, Mr. Carnegie pressed me to sit for a portrait to be presented by him to the Pittsburg Institution. . . . I willingly yielded, and agreed to the suggestion that the portrait should be painted by Mr. Ouless. . . .

But now comes a question. These leading artists ask exorbitant sums for their work, and if the cost of a por-trait is to be borne by those only who have signed the address, on each of whom the tax would then be consid-erable, I should decidedly demur. In that case the only fit course would be to commission Mr. Ouless to make a *replica* of the portrait he paints for Mr. Carnegie. The cost of this would not be excessive.

The painting of the portrait was entrusted to Mr. (now Sir) Hubert von Herkomer.

Some two days before receipt of the address he had written to Mr. Carnegie to the effect that he had stopped the action of those who were making preparations for a subscription portrait. He had now to explain his change of front.

To Andrew Carnegie.

4 *January,* 1897.

I have had to yield. A few days after I wrote to you there came to me an address of congratulation bearing

104

over eighty signatures, including those of men of eminence in various spheres, political, scientific, literary, etc., joined with a request that I would sit for a portrait. I had not anticipated anything so influential, and found myself in the predicament of having either to abandon my resolution or else to slight, in a marked and public way, numerous men whom I have every reason to respect, and bring upon myself condemnation as ill-mannered and perverse.

To F. Howard Collins.

8 *January*, 1897.

You have been victorious all along the line, as the phrase is—victorious over others and victorious over me. I did not expect to have my flank turned in such an irresistible way. However, though I have to recognise myself as in a manner defeated, there is of course, a satisfaction in the defeat, along with a small set-off the other way.

My feeling towards my fellow-countrymen (especially as contrasted with the Americans) has for years past not been a very friendly one, and my antagonistic attitude has been in part due to this feeling. Honour long delayed loses the quality of honour. . . . However, the thing is now done and well done; and having been initiated and largely urged on by you, let me offer you my hearty thanks. In you, at any rate, there has never been any tardiness of appreciation.

It is a pity that he dwelt so much on the tardiness of the honour, and so little on the cordiality and unanimity displayed in the bestowing of it. It is strange that he did not remember how for more than a quarter of a century he had persistently, and at times almost ungraciously, declined every honour that had been offered him. The warmth with which the press also supported the step his friends had taken ought to have gone far to remove any lingering feeling of bitterness for supposed past neglect. Such commendable despatch had been shown with the address that many who would have signed it came to know of it only when the report of the presentation appeared in the newspapers. The absence of their names was more than compensated for by the cordiality of their private expressions of regret at having missed the opportunity of joining in the public testimonial. As noted in a previous chapter (xx., p. 393), the letters in which he complains of neglect on the part of his countrymen have to be read along with those in which he acknowledges the sympathetic appreciation his writings had secured at home.

TO THE RIGHT HON. ARTHUR J. BALFOUR.

3 *February,* 1897.

From Mr. Howard Collins . . . I learn that I am indebted to you for much more than is implied by your signature to the address of congratulation, etc.—indebted for active aid which, noteworthy as it would have been in one having leisure, is much more noteworthy in one so much pressed by public business, and noteworthy in a still higher degree as given by one who in important matters differs in belief. And that this aid should have been given unobtrusively, too, so divesting it of any possible motive other than that of genuine sympathy, renders it still more remarkable. Pray accept the thanks which I find it imperative to offer.

My appreciation is made the greater on considering what I might myself have done under like conditions. A passive assent, would, I think, have been the limit of my adhesion. I doubt whether my generosity would have been sufficient to prompt active co-operation. Could I ascribe this difference in action to difference in creed, the belief would do much towards shaking some of my general views. But innate superiority of nature I take to be the true cause.

The first part of this letter was written in his own hand, but the effort was too much, and the rest had to be dictated.

To JAMES SULLY.

6 *February,* 1897.

Among the things which should have been done, but have not been done, is the writing to you a letter expressing my indebtedness for the efforts you have made in furthering the recent manifestation of sympathy and approval. I say " in furthering "; but remembering the steps which you took to initiate an address of congratulation—steps taken I think independently at the time when Mr. Collins proposed a portrait—the word is scarcely adequate. . . . I must not let the matter end without offering you my hearty thanks for all you have done.

As you doubtless know by experience, a writer's chief gratification is in the consciousness of work satisfactorily done, but second only to that is the manifestation of approval from the select.

Among the manifestations of approval from " the select " was the offer of the degree of D.Sc., from the University of Cambridge, and that of LL.D. from the University of Edinburgh. Both were declined. A proposal was made by the municipal authorities of Derby to mark the house of his birth with a tablet, but for reasons unknown it was not carried out.[1] As for the portrait, there were many appointments and disappoint-

---

[1] A marble tablet was put up by the Derby Spencer Society in 1907.

ments, so that nothing was done till almost the end of the year.

To F. Howard Collins.

Brighton, 6 *December,* 1897.

Who is silly enough to say that I decline to sit? I have not left this room for these six weeks. It is hard to have my misfortunes used as weapons. Herkomer was here three days ago, and would have taken photographs of me sitting in bed had the light been good. He comes again next week.

23 *December.*—Mr. Herkomer was to have been here last week, but wrote me that an attack of influenza was keeping him indoors. Yesterday he came and took five photographs; and he comes again to-morrow to take more. He talks of making the portrait wholly from photographs, but I cannot assent to this; there must be some sittings to finish from.

Who is the unfriendly friend who takes the attitude which your letters seem to imply? . . . A while ago you spoke of my " declining " to sit according to promise. . . . And then, after all, the supposition that I alone am responsible for the delay is an utter mistake. During a considerable part of the late summer months when I could have sat, had circumstances permitted, Mr. Herkomer was on the Continent, and, when I returned to town about the middle of September, I believe was still away, for I had no replies in answer to letters I wrote. . . .

Your letter reached me last night just as I was going to bed, and the irritation it caused kept me awake a good part of the night.

To Sir Joseph Dalton Hooker.

27 *December,* 1897.

Inquiries and remarks which have come round to me during the last three months, imply that the long delay

108

in the execution of the portrait has caused some adverse feeling: the delay being ascribed to perversity on my part. . . .

I dislike obligations of the kind implied by a subscription-portrait, and if there is, in any of those concerned, a lack of cordiality, my dislike becomes something stronger. . . . My present desire is that Mr. Herkomer shall be paid by me, and that the subscriptions shall be returned: each being accompanied by a copy of this letter.

Sir Joseph Hooker hastened to set his mind at rest, telling him that he was mistaken in supposing that there was any want of cordiality among the subscribers to the portrait. On receiving this assurance he wrote again.

To Sir Joseph Dalton Hooker.

30 *December*, 1897.

Your letter received. Very many thanks for it. It relieves my fears and I gladly accept your assurances, and now desire that you should keep my letter to yourself.

Mr. Collins has said on several occasions things which, it seems, I had misinterpreted.

The artist was working in circumstances of extreme difficulty, never having had a proper sitting. At length, however, in February the portrait was finished.

To Sir Joseph Dalton Hooker.

2 *March*, 1898.

Mr. Collins wrote to me a few days ago saying that the portrait is " splendid and admirable " and expressing the feeling that, as having been so largely influential in getting it done, you ought to be congratulated; if for no other reason than for the reason of having acquired

109

for the public so fine a work of art, for he speaks of it especially as a work of art which has its interest under that aspect irrespective of any interest it may otherwise have. I coincide in his feeling and gladly on public as on private grounds join in the congratulation.

Oddly enough it seems likely that I shall never see it. . . . I must be content with seeing a photograph.

When the Herkomer photogravure reproduction of the portrait was sent him he wrote:—

To HUBERT VON HERKOMER, R.A.

18 *April,* 1898.

Of course the judgments of my friends with regard to the portrait are to be accepted rather than any judgment of mine, since the looking glass, inverting the two sides, does not rightly show a man his own face, and since moreover it is impossible for him to see his face in the position you have chosen.

There is, however, one point in the face which strikes me, namely, the aquiline outline of the nose is somewhat too pronounced—perhaps not too pronounced for the position in which the head was placed, but too pronounced in respect of the average shape of the nose—I say " average " because the nose is not quite the same shape when seen from the two sides. . . .

The secret of it is that when a little child my nose was cut with a carving knife by a little sister. The wound did not leave a scar, so far as appears, but the result was that on one side the outline is more protuberant than on the other, and this gives from certain points of view an aquiline character, which is not manifest from other points of view.

I wish I had remembered this fact when the photograph was taken, for I should then have suggested an attitude giving a straighter outline, for I do not like the aquiline outline. Of course it is a considerable element in the character of the face. . . . If I had seen the photograph earlier I should have suggested a slight alteration. . . . However, though it is too late before the Academy exhibition (unless you can do it on varnishing day) it is not otherwise too late, and I should much like a slight rectification (in a double sense).

You have it seems to me succeeded well in an essential point, namely the expression. There is a far-off gaze appropriate to a thinker, and it is an *understanding* gaze, which of course I consider is not inappropriate. . . . Success in this respect is an essential success.

One other criticism occurs to me. Unfortunately I wore the dressing gown *over* a morning coat, and an impression was thereby given of bulkiness of body. This impression, moreover, is strengthened by the way in which the shoulder and right arm extend very much. The total effect of this large expanse of body and dress is somewhat to dwarf the head. To me the impression given is that of a small-headed man. Though my head is not at all specially large, still it is 22 inches round, and I think a spectator would guess a smaller size.

There, you see I have again illustrated my inveterate habit of fault-finding. However I suppose you would prefer to have my candid remarks rather than unmeaning applause. You may at any rate be quite content with the opinions of my friends.

The *Times* (30 April, 1898) notice of the Royal Academy Exhibition was severe on both Mr. von Herkomer and Spencer. Of the artist it was said: " Perhaps it is hardly his fault if that which ought to have been a masterpiece, . . . is very much the reverse." And of the sitter: " To get proper sittings from him was an impossibility; neither the wishes of illustrious admirers, nor thoughts of posthumous fame, nor any similar consideration, had any effect whatever."

111

To Hubert von Herkomer, R.A.

30 *April*, 1898.

I cannot allow myself to remain under the implied stigma which the *Times'* report of the Academy Exhibition contains, where I am described as practically disregarding " the wishes of " my " illustrious admirers," expressed though they were in so gratifying a manner and accompanied by their contributions. The utterly undeserved reflection upon me must be in some way dissipated. Will you do it, or must I? . . . I should of course prefer that you should rectify this misapprehension by distinctly specifying the causes and incidents, but if you decline I must do it myself.

Mr. von Herkomer being in Italy, Spencer himself wrote to the *Times* (5 May) pointing out that the art critic had been misled by rumour. " I feel obliged to make this statement out of regard for the feelings of the many distinguished friends and others who, having expressed their wishes in so gratifying a manner, would feel slighted did I let them suppose that those wishes had been so little regarded by me."

The portrait by Mr. Ouless for Mr. Carnegie had still to be painted. First one thing prevented a beginning being made, and then another. When the artist was ready, Spencer was too ill to sit; and when Spencer was well enough, the artist had other engagements. He was also worrying himself over the thought of what people would say if he sat to Mr. Ouless after having been unable to sit for Mr. von Herkomer. " Explanations could not easily be given, and even were they given would be insufficient." This difficulty disappeared in an unexpected way. After more than twelve months of fruitless attempts to arrange for sittings, he wrote to

112

HERBERT SPENCER.
From a painting by Sir Hubert von Herkomer, R.A.

Mr. Ouless that the painting must be abandoned altogether.

FROM WALTER W. OULESS, R.A.

13 *October,* 1899.

I am indeed sorry that, after all, the portrait has to be abandoned, but, besides other circumstances you mention, I recognise the difficulties for the sitter and the painter. The sittings could hardly fail to be a severe strain and fatigue for you, and, if that were so, it would be almost hopeless to make the portrait a success. Therefore, considering all things, I cannot but acquiesce in your view that the portrait must be finally given up, but I do so with very deep regret.

He wavered from time to time in his opinion of the Herkomer portrait, being influenced greatly by the judgments now favourable, now unfavourable, expressed by his friends. Several letters passed between him and Mr. von Herkomer about suggested alterations, but to no purpose. Being unwilling that the portrait should go into the National Gallery, he wrote to Mr. Sargent about a portrait on his own account; but the terms were too high. He then bethought him that the portrait by Mr. Burgess would be suitable for the National Gallery, and asked Mr. Ouless whether he could recommend an artist to make a copy of it for presentation to his native town. On Mr. Ouless's recommendation the work was entrusted to Mr. J. Hanson Walker. How far Spencer's mind was even at this late date from being settled about the Herkomer portrait is shown by a remark in January, 1901, to Dr. Charlton Bastian, who thought that it, rather than the Burgess portrait, should go to the National Portrait Gallery. " Thank you, too, for your opinion respecting the Herkomer portrait. It is probable I shall adopt it, but I will take the opinion of some other friends." [1]

[1] During the last year of his life, Mrs. Meinertzhagen induced him to allow Miss Alice Grant to paint a portrait of him mainly from the photograph he had taken for Mr. Sargent in 1898.

CHAPTER XXV

REVISION OF *BIOLOGY* AND *FIRST PRINCIPLES*

(*October*, 1895—*April*, 1900)

FOLLOWING his usual practice of looking well ahead, he had in 1895 ordered copies of the *Principles of Biology* to be interleaved and sent to young biologists, recommended as being familiar with recent developments of the science, with instructions to scrutinise the alleged facts and to see whether the inferences drawn from them were justified, leaving untouched the scheme of the work as well as its general principles. By the time the last volume of the *Sociology* was issued, each of the collaborators had gone through his assigned portion.

His interest in biological questions had been kept smouldering since 1867 when he completed the *Biology*. Now and again during these years the latent fire had burst into flame, as in the Weismann controversy. At other times it merely flickered. The revision for which he was now preparing furnished opportunities for giving expression to opinions of long standing, respecting the methods to be followed in biological enquiries and the attitude frequently adopted by scientific men towards them. Biologists chiefly were in his mind when he wrote to Dr. (now Sir) William Gowers that " the immense majority of writers in the special divisions of science have a horror of wide views, and prefer to

115

limit themselves to their details and technicalities.''
The largest share of adverse criticism was, however, re-
served for mathematicians.

To F. Howard Collins.

Brighton, 3 *December,* 1895.
[Lack of judgment] is a very common trait of mathematicians. Their habit of mind becomes such that they
are incapable of forming rational conclusions when they
have to deal with contingent evidences. . . .

I wish you would make . . . an inquiry bearing upon
the question of the limitation of heredity by sex. It occurred to me lately that this, for which there is so much
evidence, may be statistically tested by inquiries concerning longevity in families. If inquiry shows that in
a certain marriage the husband belongs to a family of
which the members on the average die earlier than usual,
while the wife belongs to a family of which on the average the members have lived to a good age or a great age,
then if there is limitation of heredity by sex, the
daughters of that marriage will be long-lived and the
sons short-lived. This is an inquiry quite practicable,
and might or might not serve to verify conclusions derived from other evidence.

5 *December.*—The mathematician in dealing with contingent matters does not go wrong in reasoning from
his premises, he goes wrong in his choice of premises.
He continually assumes that these are simple when they
are really complex—omits some of the factors. His
habit of thought is that of dealing with *few* and *quite
definite* data, and he carries that habit of thought into
regions where the data are *many* and *indefinite,* and proceeds to treat a few of them as though they were all, and
regards them as definite. Lord Kelvin has furnished
repeated illustrations of this.

116

9 *December.*—I am desirous in all cases to exclude superfluities from my environment. Multiplication of books and magazines and papers which I do not need continually annoys me. As you may perhaps remember, I shut out the presence of books by curtains, that I may be free from the sense of complexity which they yield. [This had reference to an interleaved copy of the *Biology* Mr. Collins had sent.]

It had been suggested that Mr. Darwin's house at Down should be acquired for a biological station, where questions relating to heredity might be rigorously tested by experiments carried out under the supervision, as it would seem, of a committee of the Royal Society. The first intimation Spencer had of this was from Professor Adam Sedgwick in December, 1896, and soon after it was again brought to his notice by Mr. Francis Galton.

To FRANCIS GALTON.

16 *January,* 1897.

The courses suggested seem to me impolitic. Everything is on too large a scale.

The purchase of Darwin's house seems appropriate as a matter of sentiment, but as a matter of business very inappropriate. The whole undertaking would be handicapped at the outset by heavy expenditure to little purpose. I should be disinclined to co-operate were any such imprudent step taken.

The thing should be commenced on a small scale by the few who have already interested themselves in it— say three or four acres with some cheap wooden buildings. . . .

Co-operation with breeders would I believe be futile. You could never get them to fulfil the requisite conditions, and selection would be certain to come in and vitiate the results.

117

Your last question, concerning my contribution and its applicability to the committee of the Royal Society, I do not understand. I do not know what you mean as to any action of the Royal Society. If it refers to the purchase of the Darwin house I should distinctly say No.

To G. H. DARWIN.

27 *July*, 1900.

Respecting the establishment for biological purposes . . . I agree with you that there is little hope of anything being done. . . .

I have never, however, myself approved of the project in the form originally suggested, commencing with purchase of the Down estate. I do not believe in big things to commence with, . . . But the management is, in fact, the chief difficulty—how to elect a fit governing body and how to ensure that they shall carry on their inquiries and report the results in a thoroughly unbiassed way. Nearly all the men available in respect of their biological knowledge are partisans, and if there were a balanced representation of the two sides, it is very probable that the administration would come to a deadlock. If otherwise, the verdict would be in large measure a foregone conclusion.

Direct references to the revision of the *Biology* are few. He had correspondence with Professor Marcus Hartog, on biological questions, during 1897-98. Of a note by the latter, about to appear in *Natural Science*, Spencer says (May, 1898): " At present, being unfamiliar with the set of facts to which you refer, I had some difficulty in following the statement. I may remark, however, that there may be a marked distinction between the process of multiplication of successive generations of cells and the sudden breaking up of cells in spores." It was probably this that suggested the send-

118

ing to *Natural Science* the relevant passages of a new chapter in the *Biology* on " Cell-Life and Cell-Multiplication," containing certain new interpretations of recent facts, which he thought it well to publish beforehand. Later in the year he sent to *Nature* a letter on " Stereo-Chemistry and Vitalism," and another on " Asymmetry and Vitalism," with reference to Professor Japp's address to the Chemical Section of the British Association. In the second of these letters he says that neither the physico-chemical theory nor the theory of a vital principle explains life, the ultimate nature of which is incomprehensible.

The congratulations on the completion of the Synthetic Philosophy stirred up criticism, sometimes in a fair, enquiring spirit, sometimes in a spirit hostile and captious. During December a correspondence was carried on in the *Times*.[1] Mr. Bramwell Booth having accused him of inconsistency, Spencer pointed out that his ideas, in common with other things, had undergone evolution. In a letter to Mr. Collins, Mr. Booth maintained that Spencer's fundamental changes of view " have been so frequent, and so radical, and if one may say so, so violent, that they totally differ from such gradual and natural developments as are, as you point out, common to all processes of thought."

To F. HOWARD COLLINS.

25 *January,* 1897.

Tell Mr. Booth that his contention is utterly beside the mark. My change from Theism to Agnosticism, to which I suppose he more especially refers, took place

---

[1] *Times,* 2, 8, 15, 17, 18 December, 1896.

long before the evolutionary philosophy was commenced, and long before I ever thought of writing it, and the change had nothing whatever to do with the doctrine of evolution. There has been no change whatever in that respect since 1860, when the writing of the philosophy was commenced. . . .
My change of opinion on the Land question, which is the other change on which he insists, is but remotely related to the doctrine of evolution, and even then is a change not in principle, but only in policy.

At a meeting of the Brooklyn Ethical Association, towards the end of 1896, he was said to have been largely influenced by the teachings of the Vedânta, through the writings of Sir William Jones. This he called a " wild idea," seeing that he did not even know the name Vedânta, and had never read any of Sir William Jones's writings. But " there are always some people who find that a man's ideas are not his own, but somebody else's."

When translating the last part of the *Principles of Sociology*, Dr. Cazelles had encountered an unforeseen difficulty. In § 849 M. Hanotaux, the French foreign minister, is represented as having made a statement " on the need there was for competing in political burglaries with other nations." Unable to take the responsibility of spreading this throughout France, Dr. Cazelles, who, during the thirty years he had been engaged in translating the *Synthetic Philosophy*, had retained Spencer's highest esteem, felt compelled to relinquish the work, to his own deep regret no less than to Spencer's.

To E. Cazelles.

6 *December*, 1896.
I greatly regret the decision expressed in your letter just received—regret it alike on personal grounds and

on public grounds. All things remembered, however, I do not greatly wonder that your attitude is that which you describe.

But, in the first place, let me point out to you that, in a preceding paragraph, England's dealings with native peoples in all parts of the world are condemned quite as strongly and much more elaborately. In the second place, let me point out that, if I remember rightly (I have not the book here), I speak of France " *vying* " in " political burglaries " with other civilised nations: the obvious implication being that all are chargeable with the same offence. Then, in the third place, let me point out that I have, if not in this last volume, yet in another volume (the *Study of Sociology*) used the expression " political burglary " in reference to our own doings especially; and I may add that, in characterising our invasion of Afghanistan as a " political burglary," I gave grievous offence to Lord Lytton, who was then Viceroy and to whom I was known personally. You will see, therefore, that my implied condemnation does not refer to the French more than to the other European peoples, and that I could not very well have omitted to condemn the one without injustice to the other.

The truth is that, of all the feelings I entertain concerning social affairs, my detestation of the barbarous conduct of strong peoples to weak peoples is the most intense. . . . To my thinking the nations which call themselves civilised are no better than white savages, who, with their cannon and rifles, conquer tribes of dark savages, armed with javelins and arrows, as easily as a giant thrashes a child, and who, having glorified themselves in their victories, take possession of the conquered lands and tryannise over the subject peoples. . . .

Elsewhere I have spoken of the nations of Europe as a hundred million pagans masquerading as Christians. Not unfrequently in private intercourse I have found myself trying to convert Christians to Christianity, but have invariably failed. The truth is that priests and people alike, while taking their nominal creed from the New Testament, take their real creed from Homer. Not Christ, but Achilles is their ideal. One day in the week they profess the creed of forgiveness, and six days in the week they inculcate and practice the creed of revenge. On Sunday they promise to love their neighbours as themselves, and on Monday treat with utter scorn any one who proposes to act out that promise in dealing with inferior peoples. Nay, they have even intensified the spirit of revenge inherited from barbarians. For, whereas the law between hostile tribes of savages is life for life, the law of the so-called civilised in dealing with savages is—for one life many lives. Not only do I feel perpetually angered by this hypocrisy which daily says one thing and does the opposite thing, but I also feel perpetually angered by it as being diametrically opposed to human progress; since all further advance depends on the decline of militancy and rise of industrialism. . . . But what the great mass of the civilised peoples in their dealings with the uncivilised regard as glory, I regard as shame.

I have not hesitated to offend my own countrymen by frequent expressions of the feelings thus indicated, and I do not at all hesitate to offend the French in the same way. If, however, it is a question of translation or no translation—if no one will venture to offend French susceptibilities by publishing in France the passage in question, then, I may remark, that the difficulty may be practically overcome by omitting the sentence and putting a number of asterisks in its place.[1]

To mark the completion of the *Synthetic Philosophy* the editor of the *Nineteenth Century* was desirous to have an article, and consulted Spencer as to the choice

---

[1] M. H. de Varigny undertook the translation of this Part, as well as of *Professional Institutions*.

of a writer. Spencer at first thought of Professor Masson, about whom he wrote as follows to Mr. Knowles:—

The only difficulty which I see is that which arises from our friendship, which has lasted now for five and forty years and from which some bias may naturally result, or may naturally be supposed to result. In fact, however, I think that both he and I are quite prepared to say what we think of one another's opinions and to accept expressions of dissent without the least ruffling of feeling. Indeed I am quite prepared for marked divergences from my views in some directions. He may, for instance, fitly comment on my extreme disregard of all authority (a trait without which, indeed, I should never have done what I have). Again he may say with truth that I undervalue the products of ancient thought and the products of ancient life in general. Then, too, there is the fact that I ignore utterly the personal element in history, and, indeed, show little respect for history altogether as it is ordinarily conceived.

To DAVID MASSON.

17 *January,* 1897.

The more I think of it the less I like it. It is clear to me that you would be continually hampered by the thought of saying too much or too little; and it would be disagreeable to me to have things said under either an *actual* or a *supposed bias.* All things considered, I think it would be best if you will regard the suggestion as not having been made.

The name of Alfred W. Benn has occurred to me as that of a fit man. He is entirely unknown to me, and, judging from what I have seen of his writing in the *Academy* and *Mind,* is quite competent.

The editor acquiesced in the suggestion as to Mr. Benn on condition that Spencer would look through the article when it was finished, and if satisfied, would give it a sort of formal approval, to be printed with it. This Spencer refused to do. The editor then gave way. But, when in the spring of 1899 the article was finished, he raised objections on the ground that it did not fulfil the condition of being " understanded of the people," and notwithstanding repeated remonstrances from Spencer, declined to publish it. Spencer was greatly annoyed: all the more so seeing that the proposal for an article had emanated from the editor and not from him. Had he been told at the very outset that the article must be written so that the man in the street could understand it, and that it must bear on its face some mark of his approval, Spencer would not have recommended Mr. Benn or any other person. " But then," says Mr. Benn in a letter to the present writer, " I should never have known Mr. Spencer's good opinion of me nor have had the advantage of his personal acquaintance." [1]

When informing Spencer that the article was finished Mr. Benn raised some questions that had occurred to him in the course of his writing.

To ALFRED W. BENN.

27 *March,* 1899.

The unanswerable questions you raise are, I think, further illustrations of the muddle which results when we attempt any solution of ultimate questions.

The idea of Cause is itself an entirely relative idea, and being so, is in the last resort inapplicable to the relation between phenomena and that which transcends phenomena, however needful it may seem to us to use

---

[1] Though Spencer wished to see the article published elsewhere, it has, in point of fact, never appeared.

the word in that relation. Cause in our conception has for its ultimate symbol the relation in consciousness between the sense of effort and any change which we produce by effort; and we use that subjective relation as a symbol for all objective relations of Cause, and when attempting to pass the limit, thought rushes out to form a relation between phenomena and that which transcends them, and inevitably carries with it this same conception of Cause. But inevitably it is a symbolic conception, and much as it seems needful for us to think of the Unknowable as Cause, yet clearly our conception of Cause, being in its origin subjective and symbolic, is essentially inapplicable.

But there is even a still deeper reply, namely, that the very idea of explanation is out of place. I have repeatedly, when dwelling on the matter and feeling at once the need for explanation and yet the conviction that no explanation is possible, ended in the thought that the very idea of explanation is irrelevant. For what is explanation? That, too, is a purely relative conception, which, if we analyse it, implies in every case the interpretation of a more special truth in terms of a more general truth; and the making of explanation behind explanation ends in reducing all special truths to cases of the most general truth. But now, what happens if we carry out this definition of explanation into the relation between the Knowable and the Unknowable? The explanation of that relation would be to include it along with other relations in a more general relation; but where is there a more general relation than that between the Knowable and the Unknowable? There is none. That is to say, the idea of explanation is excluded.

When the Trustees of the British Library of Political Science, connected with the London School of Economics and Political Science, requested him to present his works to the Library he not only embraced the opportunity of repeating his well-known views about Free Libraries, but took occasion to call in question the soundness of the policy pursued in the British Library of Political Science.

To W. A. S. HEWINS.

24 *March*, 1897.

From time to time I have had various applications akin to the one you make and have in all cases declined compliance. I disapprove of free libraries altogether, the British Museum Library included, believing that in the long run they are mischievous rather than beneficial; as we see clearly in the case of Municipal and local Free Libraries which, instead of being places for study, have become places for reading trashy novels, worthless papers, and learning the odds. I no more approve of Free Libraries than I approve of Free Bakeries. Food for the mind should no more be given gratis than food for the body should be given gratis. The whole scheme of public instruction, be it in Free Libraries or by State Education, is socialistic, and I am profoundly averse to socialism in every form.

Moreover, through the prospectus you send me there obviously runs the idea that political science is to be based upon an exhaustive accumulation of details of all orders, derived from all sources—parliamentary papers, reports of commissions, and all the details of administration from various countries and colonies. I hold, contrariwise, that political science is smothered in such a mass of details, the data for true conclusions being relatively broad and accessible.

The institution will be used by those who have in view the extension of State agencies. Alike from what I know of its inception and from what I now see of it, I am convinced that it will be an appliance not for the diffusion of political *science* but for the diffusion of political *quackery.*

126

When a similar request was made in 1898 on behalf of the Ruskin Hall, Oxford, he declined under a misapprehension as to the aims of the Hall. "I am profoundly averse to the teachings of Ruskin alike in social affairs in general and even to a large extent in art. I must decline doing anything that may directly or indirectly conduce to the spread of his influence."

Misconceptions with respect to isolated opinions of such a voluminous writer as Spencer were to be expected, but the general drift of his doctrines ought to have been well understood by this time.

To M. W. KEATINGE.

13 *April*, 1897.

I fear I cannot give you any dictum to serve your purpose, for my opinions are directly at variance with those you suppose.

There is a mania everywhere for uniformity; and centralised teaching of teachers is manifestly in the direction of uniformity. Throughout all organised existence variety tends to life, uniformity tends to death. Competition in methods of education is all-essential and anything that tends to diminish competition will be detrimental.

Your notion of restrictions put upon the teaching profession is absolutely at variance with the views I hold. It is trade-unionism in teaching—it is a reversion to the ancient condition of guilds. It is a limitation of individual freedom. It is part of a general *régime* which I utterly detest.

If, as you apparently indicate, raising the status of teachers and giving them better pay implies increase of taxation, general or local, then you may judge how far I approve of it when I tell you that, from my very earli-

127

est days down to the present time, I have been a persistent opponent of all State-education.

That he no longer looked upon his London house as his home may be gathered from the following.

To Miss ———.

1 *April,* 1897.

For practical purposes, as at present carried on, the establishment is much more yours than mine. During my long absences, now covering half the year, the house is occupied by the ——— family, yourselves and relatives; and when I am at home the social intercourse and the administration give the impression that 64, Avenue Road is the residence of the Misses ———, where Mr. Spencer resides when he is in town. . . .

All things considered I do not desire any longer to maintain our relations. . . . On estimating the advantages I derive from the presence of yourself and your sisters in the house, I find them but small—not by any means great enough to counterbalance the disadvantages.

Please therefore accept this letter as an intimation that the residence of yourself and your sisters with me will end on the first of July next.

A good deal of correspondence passed in May and June between him and a lady at whose house he spent rather less than a fortnight as a " paying guest." Through the medium of an advertisement what seemed like a rural paradise had been discovered. Things went on fairly well for a week, save for an occasional murmur; but within a few days he left. This experience as a " paying guest " seems to have prompted the following letter.

BIOLOGY AND FIRST PRINCIPLES REVISED

To Mrs. Lynn Linton.

15 *June,* 1897.

Let me suggest to you a work which might fitly be the crowning work of your life—a work on " Good and Bad Women."

You have rather obtained for yourself the reputation for holding a brief for men versus women, whereas I rather think the fact is that you simply aim to check that over-exaltation of women which has long been dominant, and which is receiving an éclatante illustration in a recent essay by Mrs. J. R. Green, which is commented upon in this week's *Spectator.*

The flattering of women has been, one might almost say, a chief business of poets, and women have most of them very readily accepted the incense with little qualification; and this has been so perpetual and has been so habitually accepted by men as to have caused a perverted opinion. . . .

The natures of men and women are topics of continual discussion, but entirely of random discussion, with no analysis and no collection of evidence and balancing of results.

If you entertain my proposal I should like very well by and by to make some suggestions as to modes of enquiry and modes of comparison.[1]

In July he went to Boughton Monchelsea, near Maidstone, where he stayed till September. On returning to town he took chambers in Park Place, St. James's, to be near the Athenæum, where he had not been since November of the previous year, and " to acquire by a more enjoyable life, the requisite strength for driving backwards and forwards from Avenue Road." After three days he broke down, went home to Avenue Road, and

---

[1] The suggestion apparently led to nothing. See *Life of Mrs. Lynn Linton,* p. 329.

did not again leave the house until he started for Brighton in October. Considering how little he had been in London, and how little happiness he had enjoyed there during recent years, one may wonder why he continued to keep up a house in town. The explanation lies partly in that hopefulness which always led him to anticipate a change for the better, and partly in his reluctance to sever his connection with the scene of his literary struggles and successes—with the great city in which had been kept up the closest friendships of his life. At length, however, the final step was taken. " The prospect of passing my last days monotonously in Avenue Road has become a dread to me, and I have decided that they may be passed much better here in front of the sea and with plenty of sun.'' He moved into 5, Percival Terrace, Brighton, soon after the beginning of 1898, hoping, as he wrote to Mr. Lecky, that his London friends would use his house as an hotel, so that he might see them as often as possible. His first concern was to get two ladies to complete his small domestic circle, musical ability being an essential qualification in one of them. His advertisement for either two sisters, or a mother and daughter, resulted in adding one more to the list of coincidences mentioned in the *Autobiography* (i., 384, 526; ii., 424). Two orphaned sisters of the name of D——— replied to his advertisement. Previously to this Mrs. Briton Rivière had recommended two sisters, also named D———; and he naturally concluded that the ladies who had answered his advertisement were the same as those recommended by Mrs. Rivière. " I should fear that these young ladies being orphans may have tended rather to the melancholy than to the joyous.'' Mrs.

Rivière then informed him that the ladies she had recommended were not orphans, both their parents being alive.

To Mrs. Rivière.

29 *January,* 1898.

In reply to a recent advertisement there came a letter from certain two Misses D—— proposing to accept the position I offered. Remembering that you had recommended certain two Misses D——, the conclusion was drawn without hesitation that they were the same two. It turns out to be otherwise. The two who replied to my advertisement are daughters of a stockbroker and are orphans. The name is by no means common. Who would have supposed that there should be bearing that name two pairs of sisters both wishing to undertake similar positions? The thing would be considered in a fiction as absolutely incredible.

Throughout 1898, and well into the spring of 1899, his domestic circle underwent many changes, owing partly to his wanting " a combination of qualities which is not very common," as several of his friends told him. With the help of Mrs. Charlton Bastian he was fortunate in the spring of 1899 in meeting with Miss Key, a skilled musician, whom he engaged for the special duty of playing the piano, which he liked to hear played several times a day; the piece he wished to be played being usually selected by himself. A month or two later Miss Killick took over the duties of housekeeper. These two ladies remained with him till his death, contributing in no small degree by their thoughtfulness and sympathy to the comfort and happiness of his closing years.

During the year 1898 he had on more than one occasion to clear up " misrepresentations." One of these was contained in a paragraph in *Literature* for January, announcing that a forthcoming work by Mr. W. H. Mallock would point out " how Mr. Spencer embodies and gives fresh life to the fundamental error of contemporary ' advanced ' thinkers in defining the social aggregate as a body ' composed of approximately equal units.' '' Spencer was at a loss to know where Mr. Mallock had found " a passage authorising this representation.''

To W. H. Mallock.

30 *January,* 1898.

After much seeking I have discovered one of the passages to which you refer, but it seems to me that its context affords no justification for the way in which you interpret it. It is a passage on p. 5 of the *Principles of Sociology,* in which, as a preliminary, the social aggregate formed by social insects is distinguished from a human society, because it is in reality a large family and because it is " not a union among like individuals substantially independent of one another in parentage, and approximately equal in their capacities.'' If here there is an implied conception of a human society, the interpretation of the words is to be taken in connexion with the contra-distinguished society: the words used should be understood in the light of this distinction. A society of ants, for example, consists of several classes —perfect males and females, workers, soldiers—and these classes differ from one another very greatly in their structures and concomitant capacities. Obviously the intention is to distinguish the *markedly unequal* capacities possessed by units of a society like this and the *approximately equal* capacities of the units forming a human society; and surely it is undeniable that, in contrast with these enormous differences in capacity among the classes of ants, the differences in capacity among

132

human beings become relatively small; *as compared* with the extremely unlike capacities of queens, males, soldiers and workers among ants, the capacities of human beings may fitly be called " approximately equal." I should have thought that it was clear that only when drawing this contrast was the expression " approximately equal " used, and that the word " approximately " is in that relation quite justifiable.

That your interpretation is unwarranted is clearly enough indicated by passages in the *Study of Sociology* accompanying those you refer to, and is quite definitely excluded by large parts of the *Principles of Sociology*. In the *Study of Sociology*, in the chapter entitled " The Nature of the Social Science " . . . [the exposition] sufficiently implies recognition of the effects of superiority and inferiority among the units, for how can there be established the differences referred to unless because the more powerful and more intelligent rise to the top? So that even here your interpretation is tacitly negatived; and then if you will turn to the *Principles of Sociology*, Part V., treating of " Political Institutions," you will find an elaborate exposition still more rigorously excluding it. . . .

So too in the *Principles of Ethics* you will see, in the division entitled " Justice," a variously-emphasised assertion that superiority must be allowed to bring to its possessor all the naturally-resulting benefits, and inferiority the naturally-resulting evils. Moreover, you will find condemnation of the socialistic ideal, with which, apparently, your representation indicated in *Literature* implies my sympathy.

Apparently this did not convince Mr. Mallock, who thought the great man theory " shows itself only accidentally and incidentally, in the body of your work. I am well aware that your sympathies are not with the Socialists; but I confess that I think your method of merging the great man in the aggregate of conditions that have produced him, has furnished socialistic theorists with many of their weapons.'' He returned to the charge in the *Nineteenth Century* for August; maintaining that in the non-recognition of '' the inequality of individuals as a cardinal social fact '' '' we have the secret of Mr. Spencer's defect as a sociologist. This great fact of human inequality, instead of being systematically studied by him, is systematically and ostentatiously ignored by him.'' To these criticisms Spencer replied in the same review the month following.

Another '' misrepresentation '' had reference to the doctrine of animism, *Literature* representing him as an adherent. This he repudiated, in the issue of February 5, showing how in the Data of Sociology '' instead of accepting the doctrine of animism, I have not only avowedly rejected it, but have, throughout the successive parts of a long argument, supplied what I conceive to be direct and indirect disproofs of it.'' In the same periodical (19 February), he endeavoured to remove the perplexity in which Mr. Andrew Lang was involved in *The Making of Religion*. Under the name of Animism or Fetichism '' there is an alleged primordial tendency in the human mind to conceive inanimate things as animated—as having animating principles or spirits. The essential question is: has the primitive man an innate tendency thus to conceive things around? Professor Tylor says Yes; I say No. I do not think it requires any ' revised terminology ' to make this difference clear.'' The matter had to be taken up again in July. The *Spectator* had classed him as one of those who believed that superstitious ideas arose from '' the universal con-

134

viction or feeling that all things in Nature are endowed with the sentient vitality and the unruly affections of mankind." " I entertain no such belief," he wrote to the editor. " This ascription to me . . . of a belief which I have emphatically rejected, is one of many examples showing me how impossible it is to exclude misunderstanding."

The war between the United States and Spain was weighing heavily on the consciences of many thoughtful Americans, among whom was Mr. Moncure Conway, who asked Spencer whether it would not be possible to form a concert of eminent men, who, whenever a peril of war arose, should meet as a " supreme court of civilization " and determine the right and wrong, before any declaration of war took place.

To Moncure D. Conway.

17 *July,* 1898.

I sympathise in your feelings and your aims, but not in your hopes. . . . In people's present mood nothing can be done in that direction.

Now that the white savages of Europe are overrunning the dark savages everywhere—now that the European nations are vying with one another in political burglaries—now that we have entered upon an era of social cannibalism in which the strong nations are devouring the weaker—now that national interests, national prestige, pluck, and so forth are alone thought of, and equity has utterly dropped out of thought, while rectitude is scorned as " unctuous," it is useless to resist the wave of barbarism. There is a bad time coming, and civilised mankind will (morally) be uncivilised before civilisation can again advance.

Such a body as that which you propose, even could its

members agree, would be pooh-poohed as sentimental and visionary. The universal aggressiveness and universal culture of blood-thirst will bring back military despotism, out of which after many generations partial freedom may again emerge.

The reader will remember how, when the Anti-Aggression excitement was on him in 1882, he had endeavoured to induce Miss Bevington to put the indignation he felt into verse. The idea occurred to him again this year.

To WILFRID SCAWEN BLUNT.

1 *October*, 1898.

For some years I have been casting about for a poet who might fitly undertake a subject I very much want to see efficiently dealt with. At one time I thought of proposing it to Mr. Robert Buchanan, who in respect of vigour of expression and strength of moral indignation seemed appropriate, but I concluded that the general feeling with regard to him would prevent a favourable reception—would in fact tend very much to cancel the effect to be produced. Afterwards the name of Mr. William Watson occurred to me as one who had shown feelings of the kind I wished to see expressed. But, admirable as much of his poetry is, the element of power is not marked: he does not display a due amount of burning sarcasm. Your recent letter in the *Times*, and since then a review in the *Academy* in which there were quotations from your poem " The Wind and the Whirlwind," lead me to hope that you may work out the idea I refer to.

This idea is suggested by the first part of Goethe's " Faust "—The Prologue in Heaven, I think it is called. In this, if I remember rightly (it is now some 50 years since I read it), Mephistopheles obtains permission to tempt Faust—the drama being thereupon initiated. Instead of this I suggest an interview and dialogue in

136

which Satan seeks authority to find some being more wicked than himself, with the understanding that, if he succeeds, this being shall take his place. The test of wickedness is to be the degree of disloyalty—the degree of rebellion against divine government.

6 *October.*—Thank you for your letter. I am heartily glad to find you entertain my suggestion. . . .

My beliefs are pretty much as pessimistic as those you express—in respect at least of the approaching condition of mankind; but holding though I do that we are commencing a long course of re-barbarisation from which the reaction may take very long in coming, I nevertheless hold that a reaction will come, and look forward with hope to a remote future of a desirable kind, to be reached after numerous movements of progress and retrogression. Did I think that men were likely to remain in the far future anything like what they now are, I should contemplate with equanimity the sweeping away of the whole race.

5 *November.*—How to put the greatest amount of feeling and idea in the shortest space is the problem to be solved by every writer, more especially by the poet, for rightly conceived (not as by Browning) poetry is a vehicle in which the friction is reduced to a minimum, and of course everything which is superfluous adds to the friction. I have often thought that nearly all our poets would have greatly benefited by restriction to one-fourth the space. Works of art in general would in nearly all cases profit by restraint. Much architecture and much internal decoration is spoiled by excess, and nearly every painter puts too much into his pictures. Composers, too, even the highest of them, as Beethoven, often spoil their works by needless expansion. To the artist each new idea seems so good that he cannot make up his mind to leave it out, and so more or less sacrifices the effect of the whole to the effect of the part.

Before the appearance of *Satan Absolved*—the title chosen for his poem by Mr. Scawen Blunt—Spencer wrote:—

To WILFRID SCAWEN BLUNT.

23 *June,* 1899.

I rejoice to hear that the poem is finished, and that its publication is not far off.

Of course I feel honoured by your proposal to preface some words of dedication to me, and accept with pleasure. Please do not, however, in any introductory words, indicate the origin of the idea which the poem elaborates. You will perhaps be surprised by this request until you understand my reason.

Already my general views, touching as they do in many places upon religious opinions, have from time to time exposed me to vilification both here and in America, and have, in consequence, raised impediments to the wider diffusion of the general philosophical views which I have set forth, and have in various ways diminished both the circulation and the influence of the books. Such being the case I do not want to again rouse, even more strongly than hitherto, the *odium theologicum* and to give it a further handle for attacks, not only upon my declared religious opinions, but also upon the system of thought associated with them, but which is in reality independent of them. It is this contemplation not of the personal, but of the impersonal effects, which makes me wish not to arouse still greater antagonism than I have already done. A further obstacle to the spread of evolutionary views would, I think, be a greater evil than any benefit to be gained.

On receiving a copy of the poem, he wrote in haste to beg Mr. Blunt to omit a passage on the first page. The description of the ante-chamber of heaven " savours too much of the earth earthy, . . . and puts the poem in too low a key.''

To WILFRID SCAWEN BLUNT.

28 *October,* 1899.

Let me first apologise for my brusquely-expressed letter written immediately on receipt of *Satan Absolved.* . . .

I did not at first recognise the fact that, by calling the poem a '' Victorian Mystery,'' you intended to suggest some analogy to the mysteries of Medieval days, and that you had adopted a mode of treatment implied by this analogy. Hence that assimilation of the divine and the human, which characterised the mystery-plays, had not been understood by me as sequent upon the adoption of the earlier mode of thought, and as a result gave me a sense of incongruity. Though I now see that the adoption of this ancient mode of thought gives consistency to the work, yet it seems to me that we (or at least cultured people) have so far travelled away from that mode of thought that the revival of it will be apt to excite in many readers an internal protest.

My chief difficulty, however, in forming a judgment arises, as I now see, from the wide difference between the general conception as embodied by you and the conception which I had myself formed and suggested. . . .

This much, however, I can say with all sincerity—that I like it much better on a second reading than on the first; and this I think is a marked evidence of its goodness. Unquestionably, Satan's description of Man and his doings is given with great power, and ought to bring to their senses millions of hypocrites who profess the current religion. I wish you would emphasise more strongly the gigantic lie daily enacted—the contrast between the Christian professions and the pagan actions, and the perpetual insult to one they call Omniscient in thinking that they can compound for atrocious deeds by laudatory words.

139

During the winter of 1898-99 he wrote two postscripts to Part VII. of the *Psychology:* one on Idealism and Realism; the other in reply to a criticism of the late Professor Green, whose article in the *Contemporary Review* for December, 1877, had recently been republished.[1] In addition to these he wrote a chapter on " The Filiation of Ideas," which he stereotyped and put away for future use.[2] A renewed attempt to introduce the metric system suggested the expediency of issuing a second edition of the brochure, " Against the Metric System," and again distributing it among members of Parliament. Under the name " A Citizen " he wrote to the *Times* four letters, which were included in the pamphlet.

With all his disregard for public opinion as far as concerned his philosophical doctrines—notwithstanding the indifference or even satisfaction with which he contemplated the shocks he occasionally gave to current orthodoxy, whether scientific or religious—he was extremely sensitive to criticism of his character, and had a rooted dislike to his private life and conversation being treated as public property. He assumed that those who enjoyed the privilege of his intimacy would respect the unwritten law of private intercourse by scrupulously refraining from making public the trivial no less than the important matters of his daily life. Himself taking little interest in personalities and gossip, he never dreamt that unpremeditated remarks made in the hearing of those living under the same roof, might be published abroad, or that the petty details of domestic life might have their pettiness intensified by being taken

---

[1] *Principles of Psychology*, ii., 505 ξ-505 π.
[2] Reprinted in this volume as Appendix B.

out of their appropriate setting and held up as a public spectacle. He had a rude awakening in the spring of 1899. Soon after the announcement of his forthcoming book on Spencer, Mr. Hector Macpherson received from a lady quite unknown to him, an offer of '' Reminiscences of Herbert Spencer.'' She and her father had lived at 38, Queen's Gardens during part of the time Spencer was there, and had been in the habit of taking notes of Spencer's sayings and doings, and these notes she now offered for ten guineas, adding that if they were not accepted she could readily find a publisher later on. On hearing of this, and on the advice of his solicitors that he had no power to stop the publication of statements concerning himself, he requested Mr. Macpherson to offer ten guineas for the MS., provided the lady would undertake not to publish any other version of the reminiscences. A legal minute of agreement and sale was drawn up and signed, and in due course Spencer obtained possession of the manuscript.

To Hector Macpherson.

25 *April,* 1899.

You bargained better than you knew. There are many absolutely false statements—false to the extent of absurdity. Here is a quotation:—'' Often (!) invited to dine at Marlborough House, but would never go.'' Imagine the Prince of Wales often repeating his invitations after being declined! The statement is absolutely baseless. Another statement is:—'' Gladstone very often came to breakfast, but this was before the Home Rule affair; also George Eliot, Darwin, Tyndall.'' Again absolutely false. With no one of the four did I ever exchange breakfast civilities save Mr. Gladstone, and instead of his often breakfasting with me I some

141

three or four times breakfasted with him. . . . Some of
Mr. ——'s quotations from his diary are, however, of a
libellous kind.

Spencer's first idea had been that the lady should be
informed by the firm of lawyers who had the matter in
hand that the publication of these reminiscences would
render her liable to prosecution. But in the end he
took a view of the matter which it seems a pity he did
not take at the outset—to treat the proposed publication
with indifference, seeing that it contained its own anti-
dote.

The health of Mr. Grant Allen was giving Spencer
much concern, his sympathies as usual leading him to
try to trace the evil to its source. A visit of some duration from his friend afforded opportunities for earnest
entreaties. These were afterwards enforced by appeals
to Mr. Grant Allen's scientific knowledge.

To Grant Allen.

BRIGHTON, 2 *June,* 1899.
I am glad to hear that your wife thinks that you have
profited by your stay here. I hope that the corner may
be by-and-by turned completely.
That it may be turned completely it is clear that you
must improve your mastication. . . . If I had to teach
children I should give them among other things a lesson
on the importance of mastication, and should illustrate
it by taking a small iron nail and weighing against it
some pinches of iron filings till the two balanced; then,
putting them into two glasses, pouring into each a quantity of dilute sulphuric acid, leaving them to stir the
two from time to time, and showing them that whereas
the iron filings quickly dissolve, the dissolving of the
nail would be a business of something like a week. This

142

would impress on them the importance of reducing food to small fragments. That you, a scientific man, should not recognise this is to me astonishing.[1]

When Mr. Grant Allen died in October following, Spencer lost one of his ablest and most chivalrous allies. Writing in June, 1900, to Mr. Edward Clodd on receiving a copy of the *Memoir,* he said:

> I was often surprised by his versatility, but now that the facts are brought together, it is clear to me that I was not sufficiently surprised. One of the traits on which I should myself have commented had I written about him was his immense quickness of perception. He well deserved this biography.

The correspondence that follows with Mr. (afterwards Sir) Leslie Stephen regarding the formation of an Ethical Lecturers Fund has an interest apart from its immediate purpose. It throws light upon the question how, with his professed dislike to reading, he was able to amass the immense amount of information contained in his earlier books. This profusion of exemplification and illustration seems inconsistent with his own repeated statements that he was constitutionally, and as a matter of fact, idle—that he was an impatient reader, and actually read little. In one of the following letters to Mr. Leslie Stephen he says that when preparing to write he read up in those directions in which he expected to find materials for his own generalisations, not caring for the generalisations of others. Under the guidance of a generalisation he picked out the relevant material,

---

[1] Mastication formed the subject of a brief essay he began to dictate a few weeks before his death, but did not finish.

ignoring the irrelevant; as a lawyer restricts his reading in preparing his brief. That he lost by this restricted reading cannot be doubted. It gave colour to the not ill-natured remark of one of his friends: " Scratch Spencer, and you come upon ignorance.'' But, taking all in all, it may be said that what he lost through lack of diligence in acquisition he made up for, or more than made up for, by the continuous exercise of his wonderful gift of organisation. If the word industrious can be so applied, then, as a thinker Spencer was pre-eminently industrious, his mind was incessantly occupied with the logical relations of things. It was the firm grasp he had of these logical relations that enabled him to retain complete mastery over the details, marshalling them at his bidding; giving, perhaps, also the impression of having unfathomable sources of information from which to draw. His literary industry was untiring. Not only were his published writings voluminous, but his correspondence was very great. The limit imposed on the writer of this volume has rendered it impossible to reproduce more than a small fraction of his letters.

To Leslie Stephen.

28 *June*, 1899.

When I received the circular asking for aid in raising the Ethical Lecturers Fund 1 at once decided to contribute. On re-reading the prospectus, however, I was brought to a pause by the paragraph requiring a University Honours degree as the minimum intellectual equipment. If John Mill had been alive and a young man, his candidature would have been negatived by this requirement. And were I a young man and proposed to adopt the career of ethical lecturer, my candidature also would be negatived.

30 *June.*—The expression which you underline does not seem to me to change the essential meaning of the passage I referred to. It implies that there shall be a standard of education substantially like that which a university gives.

I do not know what might have been the case with Mill. I can only say that were I young and a candidate, the regulation would rigorously exclude me. Not only could I have shown no education equivalent to a university honours degree, but I could have shown none equivalent to the lowest degree a university gives. . . .

Naturally, such being my position, I demur to the test specified. Moreover, not on personal grounds only, but on general grounds, I demur to the assumption that a university career implies a fit preparation.

FROM LESLIE STEPHEN.

1 *July,* 1899.

You say that when you were young you could not have shown an education " equivalent to the lowest degree a university gives.'' It is not for me to dispute that statement. I am, however, sure that when you first published books upon ethical questions, you had somehow or other attained an amount of knowledge upon such topics very much superior to that of the average " honour man,'' who satisfies the examiners in his department of study. . . . We never thought of suggesting that candidates should have passed any particular course, but that their general hold of intellectual culture should be equal to that implied by capacity to fulfil the ordinary conditions of university success.

TO LESLIE STEPHEN.

2 *July,* 1899.

Your assumption is a very natural one, but it is utterly mistaken. When *Social Statics* was written I had none of that preparation which you suppose.

145

When with my uncle, from thirteen to sixteen, my acquirements were limited to Euclid, algebra, trigonometry, mechanics, and the first part of Newton's Principia. To this equipment I never added. During my eight years of engineering life I read next to nothing— even of professional literature. Then as always, I was an impatient reader and read nothing continuously except novels and travels, and of these but little. I am in fact constitutionally idle. I doubt whether during all these years I ever read any serious book for an hour at a stretch. You may judge of my condition with regard to knowledge from the fact that during all my life up to the time *Social Statics* was written, there had been a copy of Locke on my father's shelves which I never read—I am not certain that I ever took it down. And the same holds of all other books of philosophical kinds. I never read any of Bacon's writings, save his essays. I never looked into Hobbes until, when writing the essay on '' The Social Organism,'' I wanted to see the details of his grotesque conception. It was the same with Politics and with Ethics. At the time *Social Statics* was written I knew of Paley nothing more than that he enunciated the doctrine of expediency; and of Bentham I knew only that he was the promulgator of the Greatest Happiness principle. The doctrines of other ethical writers referred to were known by me only through references to them here and there met with. I never then looked into any of their books; and, moreover, I have never since looked into any of their books. When about twenty-three I happened to get hold of Mill's *Logic,* then recently published, and read with approval his criticism of the Syllogism. When twenty-four I met with a translation of Kant and read the first few pages. Forthwith,. rejecting his doctrine of Time and Space, I read no further. My ignorance of ancient philosophical writers was absolute. After *Social Statics* was published (in 1851) I made the acquaintance of Mr. Lewes, and one result was that I read his *Biographical*

146

History of Philosophy. . . . And, shortly after that (in 1852), a present of Mill's *Logic* having been made to me by George Eliot, I read that through: one result being that I made an attack upon one of his doctrines in the *Westminster*.

Since those days I have done nothing worth mentioning to fill up the implied deficiencies. Twice or thrice I have taken up Plato's *Dialogues* and have quickly put them down with more or less irritation. And of Aristotle I know even less than of Plato.[1]

If you ask how there comes such an amount of incorporated fact as is found in *Social Statics,* my reply is that when preparing to write it I read up in those directions in which I expected to find materials for generalisation. I did not trouble myself with the generalisations of others.

And that indeed indicates my general attitude. All along I have looked at things through my own eyes and not through the eyes of others. I believe that it is in some measure because I have gone direct to Nature, and have escaped the warping influences of traditional beliefs, that I have reached the views I have reached. . . .

My own course—not intentionally pursued, but spontaneously pursued—may be characterised as little reading and much thinking, and thinking about facts learned at first hand. Perhaps I should add, that my interest all along has been mainly in the science of Life, physical, mental and social. I hold that the study of the science of Life under all its aspects is the true preparation for a teacher of Ethics. And it must be the science of Life as it is conceived now, and not as it was conceived in past times.

If you ask me what test you are to establish, I cannot answer. I simply raise the question—Is it necessary to establish any test? May not the choice be de-

---

[1] In a letter to Prof. Brough, of Aberystwith, in 1895, he said, "I never at any time paid the least attention to formal logic, and hold that for all practical purposes it is useless."

cided by the evidence furnished in each case apart from any specified standard?

While he was at Oakhurst, South Godstone, in July, Mrs. Leonard Courtney sent him an account of visits she had had from two of his admirers—Mr. Hector Macpherson and the Chinese Ambassador, Sir Chih Chen Lo Feng-Luh, whom he had entertained at lunch in June. "Of course," he replied, "I am interested in your account of Mr. Macpherson and the Chinese Ambassador. The latter's opinion that I am a resurrected Confucius is amusing, as is also his opinion that I ought to be a Duke." Writing late in the year to another friend— Mr. Carnegie—acknowledging a present of grouse, he remarks:—

Doubtless it is one of the advantages of being a highland laird that you can thus give gratifications to your friends; but I can quite believe, as you hint in your last letter, that along with advantages there are increasing responsibilities. It is not only true, as Bacon says, that when a man marries he gives hostages to fortune, but it is also true that he does this when he increases his belongings of every kind.

The letter that follows, written to a lady in Geneva, contains nothing with which the reader is not familiar. But, besides putting the evils of governmental interference and control very clearly, it bears witness to Spencer's life-long consistency with regard to fundamental opinions. It was translated into French and German and read at a Congress in Switzerland.

BIOLOGY AND FIRST PRINCIPLES REVISED

To Mrs. Josephine Butler.

3 *September,* 1899.

I learn with pleasure that you and some others are opposing the adoption of coercive methods for achieving moral ends.

Briefly stated my own views on such matters are these:—

Nearly all thinking about political and social affairs is vitiated by ignoring all effects save those immediately contemplated. Men, anxious to stop an evil or obtain a good, do not consider what will be the collateral results of the governmental agencies they employ, or what will be the remote results. They do not recognise the fact that every new instrumentality established for controlling individual conduct becomes a precedent for other such instrumentalities, and that year after year philanthropists with new aims urge on further coercive agencies, and that so little by little they establish a type of social organisation—a type which no one of them contemplated when he was urging on his particular plan.

The highest aim ever to be kept in view by legislators and those who seek for legislation is the formation of character. Citizens of a high type are self-regulating, and citizens who have to be regulated by external force are manifestly of a low type. Men, like all other creatures, are ever being moulded into harmony with their conditions. If, generation after generation, their conduct in all its details is prescribed for them, they will more and more need official control in all things. . . .

The final outcome of the policy in favour with philanthropists and legislators is a form of society like that which existed in ancient Peru, where every tenth man was an official controlling the other nine; where the regulation went to the extreme of inspecting every household to see that it was well administered, the furniture in good order, and the children properly managed; and where the effect of this universal regulation of conduct

149

was the production of a character such that the enfeebled society went down like a house of cards before a handful of Spaniards.

On completing the revision of the *Principles of Biology* towards the end of 1899, he at once took in hand the preparation of a final edition of *First Principles.* Owing to the number and importance of the alterations, he was desirous that the existing translations should be replaced as soon as possible by translations of this final edition. When the German version was completed, Professor Victor Carus wrote: " And now once more, allow me to repeat my most cordial thanks that you allowed me to translate your work anew. It was a very great treat to me." Below this Spencer has written: " This is the highest compliment I ever received, considering Professor Carus's age and position." It was with no ordinary satisfaction that, towards the end of his eightieth year, he gave the finishing touches to the system of philosophy, on which he had been engaged for forty years. His gratification was enhanced by the cordial greetings from all parts of the world which poured in upon him on his birthday—greetings which he acknowledged in a circular written by his own hand and lithographed:—

Letters and telegrams, conveying the congratulations and good wishes of known and unknown friends, have reached me yesterday and to-day in such numbers that, even were I in good health it would scarcely be practicable to write separate acknowledgments. I must therefore ask you, in common with others, kindly to accept this general letter which, while expressing my thanks to those who have manifested their sympathy, also expresses my great pleasure in receiving so many marks of it from my own countrymen and from men of other nationalities.

No one will deny that Spencer was entitled to look forward to the enjoyment of undisturbed serenity now that the task, for which he had sacrificed so much, was completed. But, ere the work of revision had been fully accomplished, events were taking place that were to cause him anxiety and vexation during the remaining years of his life. Some time before the outbreak of hostilities in South Africa he had denounced the policy that was drifting the country into war. Whatever one's opinion may be as to the right or the wrong of the war, one must admit that Spencer's attitude towards it was in complete harmony with the principles he had throughout life professed. He was invited to sign a protest.

To James Sully.

10 *December,* 1899.

Who are the " we "? I should not like to give my name in such a case without being made aware with whose names mine would be joined.

Further, I think that the protest is not sufficiently strong, and not sufficiently concise. . . . Among the facts which should be emphasised are (1) that the outlanders were a swarm of unwelcome intruders and had no right to complain of the social régime into which they intruded themselves, since nobody asked them to stay if they did not like it. (2) They were proved traitors trying to overturn the government which gave them hospitality, and, as Lord Loch's evidence shows, were long contemplating a rising and a seizure of the government of the country. Traitors cannot put in a claim to political power. (3) The Boers have done no more

151

than would inevitably have been done by ourselves if similarly placed, and in doing which we should have regarded ourselves as patriotic and highly praiseworthy. (4) The advocacy of annexation is nothing more than a continuance of our practice of political burglary. (5) We are rightly vituperated by other nations, as we should vituperate any one of them who did similar things, and as we are now vituperating Russia, for its policy in Finland, carried out in a much milder manner.[1]

TO MARK JUDGE.

2 January, 1900.

During the last week I have been in communication with the Secretary of the Anti-Vaccination League, and also with the Chairman of the South African Conciliation Committee, and this morning I have a request from the Editor of the <i>Speaker</i> to express my sympathy with the course which they are pursuing. In all these cases I am making a favourable response.

I am now nearly eighty, and it is more and more clear to me that I must cut myself off from these various distractions as much as possible for I have still something I want to do, and thinking this, I decide it will be better for me to decline taking any part in this League for Licensing Reform, even in the position of Vice-President. . . . I wish you success in your efforts.

While approving of the attitude of the <i>Speaker</i> towards the war, he declined to become a regular subscriber because its political views were " distinctly socialistic or collectivist, if you choose so to call them, and much as I abhor war I abhor socialism in all its forms quite as much." On 5 February the <i>Morning Leader</i>

---

[1] Spencer was one of the signatories of the memorial to the Czar on behalf of the people of Finland, which His Majesty declined to receive.

152

had a letter from him protesting against the spirit shown by those who shouted to the departing troops: " Remember Majuba."

To SIR EDWARD FRY.

6 *February*, 1900.

Popular passion, excited by political and financial agencies, has gagged all but one of those morning papers which expressed opposition to our war policy in South Africa. The *Morning Leader* is the only one that remains to give voice to those who reprobate the war and desire that the two republics shall maintain their independence. You will see by a copy of the paper, which you have by this time received, that, by the expression of sympathetic opinions, efforts are being made to support this organ of views properly to be called Christian, in opposition to the views of those properly to be called Pagan.

It is not to be expected that much can be done towards checking the war fever, but it may be hoped that by spreading so far as may be sympathy with equitable sentiments and reprobating those who sneer at " unctuous rectitude," something may be done towards preparing the way for a settlement not so utterly inequitable as is now threatened.

Could you help by adding some expression of your opinion to the expressions of opinions already published?

A similar letter was sent to Dr. Edward Caird, Master of Balliol College, Oxford.

To THE RIGHT HON. LEONARD COURTNEY.

24 *February*, 1900.

I daresay you will think me rather absurd in making a suggestion respecting your attitude towards your constituents.

There has grown up the altogether unwarrantable assumption that a man represents that particular part of the constituency which has elected him, and when that part of the constituency—some Conservative or Liberal Association, or what not—through whose instrumentality he was elected disapproves of his course, it seems to be thought by them, and by the public at large, that he is thereupon called upon to resign. But where is there any indication, either in the constitution or in the theory of representation, that a member of parliament represents any particular section of his constituency, any party? So far as I know, the idea of party is not recognised in the representative system at all. A member of parliament represents the constituency and the whole constituency, and not any particular section of it. . . . Hence it results that, if any Liberal or Conservative Association, or any other kind of caucus, calls upon him in a case like the present, to resign, his fit reply may be that as a representative of the whole constituency he cannot even *entertain* the proposition to resign, until it is shown to him that a majority of the whole constituency wishes him to do so.

I do not know that in your case the assumption of such an attitude would be of any advantage, since, probably, the remainder of the constituency is more against you than the part which elected you. Still, I suggest this as a general course of conduct applicable to all cases.

CHAPTER XXVI

INORGANIC EVOLUTION

In the preceding chapters little has been said as to the application of evolution to inorganic Nature. This division was passed over in Spencer's programme "partly because, even without it, the scheme is too extensive; and partly because the interpretation of organic Nature . . . is of more immediate importance." While most will admit the cogency of these two reasons, many, after reading the earlier volumes of the series, will agree with Mr. J. S. Mill in desiring to see the working out of the principles of evolution in the omitted division of the programme. Some may even think, with Dr. David Sharp, of Cambridge, that the application of evolution to inorganic Nature was of more importance than the attempt to upset Professor Weismann's theory. Be this as it may, it would be a very perverse judgment that would regard the absence of this division as telling against Spencer's work as a whole. Objection may be made if a writer fails to accomplish what he undertook to do. But, it can hardly be urged against the value of what he has accomplished that he has not done something which, for sufficient reasons, he announced at the outset he did not propose to undertake. To discredit Spencer's teaching, as has been done, now because he attempted too much, and now because he did not attempt more, does not help those who honestly wish to arrive at a just estimate of it.

155

It is, however, a mistake to assume that Spencer did not apply the principles of evolution to inorganic Nature. Not only was the subject frequently in his thoughts throughout the thirty-six years when he was writing the *Synthetic Philosophy;* but even before his programme was issued he had made two important excursions into inorganic Nature—excursions that had no small share in suggesting and developing his system of thought. The purpose of this chapter is to gather together the correspondence bearing upon evolution in its application to the inorganic world. In this way a better idea will be gained of what Spencer accomplished in this domain, than if the subject had been dealt with incidentally, and in piece-meal fashion, in the course of the narrative.

The scientific topics (other than professional ones) that first and chiefly interested Spencer, during the earlier engineering period, were Astronomy and Geology—the two departments of knowledge which, when he issued his programme in 1860, he decided to pass over, or not to treat in detail. Letters to his father during the years 1838 to 1841 contain frequent discussions of astronomical questions. Geology was taken up seriously in 1840, and, during the years he was engaged on railway surveys, he had many opportunities of acquainting himself with it at first hand. Speculation as to the change in the Earth's atmosphere consequent on the abstraction from it of carbon during the deposition of carboniferous strata, took shape in 1843-44 in a paper in the *Philosophical Magazine.*[1] In the same periodical for 1847 he had a paper on " The Form of the Earth no

---

[1] *Autobiography,* i., 624.

proof of original Fluidity."[1] A theory about nebulous matter was being worked out by the middle of 1851. He had written to Sir John Herschel and Professor Airy, inquiring " whether it had been shewn why nebulous matter must take up a rotatory motion in condensing." Their replies, so he told his father, show " that my idea is new, so I think I have made a discovery worth publishing. I shall write a paper for the *Philosophical Magazine*." He was in no hurry, however, to rush into print; for, though he told his parents in 1852 that he hoped to complete it shortly, it was laid aside for several years, owing to the writing of the *Principles of Psychology*, and subsequent ill-health. But by the spring of 1858 it began to assume a definite shape.

TO HIS FATHER.

May, 1858.

The Nebular Hypothesis works out beautifully. The article will contain a great deal that is new, and will, I think, render the argument conclusive. I have had a long talk with Dr. Tyndall on the sundry novelties, which were based upon principles in physics. *He endorses all my conclusions:* though not prepared wholly to commit himself to them, he thinks them rigorously reasoned, and well worth promulgating.

Some months after the publication of the article[2] he mentions that it " had been very favourably received everywhere. It was ascribed to Baden Powell." The early part of 1859 was taken up with a paper for the *Universal Review*, under the title " Illogical Geology."[3]

---

[1] *Autobiography*, i., 360, 641.
[2] *Autobiography*, ii., 25.   [3] *Autobiography*, ii., 50.

As the primary purpose of " The Nebular Hypothesis " was to prove that the inferences drawn from the revelations of Lord Rosse's telescope were illegitimate, so that of " Illogical Geology " was to direct attention to the inconsistency of the reasonings of geologists. The writing of these two articles, which touched upon the two divisions of Inorganic Evolution as he conceived it, played an important part in the evolution of the scheme of philosophy, which had gradually been growing in extent and definiteness. In the outline sketched during the early days of 1858, the first volume is represented as including, after Parts I. and II., dealing respectively with " The Knowable " and " The Unknowable," Part III., Astronomic Evolution, and Part IV., Geologic Evolution.

Another outline of this first volume, of what he calls the *Deductive Philosophy*, presents the contents of Parts III. and IV. with more detail.

Part III.   The Principles of Astrogeny.
   Chap.   I.   Primitive Cosmogonies.
      "   II.   A Priori Probabilities of Evolution.
      "   III.   Where are the Nebulæ?
      "   IV.   What are the Nebulæ?
      "   V.   The Comets.
      "   VI.   Motions of the Sun and Planets.
      "   VII.   Specific Gravities of the Sun and Planets.
      "   VIII.   Temperature of the Sun and Planets.
      "   IX.   Our Sidereal System.
      "   X.   The Future.

INORGANIC EVOLUTION

The omission of Astronomic and Geologic Evolution from the programme issued two years later did not mean that the inorganic world was to be entirely passed over, but only that it would not receive the detailed treatment accorded to Life, Mind, Society and Morality. Readers of *First Principles* are aware of the course followed in the exposition. " The Transformation or Equivalence of Forces," " The Direction of Motion," and " The Rhythm of Motion " are each exemplified, firstly, in astronomical and secondly, in geological transformations, before their operation in organic and superorganic transformations is discussed. The same course is followed in the exposition of " The Law of Evolution," " The Instability of the Homogeneous," " The Multiplication of Effects," " Segregation " and " Equilibration." When treating of " Dissolution " the exposition naturally follows the reverse order. Putting all these expositions together one may obtain a general idea of what the *Principles of Astrogeny* and the *Principles of Geogeny* would have been like had time, energy, and knowledge sufficient been vouchsafed to him.

What he described as " a further development of the doctrines of molecular dynamics " appeared in the *Reader* (19 November, 1864) under the title—" What

159

is Electricity?'' Nine years later, when writing to Dr. Youmans (12 November, 1873) he said:

> Since I began this letter there has dawned upon me, after this long delay, an extension of that theory of electricity set forth in the *Reader* and published in the *Essays*. I am busy writing a postscript which, when it is in print, I shall submit to Tyndall and other authorities, and, if they do not disprove it, will send you a copy for addition to the American volume.

From John Tyndall.

ATHENÆUM CLUB [1873].

I have glanced over your paper, rather than read it critically. It shows the usual penetration; but will you bear with me if I advise you not to publish it as it now stands. Its aim is ambitious, and I frankly think it fails in its aim. If you publish it as a speculation, not as an '' explanation,'' no harm can accrue. But I think harm would accrue if it were published in its present garb.

I often wished to say to you that your chapters on the Persistence of Force, etc., were never satisfactory to me. You have taken as your guide a vague and to me, I confess, altogether unsatisfactory book. The greater part of your volume I consider to be of such transcendent merits, putting one's best thoughts into the clearest language, that I feel all the more the transition to the chapters to which I have referred. I expressed, I think, the opinion to you some time ago that they ought to be rewritten.

If you have considered how the disturbance of molecules can generate attraction and repulsion at a distance, you ought to state the result of your thought. If you have not thought of this question, then I think you have omitted the fundamental phenomenon of electricity.

I am hard pressed, and therefore write briefly. You

will excuse my frankness. I certainly should grieve to see anything with your name attached to it that would give the enemy occasion to triumph.

To JOHN TYNDALL.

22 *December*, 1873.

I quite agree with you as to the undesirableness of publishing this postscript as it stands: indeed, I sketched it out with the expectation that criticism would probably oblige me to remodel it. I quite intended (but I see that I must make the intention more clear) to put forth the hypothesis simply as a *speculation:* apparently having such an amount of congruity with physical principles as made it worth considering—especially in the absence of anything like a satisfactory explanation.

I have had another letter from Clerk Maxwell, which considerably startles me by its views about molecular motion. I should like to talk to you about them. They seem to me to differ from those which I supposed you to hold, and which I supposed were held generally.

Thank you for your reminder respecting the chapter on the " Persistence of Force." I hope to make it worthy of your approval. I am now remodelling it, and the two preceding chapters.

When sending the paper to Professor Clerk Maxwell reference seems to have been made to a remark made to Professor Kingdon Clifford regarding Spencer's views about nebular condensation.

FROM J. CLERK MAXWELL.

5 *December*, 1873.

I do not remember the particulars of what I said to Professor Clifford about nebular condensation. The occasion of it was I think a passage in an old edition of your *First Principles,* and having since then made a little more acquaintance with your works, I regarded

161

it merely as a temporary phase of the process of evolution which you have been carrying on within your own mind. Mathematicians by guiding their thoughts always along the same tracks, have converted the field of thought into a kind of railway system, and are apt to neglect cross-country speculations.

It is very seldom that any man who tries to form a system can prevent his system from forming round him, and closing him in before he is forty. Hence the wisdom of putting in some ingredient to check crystallisation and keep the system in a colloidal condition. Candle-makers, I believe, use arsenic for this purpose. . . . But you seem to be able to retard the crystallisation of parts of your system without stopping the process of evolution of the whole, and I therefore attach much more importance to the general scheme than to particular statements.

After describing several experiments, which he would not say were inconsistent with Spencer's theory, but which were very important and significant, Professor Clerk Maxwell continues: " As I observe that you are always improving your phraseology I shall lay before you my notions on the nomenclature of molecular motions." One of the terms defined was " the motion of *agitation* of a molecule," namely " that by which the actual velocity of an individual molecule differs from the mean velocity of the group."

On receipt of some remarks by Spencer on the word " agitation," Professor Clerk Maxwell wrote again (17 December, 1873) :—

The reason for which I use the word " agitation " to distinguish the local motion of a molecule in relation to its neighbours is that I think with you that the word

" agitation " conveys in a small degree, if at all, the notion of rhythm.

If motion is said to be rhythmic when the path is, on the whole, as much in one direction as in the opposite, then all motion is rhythmic when it is confined within a small region of space.

But if, as I understand the word rhythmic, it implies not only alternation, but regularity and periodicity, then the word " agitation " excludes the notion of rhythm, which was what I meant it to do. . . . A great scientific desideratum is a set of words of *little* meaning—words which mean no more than that a thing belongs to a very large class. Such words are much needed in the undulatory theory of light, in order to express fully what is proved by experiment, without connoting anything which is a mere hypothesis.

To J. CLERK MAXWELL.

30 *December*, 1873.

I must confess that I was taken somewhat aback by the statement that you deliberately chose the word *agitation* because it negatived the notion of rhythm. For I had hardly anticipated the tacit denial that the relative motions of molecules as wholes have rhythm. I feel fully the force of the reason for supposing that, when molecules are irregularly aggregated into a solid, the tensions due to their mutual actions will be so various as to produce great irregularity of motion; and I have, indeed, in the first part of the speculation concerning electricity, indicated this as a possible cause for the continuity of the spectrum in solids. But, admitting this, there seem to me two qualifying considerations. If, as shown in the lecture you were so kind as to send me, molecules of different weights have different absolute velocities in the gaseous state; then, must it not happen that when such differently-moving molecules are aggregated into solids, their *constitutional differences of mobility* will still show themselves? Such constitutional differences cannot well disappear without any results; and if they do not disappear, must there not result characteristic differences between their motions of agitation in the two solids they form—must not the two agitations differ in the *average periodicities* of the local motions constituting them? The second qualifying consideration which occurs to me is this. Though molecules, irregularly aggregated into a solid, may be expected to have motions more or less confused by the irregularities of the tensions; may we not say that, when they are *regularly* aggregated into a solid (as in a crystal), they will be subject to *regular* tensions, conducing to regular motions? Do not the formation and structure of a crystal imply that its units are all so homogeneously conditioned that they must have homogeneous motions?

The original draft of the postscript to the article " What is Electricity "? was amended in the light of the criticisms, oral and written, to which it had been subjected at the hands of Professor Tyndall, Professor Clerk Maxwell, and others. Admitting that the hypothesis had received no endorsements, he held that it had not been proved untenable. He published it, therefore, as a speculation only, adding to the postscript another postscript containing suggestions arising out of the criticisms.[1]

The constitution of the Sun, which had formed the subject of a paper in the *Reader* early in 1865, came up again in 1874.

To E. L. YOUMANS.
16 *October,* 1874.

Proctor, in the last number of the *Cornhill,* has been drawing attention to the conclusions of your astronomer

---

[1] *Essays,* ii., 176-187.

164

Young that the sun is a hollow sphere. . . . His reasonings are in great measure the same as those set forth in my essay on the " Constitution of the Sun "—reasonings which I have been for the last year past intending to amend in respect of the particular process by which the precipitated matters form the molten shell. There are mechanical difficulties, named to Clifford by Clerk Maxwell, to the mode of formation as originally described. But, on pursuing the results of the process of precipitation into vapour and then into metallic rain, perpetually ascending and perpetually thickening as concentration goes on, I reached a conclusion respecting a formation of the shell, to which no objection has as yet been made by the authorities with whom I have discussed it. Apart however from this particular portion of the hypothesis which needs amendment, Professor Young's conception of the Sun's constitution and the progress going on in the Sun, are essentially those which I set forth.

He at once set about amending his reasonings " in respect of the particular process by which the precipitated matters form the molten shell." A slip proof of the amended hypothesis was sent to Professor Clerk Maxwell, who, admitting that he did not " quite understand the principal features " of the hypothesis, adduced reasons to show that " a liquid shell supported by a nucleus of less density than itself, whether solid, liquid or gaseous, is essentially unstable." On Professor Clerk Maxwell's letter (December 17, 1874) Spencer has pencilled: " This argument at first convinced me that my hypothesis was untenable. But subsequently the corollaries from Andrews's investigations concerning the critical point of gases, implying that a gas might become

165

denser than a liquid and yet remain a gas, led me to readopt the hypothesis.''[1]

This point with others is touched upon in correspondence with his French translator.

To E. CAZELLES.

12 May, 1875.

I enclose impressions of some passages which will be substituted hereafter for certain parts of the essay on the '' Nebular Hypothesis.'' [One of the alterations] is made as an abandonment of an hypothesis which Professor Clerk Maxwell has clearly proved to me is not tenable.

Respecting your question concerning the calculation of Tait, or rather of Sir William Thomson, I will write to you shortly, when I have refreshed my memory about it. Meanwhile I may say that I believe it to be wholly untenable; for the reason that it sets out with assumptions that are not only gratuitous, but extremely improbable.

20 July.—I sent you the other day Huxley's address in which he controverted the conclusions of Sir William Thomson respecting the age of the Earth and of the Solar System. I meant before now to have written to you, giving my own further reasons for rejecting the inference drawn from his assumptions—or rather for rejecting his assumptions.

8 March, 1876.—I referred the other day to Sir William Thomson's paper on the solar heat, published in Macmillan's Magazine for March, 1862. The aim is to show that the Sun cannot have been radiating heat at its present rate for anything like the time required by the inferences of geologists. The fallacy in his argument, which I remember to have observed when read-

---

[1] Essays, i., 164.

ing, I find to be this:—the calculation which lands him in his conclusion that radiation at this rate cannot have gone on for the required period, tacitly assumes the bulk of the sun to have been something like what it is now; whereas, on the hypothesis of nebular condensation, the implication is, that for vast periods before the Sun reached his present degree of condensation, he was slowly contracting from a larger size, and was all the while radiating heat. Helmholtz has calculated that since the time when, according to the nebular hypothesis, the matter composing the Solar System extended to the orbit of Neptune, there has been evolved by the arrest of sensible motion, an amount of heat 454 times as great as that which the Sun still has to give out. Now since a considerable part of this concentration and radiation must have taken place during the period in which the Sun's mass was receding inwards from the limits of the Earth's orbit; and, as during all the latter stages of this period (say from the time when the Sun filled the orbit of Mercury) we may assume that the Earth has reached its concentrated form; it is clear that, during all the remaining period of the Sun's contraction, the Earth must have been receiving its radiations, though in these remote periods the radiations must have been far less intense, *yet since they emanated from a relatively enormous surface subtending at the earth a relatively immense angle,* the total amount of radiation received by the Earth may have been as great or greater. Remembering that, were the Sun double its present diameter, it would need to radiate at but one-fourth its present rate to give us the same amount of heat, and that, did it subtend an angle of $5\frac{1}{2}$ degrees, one hundredth of its present radiation for a given portion of surface would suffice; we see it to be not only possible, but on the nebular hypothesis quite certain, that the Earth has been receiving light and heat from the Sun, adequate for purposes of life, for a period immensely greater than is inferable when the calculation is made on the assumption that the Sun's bulk has been during the time something like the same.

The dispute between the physicists and the geologists as to the age of the Earth and the Solar System has changed its aspect during recent years. Until a few years ago the temperature of the Sun was supposed to be due solely to concentration of gaseous matter and the fall of meteoric stones. Sir William Thomson estimated that the Sun has been giving out heat for a period of some twenty or thirty millions of years, and that geologists must limit their time demands accordingly. But recent discoveries in regard to radio-activity point to the possession by the Sun of other sources of heat. The duration of the solar heat may therefore be indefinitely extended—extended at any rate as far as is necessary to satisfy the geologist, with his indefinite, and, some think, not very modest, claim of from one to five or six thousand millions of years, as the period during which the Earth has been sufficiently cool to permit of the appearance of living things on it.

Across a correspondence with Dr. Charlton Bastian, Spencer has written: '' This refers to the fact that Lockyer's speculations concerning the compound nature of the elements, as shown by the changes of the spectra, were pursuant on a remark I made to him expressing that belief.''

To H. CHARLTON BASTIAN.

25 *November,* 1878.

One Sunday afternoon some four or five years ago, you and I called together upon Lockyer. . . . We chatted with him for some time in his laboratory, and our conversation turned upon Spectrum Analysis. . . . Have you any recollection of this conversation? and can you recall any opinion which I expressed respecting the implications of spectrum phenomena—what I thought was to be necessarily inferred from the more or less numerous lines contained in the spectrum of each element, and what I thought was to be inferred from that transformation in the spectrum of an element, which takes place under certain physical conditions? . . . As we walked away something passed respecting the bearings of what I had been saying upon the views contained in that work [Bastian's *Beginnings of Life*, recently published], leading to the remark that had you entertained the view, you might have begun your exposition somewhat further back.

FROM H. CHARLTON BASTIAN.

27 *November*, 1878.

I recollect the walk quite well to which you refer, our call upon Lockyer, and that there was a conversation in his laboratory in reference to the different spectra yielded by so-called elements, under different conditions of temperature, etc. I know that Lockyer told us about some of his recent results, and that you expressed some opinions in interpretation of the evidence, and concerning the transformations of the spectra to which he referred—but, unfortunately, beyond that I cannot go. The details have slipped from my memory.

I recollect the conversation afterwards to which you refer, and know that the general conclusions from the conversation with Lockyer favoured the view that the so-called elements were themselves products of evolution.

This view of the elements came up again some twelve years after.

FROM HENRY CUNYNGHAME.

30 *May*, 1891.

A short time ago, being in the company of Mr. Crookes, he was good enough to explain to me his theory as to the composition of the elements, which he thinks have been formed by a process of evolutional segregation. He has devoted some years to experiments upon this question, and the behaviour of the rare earths, such as yttrium under the spectroscope, strongly confirms these views. For by long continued fractionation, different sorts of yttrium seem to present themselves, differing, as different breeds (say) of cows differ from one another. Of course the persistence of type, when once developed makes it practically impossible to transmute metals, just as, to use his own simile, you cannot, without returning to some primitive type, make a cow into a horse.

I said that I thought these experiments would be highly interesting to you as, in one of your works this view had been clearly foreshadowed. Mr. Crookes said that was so, and he had quoted your words in several of his lectures.[1]

On looking through Mr. (now Sir William) Crookes's pamphlets, Spencer wrote of them to Mr. Cunynghame as " yielding verifications of the view I have long entertained, and as tending to show how much more completely evolutionary the genesis of compound matter has been than I supposed. It is marvellous to trace in this field a parallel to the genesis of varieties and species." And to Mr. Crookes he wrote (8 June): " Your views—especially in respect of the development of varieties and species—carry out the evolutionary idea in this field very much further than I have ever dreamt it could be carried." It is doubtless true that if *First Principles* were to be written in the light of recent advances in physics and chemistry, it would in many important respects differ from the book as we know it even

---

[1] Also in his address as President of the Chemical Section of the British Association of 1886.

in its final form. At the rate of progress of recent years a book on physics, it has been said, cannot appear " that is not already out of date a week after the author returns his proofs." Spencer was aware that his outline of Inorganic Evolution had reference to the knowledge of the time and was subject to modification with every increase in our knowledge. Granted that " he did not fully nor always rightly utilise the chemistry and physics of his time " (and who has ever done so?), he has the incontestable merit of having foreshadowed some of the most striking chemical and physical discoveries of recent years. The theory that the so-called elements are products of evolution was both novel and startling in the seventies. Now-a-days it may be said to be an accepted doctrine. Not only are the atoms no longer considered indivisible, but estimates are made of the number of corpuscles or electrons contained in a so-called atom; and descriptions are given of the struggle for existence continually going on among the communities of corpuscles, ending in the overthrow of the unstable and the continuance of the stable. Like species in the organic world, the atoms are evolutionary products, the result of competition and survival of the fittest.

Writing in July, 1880, to Dr. Youmans, he mentions having met Mr. Moulton.

He told me that there had lately been made a discovery which tended to verify my hypothesis with regard to the interior constitution of celestial bodies: the discovery being that made by a Professor Ramsay of Bristol,[1] who, it turns out, is a very competent experimenter. He contributed a paper to the Royal Society, giving re-

---

[1] Now Sir William Ramsay, of University College, London.

sults respecting the transition from the gaseous to the liquid state, in which he made it manifest that, at the stage of pressure in which the gas becomes equally dense with the liquid, the line of demarcation of the two gradually becomes hazy and vanishes into a fog, and that, eventually, the liquid and the gas mingle so as to be no longer distinguishable. And Moulton drew my attention to the fact that this makes quite feasible, and in fact almost necessary, my supposition with regard to the gaseous nuclei of the Sun and planets. The result of this will be that I shall have to alter afresh that passage in the essay on the nebular hypothesis which I erased, and shall have to re-instate part of it and modify the remainder so as to incorporate with its arguments this revelation.

No article of Spencer's was subjected to so many revisions as that on " The Nebular Hypothesis." During January and the first half of February, 1883, he embraced the opportunity of a new edition of the *Essays* being called for to subject it to further revision.

To E. L. YOUMANS.

8 *March*, 1883.

At length I send you the portions of the revision of the article on the " Nebular Hypothesis." They have given me an immensity of trouble, and I am heartily glad they are out of hand.

The trouble has been in part caused by the fact that I have subjected them to various criticisms, and on minor points have taken advantage of these. As a result I feel quite safe as to the legitimacy of the speculation. Of course it is a case of Speculation *versus* Speculation; and the physical arguments being admitted to be tenable, the thing has as good a basis as can well be given to it.

172

Towards the end of 1889 he again revised and added to the article, before incorporating it in the final edition of the *Essays,* being assisted by Mr. W. T. Lynn, of the Greenwich Observatory. Copies were sent for criticism to Lord Rayleigh, Sir William Thomson, Dr. Isaac Roberts, Lord Crawford, Mr. Huggins, and to Professors Dewar, Darwin, Williamson, Frankland, and Tyndall. Writing in reply on January 1, 1890, Sir William Thomson said that he felt quite lost when he tried " to think of anything that can be imagined as a *primitive* condition of matter. Of antecedent conditions we may freely reason, and with fairly sure judgment. But of a condition which can come, under known law, from no antecedent, or of a chaos which existed through infinity of past time till a declension of atoms initiated the evolution of kosmos, I can form no imagination. Yet we seem to require a *primitive* condition of matter." Whenever he had thought of it, he had " been led to think of uncombined separate atoms as the primitive condition of matter." " But assuming this to be the case, we see by perfectly definite calculations, that the heat of chemical combination from the condition of detached atoms to the actual state of matter . . . is *very small* in comparison with that due to gravity."

To Sir William Thomson.

3 *January,* 1890.

I am very much obliged by your letter of yesterday, giving me your criticism in such clear detail. Let me, while thanking you, express my regret that I should have entailed upon you so much trouble. I had not supposed that you would write so fully, or my conscience would scarcely have let me write to you at all, for I should not have liked to intrude so much upon the time of one to whom time is so precious, knowing as I do by experience how terribly correspondence displaces matters of much importance.

I quite follow and fully appreciate the drift of your remarks, and more especially perceive that which I have not before recognised—the relatively small amount of heat evolved by chemical combinations among the ultimate units of matter, in comparison with the heat evolved by gravitation. It is clear that the amount of molecular motion possessed by each of such ultimate units must be transcendently great, before the quantity of motion lost by unions among them can be comparable in amount to the quantity of motion lost in the course of the journey to their common centre of gravity. Still, I suppose, one may infer that, if preceding unions of such kind had generated a high temperature in the nebulous mass, at a time when it filled the orbit of Neptune, a considerable increase in the time required for concentration into the present solar mass would be implied.

I am much obliged by the copy of the paper which at your request was sent to me by your secretary. I perceive that it contains much matter of interest to me. A good part of it will I fear lie out of the sphere of my comprehension; my mathematics, never very extensive, having become rusty.

Some years before he had urged Professor Tyndall, by way of change of work and scene, to '' take up the general question of the condition of the Earth's interior. Recently, the numerous earthquakes and eruptions in various and remote parts of the Earth, sundry of them nearly or quite simultaneous, seem to me to be quite irreconcilable with the Thomsonian view that the Earth's interior is as rigid as steel. Further contraction of this rigid mass, the only possible cause assignable by Thomson, appears to me to be one quite incapable of explaining the facts.''

To J. W. Judd.

23 June, 1890.

I recently read with much interest the report given in *Nature* of your lecture to the Chemical Society on the '' Chemical Changes in Rocks under Mechanical Stresses.'' Especially was I struck by the paragraph which states that the '' volcanic glass known as *marekanite* '' '' will, when heated, swell up and intumesce,'' and that '' the brown glass ejected from Krakatau, during the great eruption of 1883, if heated, increases to many times its original bulk, and passes into a substance which, macroscopically and microscopically, is indistinguishable from the pumice thrown out in such vast quantities during that great eruption.''

I am reminded, by this paragraph, of certain conclusions concerning volcanic eruptions which I reached after an excursion up Vesuvius during the eruption of 1868. Inclosed is a passage written some years ago, briefly setting forth these conclusions. Though not named in this interpretation (which is simply a note appended to the account of the excursion)[1] the character of pumice-stone had occurred to me as one of the evidences, since the liberation of water and its assumption of the gaseous state under diminishing pressure would, besides producing the effects above described, produce in many cases masses of vesicular substance. It matters not to the hypothesis whether the contained water is mechanically distributed only, or whether it is water of crystallization, or water chemically combined. In any of these cases, if it assumes the gaseous state the effects will be of the general nature described.

But my more immediate purpose in writing to you is to ascertain what is now regarded as the most feasible

---

[1] *Autobiography,* ii., p. 211, note.

interpretation of such vast catastrophes as that of which Krakatau was the scene. On glancing at the summary of conclusions contained in the report of the committee appointed to investigate it, I find to my surprise that the eruption or explosion was ascribed to the intrusion of the sea: the implication being that action of a large body of water on a large body of lava would generate an adequate force. Is this probable? Such a co-operation would be limited to the surface of contact of the water and the lava. How could the evolved steam, quickly checked in its genesis by the chilling and solidification of the adjacent molten matter, move so vast a mass? In the first place how is the entrance of sufficient water to be accounted for? Its entrance could be effected only by a pressure greater than the pressure of the body of the lava, part of which extended above sea level. Considering the relative specific gravities of the two, such an intrusion would be unaccountable, even in the absence of greater hydrostatic pressure on the side of the lava. In the second place, apart from mechanical obstacles, I cannot see how intrusion and spread of the water, taking an appreciable interval of time, could have the consequence supposed. The probability appears rather to be that, by the steam first generated, local fissures would be formed, allowing of escape and preventing the requisite accumulation of steam, even could a sufficient quantity be evolved.

If, on the other hand, we suppose a state of things like that implied by the above hypothesis and implied, too, by certain results of the researches you have summarised, we have a force that is both adequate and of the kind required to account for the various effects. On this hypothesis, the molten matter within the volcano, forming in the midst of its cone a column of, say, several thousand feet high, contains water which can assume the gaseous state only towards the upper part of the molten column, where the pressure is relatively moderate. Suppose that, at some place towards the lower part of the cone, some considerable area of its side has been thinned away by contact with the contained lava; and that, instead of emitting through a fissure a small stream of lava, as commonly happens, it suddenly gives way and collapses over, say, many acres, what must happen? Everywhere throughout the lava which rushes forth, the water and carbonic acid, relieved from pressure, become gaseous. The column of lava, extending high up the cone, suddenly falls perhaps a thousand or two feet, and relieves, from the greater part of the immense pressure it was subject to, the entire body of lava which filled the lower part of the volcano. The water and carbonic acid, imprisoned in every part of it, are liberated; and a mass of matter, of perhaps half-a-mile cube, suddenly explodes.

All the effects produced appear to be natural consequences. Once being ruptured, the sides of the cone, subject to the tremendous force of the escaping gases, would be likely to collapse and be in large measure blown away. Those parts of the molten matter which, not being very far below the crater, had parted with considerable portions of their water and carbonic acid in the shape of ascending and exploding bubbles, would, when wholly freed from pressure, expand in but moderate degrees, and so would form vesicular masses of pumice-stone, which, ejected in large quantities, would cover neighbouring regions, as the sea was covered round Krakatau. Further, the lower portions of the lava, which, subject to high pressure, had, until the moment of the explosion, retained all their water and carbonic acid would, when these were suddenly changed into gases, explode in such a manner as to dissipate their solid substances in small fragments, down to minute particles. Whence would result enormous volumes of dust, such as were produced by the Krakatau eruption and so widely pervaded the atmosphere.

Probably had not other occupations prevented me from being *au courant* with geological speculation I might have learnt that kindred interpretations had been given; but not having met with such, I am prompted by the bearings of your late lecture to inquire what is the present state of opinion on the matter.

In answer to the enquiry as to the present state of opinion, Professor Judd wrote (25 June, 1890):

While a few geologists still maintain that Volcanic Eruptions are produced by the penetration of masses of water to highly heated rocks—many, and I think the majority—following the late Mr. Poulett Scrope, hold that the gradual disengagement of water-gas and other gases *in the midst of a molten mass* (as the pressure is continuously relieved by each ejection) are the really efficient cause in a volcanic outburst.

In 1894 he thought of again calling in question the calculations as to the age of the Earth, made by Sir William Thomson (afterwards Lord Kelvin).

To T. H. Huxley.

1 *October,* 1894.

Has anything of late been said apropos of the controversy between yourself and Lord Kelvin concerning the age of the Earth? I am about to send for his volume of republished essays, but my impression, though a vague one, is that some of his data are inadmissible. I fancy that he is rather famous for reasoning mathematically from assumptions which are of a questionable kind, and then affirming positively the truth of his conclusion; and the world at large have that superstition in regard to mathematicians that they accept as a matter of course a conclusion mathematically reached, forgetting that its validity depends upon the truth of the data.

INORGANIC EVOLUTION

From T. H. Huxley.

3 *October*, 1894.

Kelvin and I have made no progress that I see. It is as much as I can do to get him to understand that the fact of evolution being proved by fossil remains, the time it may have taken is a question of quite secondary importance.

This information was asked for in view of a letter for *Nature* on " The Cooling of the Earth," which he wrote in the beginning of 1895, Mr. (now Sir) George H. Darwin being consulted. The letter, which was immediately withdrawn lest it should provoke a controversy, was as follows:—

One who is quite incompetent to criticise a chain of high mathematical reasoning may be not incompetent to form an opinion concerning the validity of the premises from which the reasoning sets out. Such premises may be entirely non-mathematical, and, if so, the mathematician cannot claim special authority for them: his assumptions remain open to criticism by others than mathematicians. Thus looking at the matter, I venture to make a suggestion respecting the calculation of Lord Kelvin and the question at issue between him and Professor Perry.

The reasoning of the one and the criticism of the other are concerned exclusively with processes which have gone on within the body of the Earth. In the one case, a certain interior constitution is assumed, and from the rate of increasing temperatures at increasing depths below the surface, an inference is drawn respecting the time which has been occupied in cooling. In the other case, a question is raised as to the validity of the assumptions in regard to the Earth's interior constitution, and a consequent scepticism about the inferences drawn

179

is expressed. But, in both cases, it appears to be assumed that the condition of things outside the Earth's body has all along been the same as now. It is assumed that whatever may have been the past temperature of the Earth's mass and of its solid or liquid surface, there have been the same facilities for the escape of its heat into space as there are at present. Must this assumption be accepted as beyond doubt? Are we not warranted in demurring to it? May we not even conclude that it is far from being true?

Since the existing heat of the Earth, and that much greater heat which the argument supposes it once to have had, are not otherwise accounted for, it might be contended that the nebular hypothesis (or the hypothesis of dispersed matter in some form), which alone yields an explanation, is tacitly assumed; and it might be fairly held that, if we are to go back upon the nebular hypothesis (or the hypothesis of dispersed fragments) at all, we must go back upon it altogether. Passing over, as not immediately relevant, the early gaseous state (either primordial or produced by collision), and coming at once to the condition in which the elements now mainly composing the Earth's crust were unoxidised, the inference might be that the uncombined oxygen and other gases must at that time have constituted a very voluminous atmosphere, and that the escape of heat through such an atmosphere, especially if it contained any compounds having the form of condensed vapours, must have been extremely slow. But without going back thus far, sufficient reason may be found for a demurrer to the current conclusion.

Let us grant the assumption made that the Earth's body has all along consisted of solid matter, if not such as we now know, yet akin to it in respect of density and conducting power. Evidently the inference drawn from the observed gradient of increasing temperature as we descend, itself implies the belief that the matter of the surface was once, if not at as high a temperature as the interior, still at a high temperature. Suppose we go back to a time when its temperature was 152° C. At that temperature water boils under a pressure of five atmospheres (four plus the normal). The implication is that maintenance of the Earth's water, or rather part of it, in a liquid form on the Earth's surface, necessitated the existence of a quantity of aeriform water equivalent to more than a hundred feet of liquid water; that is to say, assuming the mean pressure of $2\frac{1}{2}$ atmospheres, the stratum of steam must have been over 70,000 feet deep, or more than 13 miles—an estimated depth which, taking into account the great expansion and indefinite limit of the outer part, would be much less than the actual depth. Even supposing this vast mass of water to have existed as transparent gas, the escape of heat into space must have been immensely impeded: the absorption of radiant heat by the vapour of water being so great. But the water could not have wholly existed—could not have mainly existed—as a transparent gas. It must in large measure have existed as a dense cloud of vast depth. The implication seems to be that, next to the heated surface of the Earth, there was a transparent stratum, but that above it came an opaque stratum of far greater thickness, at the outer limit of which went on condensation into rain. Under such circumstances the escape of heat must have been effected by convection-currents, ascending, expanding, falling in temperature, precipitating at the periphery, and there parting with heat into space. Must we not conclude that during this period the cooling of the Earth went on at a rate relatively small?

During stages thus exemplified the changes in the Earth's crust, at first of igneous origin only, would begin to be complicated by others of aqueous origin; and the geological processes which have brought about its present state would be initiated. But, manifestly, throughout the enormous period required for the tolerably complete deposition of the water, and the clearing of the air from its vast stratum of cloud, the rate of escape of heat would be still relatively small, and it would go on only slowly increasing, until there was reached some such escape as that which now takes place through an air often cloudless, and at most times only moderately charged with water. During this era, the geologic changes would be actively proceeding, and there would be time for the deposit of a vast series of azoic strata—a time to which the present gradient of internal temperature gives no clue.

A long and complicated series of biologic changes would become possible after the temperature had fallen to 100° C. It is true that though some forms of *Protozoa* can exist at that temperature, or even a little above it, we may not infer that therefore life might then have commenced, for the agency of light may have been lacking. Though, with seas at a temperature of 212° F., the stratum of cloud may not have been so dense as to prevent the passage of some light—though the darkness may not have been as great as that which exists at the bottom of the ocean, where nevertheless there is a large amount of life, not only of *Protozoa,* but of *Metazoa* considerably elevated in type—yet it may be contended that, as the life at the bottom of the ocean is dependent on nutritive matter present in sea-water, which has somewhere and at some time resulted from the decomposition of carbonic acid by chlorophyll with the aid of light, we cannot assume that light was not essential. Still the inference may fairly be that when the process of cooling from 212° downwards had gone so far that the universal cloud allowed a certain amount of light to pass, life became possible, and that biologic changes might have commenced at a time when the cooling process was not going on at anything like its present rate, and might have gone through many of their earlier stages before anything like the present rate was reached.

If it should be said, as seems possible, that the inference from the gradient of internal temperature stands by itself, and may be held valid without regard to changes in the Earth's atmosphere, this reply may be made:—Let us assume that the mass of the Earth once had an absolutely non-conducting envelope. Its temperature would then be the same at the centre and the surface, and there would be no thermal data from which its age could be inferred: nothing would negative the inference that it had so existed for an infinite time. Now, suppose the absolutely non-conducting envelope taken away and the Earth left bare. The cooling then commenced would, in course of time, produce a gradient of temperatures analogous to that which is found existing. But the data furnished by this gradient would give no clue whatever to the duration of the pre-existing period, throughout which the escape of heat was prevented. Any inference drawn as to age would be delusive. And if this must be admitted in the case of a sudden change from absolute prevention of radiation to absolute permission of it, then it must be admitted that a gradual change from great prevention to small prevention will also vitiate the inference. The observed gradient when the obstacle to radiation is small will be delusive, if supposed applicable to a time when the obstacle to radiation was great.

To state the case briefly in figurative language—the Earth had once a very thick blanket; its blanket has in the course of immense epochs gradually thinned away; and hence it would seem that an estimation of its age from thermal data, which assumes its present thin blanket to have always existed, is open to grave doubt— to say the least.

His last contribution to the Nebular Hypothesis was made in 1900, when preparing the final edition of *First Principles*. When writing section 182*a* [p. 485] he was in correspondence with Dr. Isaac Roberts, whose *Photo-*

graphs of Stars, Star-clusters, and Nebulæ he found very instructive. A month or two after the issue of this edition of *First Principles* he returned to the subject in a short paper on "The Genesis of Gaseous Nebulæ," which he intended to be added as Appendix D.[1]

In a short letter to the Editor of the *Fortnightly Review* (April, 1900) on "Professor Ward's Rejoinder," Spencer thus refers to the criticism arising out of the omission of Inorganic Evolution from detailed treatment in the *Synthetic Philosophy*:—

He continues to harp upon the fact that the two volumes treating of Inorganic Evolution were omitted by me; insisting that the fabric of conclusions drawn is vitiated by the omission. Observe the alternative implied by him. Execution of the works dealing with Organic and Super-organic Evolution was thought by most to be impossible, and if preceded by works dealing with Inorganic Evolution would have been quite impossible. But in the absence of the part dealing with Inorganic Evolution the rest, according to Professor Ward, lacks "adequate foundations" and is valueless. Thus, it was useless to try the one course; it was useless to pursue the other; therefore, nothing should have been attempted. It was not allowable to leave the earliest stages hypothetical; and, beginning with the chemical elements as we know them, to trace out later stages of evolution as conforming to one law. And then, when it was pointed out that the gap was not wholly vacant, but that (in addition to the sketch of Inorganic Evolution in *First Principles*) five sets of evidences I had given implied that the chemical elements have been evolved [*Essays*, i., 155-9], these are cavalierly passed

---

[1] See *First Principles*, p. 538.

over as having been set forth in three pages of a " fugitive essay." [1]

---

[1] Fugitive, in the sense of being a review-article, but not otherwise:—not fugitive, since it contained disproofs of the belief then current among astronomers, but now abandoned, that the nebulæ are remote galaxies (see Proctor's *Old and New Astronomy*, p. 726) :—not fugitive, since the conclusion drawn respecting the Sun's photosphere (at variance with conclusions then held) was, two years after, verified in chief measure by the discoveries of Kirchoff and Bunsen.

CHAPTER XXVII

HIS LAST BOOK

(July, 1900—*April,* 1902)

At the age of eighty, and with the purpose of his life achieved, Spencer had established an indisputable claim to complete mental repose during the few remaining years. But, as had been his wont, ere the work was completed on which he was engaged, he was planning another book. In September, 1899, he wrote to Mr. Appleton, of New York, that he wished to have the revision of *First Principles* out of hand " because I want to devote myself to some further work. I have still a little energy left, and still some things to write, which will, I think, make a volume not unlikely to be popular." As he wrote to a correspondent in the following year, mental occupation had become a second nature. " It is difficult after fifty years of writing to emancipate oneself from the habit. Life would be too dreary were the setting-down of ideas brought to a sudden rest."

Had he reflected he would have seen that there was little ground to fear that time would hang heavy on his hands. The widespread, varied, and prolonged influence he had exerted afforded a guarantee that the remaining years of his life would be well filled with the interests his writings and his personality had created or fostered. His characteristic impatience with intellectual error, moral delinquency, or remediable physical evil,

186

would, despite good resolutions to keep out of the fray, continue to plunge him unwittingly into the thick of the fight. Correspondence, never light, had also to be reckoned with. Many of his correspondents were personally unknown; and not a few of them, though ostensibly anxious enquirers for information, were in reality only commonplace autograph hunters. Besides begging letters and applications for interviews, there was a continuous stream of requests for photographs, autographs, mottoes, sentiments; for advice on the bringing-up of children, on the organisation of schools, on the management of debating societies; for expressions of his matured opinions on all manner of topics, ranging from the industrial situation in New Zealand to divorce in Italy. The octogenarian was expected not only to favour authors with an authoritative judgment on their books, but to justify this doctrine and to explain that doctrine contained, or supposed to be contained, in one or other of his own writings, extending over half a century. Mr. Andrew Lang says that bores fall into well-defined categories, and that a general lithographed reply should be framed for each category. Spencer had for years adopted some such measure of relief : his lithographed or printed forms having in some cases a space at the end for a sentence dealing with any special feature of the communication replied to. But Mr. Lang admits that it is not so easy as it seems to devise proper replies to some correspondents without employing profane language. From help of this kind Spencer was constitutionally and on principle debarred [1] To certain requests the only suitable course was to make no reply. What could

---

[1] See, however, *Autobiography*, i., p. 570.

he say, for example, to the members of a literary institution in India, who asked for a present of all his books? How was it possible to write a satisfactory answer to a Hindu, absolutely unknown to him, and without credentials, whose business had been ruined by the famine, and who asked for a loan of £200? How could he, with his dread of visitors, give a favourable reply to a young Syrian who wished to spend the summer with him: '' To accompany you in your daily walks, to hear what you speak, to observe how you act in all the common affairs of life ''? While ignoring without compunction the general autograph hunter, he was always willing to send his autograph or photograph to friends. The claims of kinship, even though distant, were responded to, as in the case of a great-granddaughter of his uncle John, to whom, though he had never before heard of her, he sent three autographs for her three children. Even bearers of the same name, without any bond of kinship, were occasionally favoured by these small attentions.

In addition to the customary requests from editors for articles, or paragraphs, he had in these later years to meet special requests suggested by special events. For example,—to send '' some brief message of congratulation and counsel for the Federating Colonies '' at the opening of the first parliament of Federated Australia; to write on '' The Guiding Principle of Mankind in the Twentieth Century; '' '' to rewrite for the common people these two quotations from your admirable works; '' to answer the question: '' What is the chief danger, social or political, that confronts the coming century? '' to send '' a brief New Century message to English-speaking women ''; to name his favourite author, which of

188

this author's books he liked best, and his reason for the choice; to join in a symposium dealing with the ultimate settlement in South Africa; to write for a Fourth of July number " something in the way of an expression of your opinion regarding Peace amongst men "; to contribute towards a review of the year 1901, an article on " The Parliament of Man, the Federation of the World—to what extent do the Events of the year 1901 foreshadow the realisation of this Ideal in the Twentieth Century "; to express his opinion on " Lord Rosebery's letter announcing his ' Definite Separation ' from the Liberal Leader." Not only did the infirmities of age negative compliance with such requests, but the very idea of writing on a text prescribed by others was one which he never could entertain.

The place selected for the summer was the Rectory at Bepton, just under the Downs, to the south of Midhurst in Sussex. " It was," writes Mr. Troughton, " a most charming spot, just the sort of place, in fact, to appeal to a man so passionately fond of the country as Mr. Spencer was. . . . It was here, amid this delightful Sussex scenery that he pondered over ' Ultimate Questions ' and put into words the reflection which had more than once occurred to him as old age crept on apace— ' Shall I ever again be awakened at dawn by the song of the thrush.' " [1]

Letter writing was easier for him than personal discussion: for this, if for no other, reason that he could choose his time better. Animated conversation, as years went on, more and more upset him. Insomnia became more persistent; yet, so sound was his constitution, that

---

[1] *Facts and Comments*, p. 207.

his medical attendant remarked that "old age had scarcely touched him." The restrictions on personal intercourse made him all the more keenly alive to written expressions of sympathy. Thus he acknowledges congratulations from the South Place Ethical Society in July, 1900.

Declining years have their pleasures as well as their pains, and among the pleasures may be named expressions of sympathy, such as those contained in the address you send me on behalf of the South Place Ethical Society. Many, who have spent their lives in the development of their ideas, have not had the satisfaction of meeting with recognition. Only after their deaths have their ideas been appreciated. I have been more fortunate, and, having lived long enough to complete my work, have also lived long enough to see that it has not been without its effect. Thank you for your kind words, and for the expression of your good wishes.

The book he was writing clearly shows how deeply his soul had been stirred by the war in South Africa and the policy that led to it. Probably no political event in the whole course of his life moved him so profoundly. "I am ashamed of my country," was his frequent remark. Liberals equally with Tories were, in his opinion, responsible for the deplorable condition into which the country had drifted. For this, as well as for other reasons, he declined to join the League of Liberals against Aggression.

To A. M. Scott.

26 *July*, 1900.

I do not desire to be classed among those who are in these days called Liberals. In the days when the name came into use, the Liberals were those who aimed to extend the freedom of the individual *versus* the power of the State, whereas now (prompted though they are by desire for popular welfare), Liberals as a body are continually extending the power of the State and restricting the freedom of the individual. Everywhere and always I have protested against this policy, and cannot now let it be inferred that I have receded from my opinion.

Nor did he desire to be classed with the party that had seceded from the Liberals. In June, 1901, he instructed his secretary to write to the editor of one of the London papers:

When the Liberal Unionists seceded they were never weary of declaring that in all questions save one—the Home Rule question—they remained Liberals; and so long as this question was prominent they were entitled to stick to the name. But things have changed since then, and their *raison d'être* as ' Unionists ' has long since disappeared. . . . They have now nothing in common with the Liberals and everything in common with the Tories. Then why not . . . invariably call them Conservatives or Tories?

To Moncure D. Conway.

15 *August,* 1900.

Waves of human opinion and passion are not to be arrested until they have spent themselves. You appear to think, as I used to think in earlier days, that mankind are rational beings and that when a thing has been demonstrated they will be convinced. Everything proves the contrary.[1] A man is a bundle of passions which severally use his reason to get gratification, and the re-

---

[1] To Spencer might have been applied the words of the *Times* regarding a Russian statesman: "His has been that untimely fate—the unhappiest that can befall a reformer—to sit helplessly by while reaction triumphs."

sult in all times and places depends on what passions are dominant. At present there is an unusual resurgence of the passions of the brute. Still more now than a generation ago, men pride themselves, not on those faculties and feelings which distinguish them as human beings, but on those which they have in common with inferior beings—pride themselves in approaching as nearly as they can to the character of the bull-dog.

To WILFRID SCAWEN BLUNT.

5 *September*, 1901.

When is this dreadful state of things to end? I hope that there may come a severe financial crisis, for nothing but the endangering of their personal interests will open the eyes of the war party.

7 *October*.—You are doubtless rejoicing, as I am, that the aspect of affairs is black for the Government and for the country. A little pressure on the market, a bank failure or two and a consequent panic, may open people's eyes and make them repent. However heavy the penalty they may have to bear, it cannot be too heavy to please me.

About this time he wrote (by way of suggestion, not for publication) to the editor of one of the London papers.

A strong point might be made against our proceedings in South Africa by quoting a passage from the charge of the Grand Jury, delivered by Lord Chief Justice Cockburn in the case of Governor Eyre and the Jamaica business. In that charge he emphatically asserted that the English constitution knows no such thing as martial law; saying that martial law has no independent basis whatever, but is an agency which comes into action only when the ordinary agency for maintaining law has broken down—is, in fact, nothing else than an armed servant of the ordinary law, which is called in when the ordinary servant is not strong enough to carry out its injunctions. This passage should, I think, be continually emphasised.

To THE RIGHT HON. JOHN MORLEY.

10 *November,* 1901.

I enclose you a copy of a letter written a little time ago, which had not the intended effect.

I enclose it because I see that in your speech the other day you quoted another distinguished lawyer on the question of martial law; and it occurs to me that if, as I see stated, you propose to bring up the question before Parliament this next session, it will be desirable to add Cockburn's opinion to Campbell's. . . . Martial law as properly understood ought to be nothing more than the calling in of the soldiery, with its accompanying discipline, when the police fails: the whole thing being done under command of the civil power, and ceasing when the civil power withdraws its command.

An interchange of letters took place with Dr. E. B. Tylor touching the controversy of 1877.[1] Spencer had drawn attention to a passage in *First Principles* (chap. ii., § 14, para. 2) in which occur the words " be it in the primitive Ghost-theory, which assumes a human personality behind each unusual phenomenon "—words showing conclusively that his own ideas had been formed before the promulgation of Dr. Tylor's opinions. Soon after, however, his secretary discovered that the passage cited was not in the earlier editions of *First Principles,* having been first introduced as late as 1890. Dr. Tylor was at once informed of this, and a long letter was after-

---

[1] See vol. i., chap. xiv., p. 252.

wards written giving an account of the genesis of his beliefs, going back to 1853 and concluding thus:—

I feel bound to recall these evidences, as already said, because I cannot leave you under the impression that I accept your version of the matter, but I do not suppose your opinion will be altered. An idea fixed for thirty years is not easily changed, and it is impossible to change my own conviction, conscious as I am of what the facts were; so the matter must now drop.

Professor Knight's article in the *Bookman* for January, 1901, was a welcome introduction to the new year. Its very sympathetic and appreciative utterances he prized all the more as coming from one who was in antagonism on more than one point. " In England (though not elsewhere) manifestations of approval have usually been so tepid that yours, being so exceptional, give me much pleasure." In May he was both " surprised and gratified " by an application from Mr. Brant-Sero (an Iroquois) for permission to translate *Education* into the Mohawk language. As if in answer to his complaint that manifestations of approval in England had been tepid, there appeared an article " On the Last of the Great Victorians," in *Black and White* (18 May, 1901) —an article pervaded by a tone of " deep and heartfelt sympathy."

Incidents like these belong to the bright side of 1901. On the dark side were not only the war and the alleged national degeneration; there was also the continued shrinking of the already narrow circle of his friends: death having recently removed Dr. W. J. Youmans, Mr.

John Fiske, Dr. Lewis G. Janes, and Mr. Robert Buchanan.

Occasionally one comes across a letter which shows how he was progressing with his last book.

To Sir Robert Giffin.

17 *May*, 1901.

Is it possible to state in a rough way—of course in a *very* rough way—what is the amount per head entailed on producers by £100,000,000 of national expenditure in terms of working days? . . . I have in view the extra work entailed on those who are either manually occupied or are necessary regulators of those manually occupied, and on whom extra taxation entails so much the more labour. I want to state how many extra days work in the year £100,000,000 of expenditure entails on these.

20 *May.*—I am immensely obliged to you for your note and memorandum. It tells me all I wanted. Nothing more than a rough estimate is possible or is requisite for my argument—an argument directed towards showing people that, as in all cases throughout history, those who enslave other peoples enslave themselves.[1]

To Right Hon. Arthur James Balfour.

Petworth, 19 *June*, 1901.

I believe it has been announced that you propose to drop the Copyright Bill. It is now 24 years since I gave evidence before a Royal Commission which sat in 1877, and among the recommendations agreed upon was one that the duration of copyright should be for life and 30 years after death, instead of being as now; and I believe the report of the Commission recently sitting endorsed that recommendation, omitted in the Bill now before Parliament. . . .

---

[1] *Facts and Comments*, p. 122.

Would it not be possible to introduce a short bill doing nothing more than change the duration of copyright, leaving all detailed matters to be hereafter dealt with?

The matter is very important to needy authors who have families, since it is very much a question of leaving a good provision for children or leaving very little.

To me it is a matter of no personal interest, but only of public interest. I have bequeathed my property for the purpose of carrying on the *Descriptive Sociology* after my death. The returns from my books will form part of the revenues which will be available for the undertaking. Under the existing law a large part of these revenues will lapse seven years after my death.[1]

I have, however, a further reason for being anxious that the present law respecting duration should be changed, namely that as the law now stands it will be possible seven years after my death for anybody to publish the imperfect versions of my books of which the copyright has expired, though the perfect versions are still copyright. . . . This I should regard as a disaster.

To SIR JOSHUA FITCH.

PETWORTH, 1 *July*, 1901.

In something I am writing I want briefly to enumerate the various ways in which the militant spirit is infusing itself into our teaching institutions of all grades—military discipline, military teaching. . . .

I want to indicate also the way in which the tendency

---

[1] In his will Spencer provided that the residuum of his estate should be devoted, under the direction of Trustees, to carrying on the publication of the series of volumes of the *Descriptive Sociology*, commenced in 1867 and stopped in 1881. Mr. H. R. Tedder, Secretary and Librarian of the Athenæum, was appointed general editor of the series. The following volumes are now in preparation:—Chinese, compiled and abstracted by Mr. E. T. C. Werner, H.M.'s Consul, Kiu Kiang, China; Hellenic Greeks, by Dr. J. P. Mahaffy and Prof. W. A. Goligher; Hellenistic Greeks, by the same; Romans, by Mr. E. H. Alton, F.T.C.D., and Prof. Goligher. Arrangements are also being made for a volume on the Ancient Egyptians.

to unification in teaching has been growing. It was shown in the medical profession some years ago by an agitation for some uniform system of examination, but I do not know how that ended. Then there is the present Government's Education Bill, dropped for the time being, which takes away such small variety as arose from school-board management. And there is the endeavour to unify by introducing the ecclesiastical element more widely or, indeed, universally. Private schools are being put more and more to disadvantage, so that they are in course of being crushed out, and there results an increase of uniformity. Moreover, I remember a while ago there was a meeting of Head-masters of public schools, at which something like an appeal was made to the Government to bring them all under some kind of State control—again to unify the system. I wish to illustrate the universal tendency towards regimentation.[1]

He returned to Brighton early in September, feeling so much stronger that he contemplated taking a fortnight in London—an idea which, however, he had not strength to carry out.

A letter from Mr. Leslie Stephen (September, 1901), introducing Dr. Stanton Coit, the editor of *Ethics,* induced Spencer to subscribe towards the Ethical Lectures Fund, while adhering to the view expressed in 1899 as to the qualifications of the lecturers.[2] He even assented to allow his name to be given to one of the lectureships. His misgivings about the scheme presently re-appeared in another form, as one learns from a letter to Dr. Coit in November.

---

[1] *Facts and Comments,* p. 140. In April following he wrote to several London papers, recalling a saying of Lord Salisbury's that "their aim must be to capture the Board Schools." "That which was then set forth as an aim is being now carried out."

[2] *Supra,* chap. xxv., p. 144.

The drift of the articles in your periodical, *Ethics* . . . opens my eyes to the certainty that there will be no sufficient agreement in the ethical views to be propagated by ethical societies. . . . So clearly do I see that some of the views enunciated will be views from which I profoundly dissent, that I must ask you for an abandonment of the proposal to give my name to a lectureship.

In another letter to Dr. Coit (1 March, 1902) he says: " I cannot without self-stultification continue to co-operate in any way, and I must therefore request that my name may be erased from the list of subscribers to the fund." But he was careful to add that his " dissent from the social ideals, which the Ethical movement, as now directed, will diffuse, must not be taken as evidence of contentment with present social arrangements."

His impatience as a reader, to which he so frequently alludes, was sometimes traceable to intellectual dissent, as in the case of Kant's *Critique,* sometimes to emotional or moral aversion, as in the case of Carlyle. In whichever of those two ways his further acquaintance with a book was put a stop to, the result, as far as concerned his estimate of the author's works, was the same. Instead of keeping his judgment in suspense, he was apt to form a very decided opinion, which in after life he seldom reconsidered. This trait was exemplified when Mr. Collins asked what he thought of Robert Louis Stevenson.

To F. Howard Collins.

18 *October,* 1901.

Your question about Stevenson I answer just after having listened to a review of his life in the *Times.* I have read very little of him. I began to read many

198

years ago *Travels with a Donkey in the Cevennes,* but
was so disgusted with his treatment of the donkey that
I gave it up quickly and never looked into another of
his books for many years.

His opinions as to the value of learned Academies had
long been well-known. It was, therefore, from a feeling
of the courtesy due to an author of distinction, rather
than from any expectation of receiving a favourable
response, that he was invited to join the movement for
the institution of a British Academy of Letters.

To Sir E. Maunde Thompson.

20 November, 1901.
I am obliged by the invitation made by the sub-com-
mittee you name to be one of those to receive the charter
of the proposed British Academy of Letters. I must be
excused, however, if I do not accept the invitation. . . .
I have, in contesting the views of Mr. Matthew Arnold,
who wished for an English Academy, given expression
to sundry objections, and I still hold those objections to
be valid.

Sir Joseph Dalton Hooker, Lord Avebury, and Spencer were the sole survivors of the X Club; but they
rarely met in these years. Occasionally letters passed
between them.

To Sir Joseph Dalton Hooker.

16 November, 1901.
It is a long, long time since any news passed between
us—a year and a-half, I think. Superfluous letter writing is at your time of life, and even at mine, a thing to
be avoided; but still, I should like to have a few lines
telling me how you fare in your contest with the inevita-

ble. . . . I am taking my daily drives and doing a fair
amount of work.

A sentence in Sir Joseph Hooker's reply—'' You have
held, and still hold, a big grip on my life ''—shows how
strong the bond of their friendship was.

FROM LORD AVEBURY.

25 January, 1902.

You may have seen that the Committee of the Society
of Authors, over which I have the honour of presiding,
have suggested your name as the one we should put forward from England for the Nobel prize.

The suggestion I may add has been cordially received.

As one of your oldest friends it has been a great pleasure to me to take a part in endeavouring to secure for
you this well merited recognition.

Spencer's name was forwarded to the Swedish Academy, but the prize was not awarded to him.

He was trying to answer the question, '' What should
the Sceptic say to Believers? '' [1]

TO MRS. SIDNEY WEBB.

14 February, 1902.

My special motive for writing is to ask whether you
did not once tell me that your girlhood was often made
miserable by your religious convictions—by the thoughts
of hell which had been instilled into you.   And my reason for asking this is that I am just now about to say a
little upon the difficulty of the agnostic in dealing with
others—when to leave them alone and when to attempt
to change their convictions.   There are various cases,

---

[1] Facts and Comments, p. 292.

and I want to say a little about each kind.   There is, I
believe, a good deal of religious despondency, and not
a little religious insanity, and all this evil has to be set
off against what may be said on the other side.

Facts and Comments was published in London and
New York on April 25, 1902.

To ALEXANDER BAIN.

25 *April,* 1902.

I bait my hook with a book in the hope of catching a
letter. You either have received or will shortly receive
a copy of *Facts and Comments,* which is my last book,
written during these two years at the rate of ten lines
a day.

I have heard nothing of you for a long time save the
accounts which Duncan has given me on the occasions
of his visits down here. You, too, as I gather, are much
invalided, but are still able to take a drive daily. This
unfortunately I cannot do. . . .

I not unfrequently think of the disgust you must feel
at the fate which has overtaken *Mind.* That you, after
establishing the thing and maintaining it for so many
years at your own cost, should now find it turned into
an organ for German idealism must be extremely ex-
asperating. . . . Oxford and Cambridge have been cap-
tured by this old-world nonsense. What about Scotland? I suppose Hegelianism is rife there also.

As friend after friend was removed by death, Dr.
Bain, like Spencer, cherished all the more warmly tokens
of fellowship from those that survived. '' I never saw
such a beaming smile on Dr. Bain's face as when he
showed it [the above letter] to me,'' said his wife to the

201

LIFE AND LETTERS OF HERBERT SPENCER

present writer. " He was evidently extremely pleased to hear from Mr. Spencer, and Mr. Spencer's sympathy in connection with *Mind* was most highly valued."

Next day Spencer wrote to Professor Masson in a similar strain.

I suppose Hegelianism is rife in Edinburgh as it is in Oxford and Cambridge. This is one of those inevitable rhythms which pervade opinion, philosophical and other, in common with things at large. But our Hegelianism, or German Idealism in England, is really the last refuge of the so-called orthodox. As I have somewhere said, what could be a better defence for incredible dogmas than behind unthinkable propositions?

In December previous he had written to the Editor of *Mind,* with reference to the promise made to Professor Sidgwick at the time *Mind* changed hands, guaranteeing his financial support.

Since that time *Mind* has been becoming more and more conspicuously an organ of the Hegelians, or of German Idealism. The result was that, just before my first annual subscription became due, I wrote to my bankers to erase my name as a subscriber. Of course I should regard it as quite appropriate that each school of philosophic thought should have its say, but of late one school has been having very much more say than the rest. It cannot be expected that I should aid the survival of a periodical so largely devoted to the expression of views diametrically opposed to my own.

The appearance of his last book just two days before his eighty-second birthday lent additional meaning and

202

fervour to the annual greetings.[1] Thus Lord Hobhouse wrote:—

Though, alas! the generation is froward; and some of your good seed has been devoured by fowls of the air; and some fallen on barren rock; and some choked by thorns; a great deal has fallen on good ground, and has brought forth fruit manifold, and will assuredly bring forth more in more favourable seasons.

To Lord Hobhouse.

4 May, 1902.

Among the many congratulations received on the occasion of my eighty-second birthday I can say very sincerely that none have been so appropriate, and therefore so pleasurable to me, as that for which I have to thank you.

It is, as you say, doubtful whether the event itself is one to be rejoiced over, but you express my own feeling fully, when you say that it is a matter of rejoicing to me that I have lived long enough to complete the work, which half a century ago I conceived and soon after definitely undertook. Some small aims of no great moment remain unfulfilled; but, passing these by, I have the satisfaction, which I suppose is rare, of having done what I proposed to do; and it adds to this satisfaction to receive this expression of your sympathy.

You too have been working towards ends which the course of things is thwarting, and we must both be content with contemplating a remoter time when good efforts made now will have some effects, though they may be infinitesimal.

---

[1] Among the greetings from abroad was the usual letter and birthday gift from M. Geza Schulek, of Buda Pesth. Three years before this date he and his wife had come to England expressly to see Spencer for a few minutes.

An envelope, containing a lock of his hair, encloses also a note, of which the following is a facsimile:—

My hair cut on
my 82nd birthday
still retains some of
the original colour. I
write this without
spectacles and without
feeling the need for
any.

H. S.

CHAPTER XXVIII

THE CLOSE OF LIFE

(*April*, 1902—*December*, 1903)

Facts and Comments had been definitely announced as his last book. This circumstance, together with the varied nature and contentious character of the work, tended to excite more than the usual interest. Professor Masson thought it " eminently readable and interesting —none the less that much of it is provocative of dissent, and is sure to be protested against in various quarters. I refer especially to the questions concerning the war and other present-day questions. If I say that here and there I am among the dissenters in this department, that will not, I am sure, distress you much." Sir Joseph Dalton Hooker was a dissenter, or at least a partial dissenter, about the war. Professor Bain thought the " showing up of Matthew Arnold's absurd claim for the State-Church as the exclusive nursery of men of genius was a very deserved and important correction. But perhaps the part of the book that aroused my deepest interest was your concluding remarks on Ultimate Questions." While recognising it as " the conclusion of strenuous, honourable, consistent work," the *Times* noted in these " slight, sketchy, and imperfect " utterances " a tone of persistent egotism," too great to be quite excusable. The essay on " Some Light on Use-Inheritance," " has the charm of copious and felicitous

205

illustration in which Mr. Spencer is unsurpassed.''
'' We should have liked the latest words of one who has
deeply influenced his generation to be measured, calm,
equitable, peaceful. In some of these essays are present
these qualities. . . . But in too many of the *Facts and
Comments* is a tone of acerbity.'' The *New York Saturday* of May 17 was gracious enough to excuse this
'' excursion into the domain of fads,'' on the ground
that '' a man of eighty-two is too old to work and may
play if he likes. If in setting his desk in order he comes
across scraps of disconnected literary output, which did
not fit anywhere in his earlier books, and he chooses to
gather them into a haphazard collection . . . why
should he not do so?'' Readers in the United States
were naturally interested in '' A Few Americanisms,''
and were not unwilling to avail themselves of the invitation, conveyed in the last paragraph of the article, to
expose deteriorations in the English language as spoken
in Great Britain. Among the causes that contributed
to create more than the usual demand for the book on the
Continent, not the least were its denunciations of the
South African War: these denunciations seeming to
afford a justification for the general dislike to Great Britain during those years. So popular was it in France
that three translations were offered. In Germany more
than one version was proposed; but, instead of translating the whole book, selections were made from it and
from *Various Fragments*. At one time it looked as if
there would be no Italian translation, Spencer having
intimated that rather than tolerate the persistent repudiation of an author's rights he would prefer to let the
book remain untranslated. '' It is not that I care about

the actual amount receivable.'' In proof of this he handed over to the translator his own share of the amount paid by the publisher. Russia, so long in the front rank, had years ago fallen behind. Spencer's books continued to be objects of suspicion to the Russian authorities, whose blundering ignorance is shown in the *Times* of July 28, 1903. A student, on being examined for admission to the University, was charged with being a socialist, on the ground that he had been seen in the street at the age of 15 with Spencer's *Sociology* under his arm! Nevertheless, *Facts and Comments* appeared in a Russian dress before it was published in French or German.[1]

In May, 1902, he went on what was to be his last visit to the country, Leith Vale, Ockley, in Surrey, being the place selected. How he enjoyed himself was thus described at the time by Mr. Troughton: '' Above all he is delighted with the multitude of song-birds hereabouts. Listening to the birds the other day, while sitting outside under the verandah during a short spell of sunshine, Mr. Spencer said, ' This is what I have been looking forward to for the last six months.' '' His absence from Brighton deprived him of the pleasure of meeting one with whom he had corresponded a great deal, but whom he had never seen—the Dowager Countess of Portsmouth, who first became interested in him through her brother, the Hon. Auberon Herbert.

---

[1] Since the year 1865, when proposals to translate his books were first thought of, most of Spencer's principal works had been rendered into Russian, French, German and Italian. Portions of them had also been translated into almost all the other languages of Europe, as well as into the chief languages of India and into Japanese and Chinese. During his last years translations of *Education* into Arabic and Mohawk were mentioned.

To the Dowager Countess of Portsmouth.

6 *June,* 1902.

I am very unfortunate. Some years ago you honoured me with a call at Avenue Road, and I was out. And now that you are about to visit Brighton I am away from there. . . .

The contretemps is very provoking, since I should have been greatly pleased to see one from whom I have received so many kindnesses. I fear I thus lose my last chance, for being now eighty-two, the probability that you will again visit Brighton during my life is but small.

To Mrs. Bray.

6 *June,* 1902.

Allow me at eighty-two to shake hands with you at eighty-eight! I say shake hands rather than offer congratulations, since you know as well as I do, or better, that the infirmities and weariness of advanced years are such as render continuance of them not a cause for congratulation. . . .

I managed three weeks ago to get to this place, which is in all respects charming, and I am on the average profiting by the change.

The requests for contributions from his pen were varied and numerous. He was invited by the Danish Minister of the Interior, through Mr. Goschen, the British Minister, to write a short article for a journal which was to be issued weekly during the Exposition Historique de la Presse Danoise, the subject prescribed being an inquiry as to the direction in which social development was tending—whether towards socialism or individualism. This invitation was declined " because the amount of thought required would be too great a tax." The approaching Coronation brought many such appeals.

THE CLOSE OF LIFE

A few lines " on the subject of the Trust in Atlantic
Steamships " were solicited by one of the London daily
papers. *The Neue Freie Presse* was eager to get a contribution for its Christmas number—" Antisemitism "
being suggested as a topic. Mr. Spielmann begged for
a few words on the condition of the Jews in Roumania.
The *Giornale d'Italia* sought his opinion about the sup-
pression of the Religious Orders in France. " A few
words of sympathy and support " were sought by a
small number of people in Melbourne, who were forming a society bearing his name.

Peace had been proclaimed and there had now to be
faced the consequences of the war. The condition of
the sufferers, whether Boers or Britons, aroused the
active sympathy of all parties. Among those who had
suffered most was Ex-President Steyn, whose fortune
and health were completely shattered by his heroic efforts to save the independence of his State. While Mr.
Steyn was on his way to Europe, to obtain the best available medical assistance, Spencer was asked to give his
name to a movement to send some token of the sympathy
and admiration of well-wishers. He readily assented on
condition that the matter would be kept entirely private,
and that the secretarial work would be done by the
friend who had made the suggestion.

The gift was transmitted with the following letter:—

To Ex-President Steyn.

10 *August,* 1902.

A few friends in England have paid me the compliment of making me the medium for transmitting to you
the accompanying testimonial of their sympathy and

209

high admiration. They believe, as I do, that nowhere among historic characters is there to be found one whose persistence in upholding a cause he believed to be right has been more conspicuous. Even enemies must admit that sacrifices of position, property, and health, which have ended in a prostration so extreme as that which you now suffer, imply a heroism rarely to be found among men. To emphasise their belief and accompanying admiration, they beg your acceptance of this proof of their great regard, joining to it the hope that with care, and the attention of sympathetic friends, you may yet recover.

Needless to say, this spontaneous recognition of his honesty of purpose and of the self-sacrificing devotion with which he had pursued the course he believed to be right, was gratefully appreciated by Mr. Steyn. The value of the gift was enhanced by the medium through whom it was transmitted, Spencer's having been an honoured name in South Africa, long before the outbreak of the war.

Spencer was eagerly waiting for public intimation of some centre of co-operation for the collection of subscriptions to the Boer Fund, and represented to General Botha and his colleagues, who were then in London, the impolicy of delay.

To General Louis Botha.

24 *October,* 1902.

I have been both astonished and greatly annoyed by the way in which the Boer Relief Fund has been managed in England. We have a maxim, " Strike while the iron is hot "; whereas the course pursued seems to have been " Wait till the iron is cold "!

If, immediately after your interview with Mr. Chamberlain, there had been an advertisement, naming a committee of some three or five, with an indication of the bank to which subscriptions might be paid, there would at once have been a response from a great many who now have become almost indifferent from mere lapse of time. Two months have passed, and the feelings of the sympathetic have been allowed to die away before anything practical has been done. . . . The whole thing, in my opinion, has been dreadfully bungled. Pray have the thing put in such business form as is always taken by any body which proposes to raise subscriptions.

General Botha shared Spencer's regret that so much precious time had been lost. But being without experience in circumstances entirely new, he and his brother delegates had to be guided by the advice of their friends.

A request made by the Rationalist Press Association for permission to publish a cheap reprint of the first part of *First Principles* was declined for reasons stated in the following letter.

To GEORGE J. HOLYOAKE.

26 *August*, 1902.

Two mischiefs are apt to arise from reading separately the first part of *First Principles:* (1) Those who are opposed to its views conclude that the second part, being as they think based upon the first, must be equally opposed to their views, and even when they have the whole volume before them they read no further. I have direct evidence that this happens. (2) Those who read sympathetically are liable to draw the utterly erroneous conclusion that in Part I. is contained the substance of the Synthetic Philosophy, and that having read it they need read no further.

There is a mischief of another kind from presenting the " Unknowable " apart from the general system of things set forth under the title of "The Knowable." Those who are led to abandon the current creed, and whose lives have given them no knowledge of the natural order of things to fill the gap left, remain in a state of unstable equilibrium, and are apt to lapse back into one or other kind of superstition—Roman Catholicism usually. I personally know two instances of this.

A month or two later he assented willingly to the issue of a sixpenny edition of *Education*. The Northumberland Society for the Liberation of Education from State Control, was also permitted to reprint the chapter on "National Education" in *Social Statics*.

The quantity of miscellaneous correspondence got through during the three months spent in the country is astonishing, when one remembers his increasing infirmities—aggravated by the "unsummerly summer," as he calls it: "winter" is the term by which he describes it to Mr. Carnegie. "During this sojourn at Leith Vale," writes Mr. Troughton, "it became more manifest than it had been before that he was breaking up, physically, certainly, and also mentally; but the decay of mental faculty was less marked than the bodily decrepitude, which seemed now to be advancing with rapid strides."

Points of resemblance between Spencer's views and those of Rousseau had been touched upon in the past more frequently than Spencer liked, owing to the suggestion conveyed that he had borrowed some of his characteristic doctrines about man, society, and education from the French writer. With regard to education he had been at pains to point out to M. Gabriel Compayré in October, 1901, that he had never read *Emile*, and

212

owed none of his ideas on education to it. And, now, when Mr. Hudson sought permission to dedicate a forth-coming book on Rousseau to him, he felt constrained to refuse.

To W. H. HUDSON.

7 *January,* 1903.

I regret to say " No " to any proposal you make, but I cannot consent to the dedication of your book on Rous-seau to me. There are several kindred reasons for this.

You probably remember the controversy with Huxley in the *Times* ten years ago or more. . . . One of his letters contained the assertion that I had adopted my political views from Rousseau. Such a dedication as you name would tend to verify this wholly baseless as-sertion. . . . His cardinal political principle, so far as I know it at second hand, I reject.

He is said to have taught the primitive equality of men. This I hold to be absurd, and my own doctrine implies no such belief, which is quite inconsistent with the evolutionary doctrine—the struggle for existence and survival of the fittest.

Not the equality of men, but the equality of their claims to make the best of themselves within the limits mutually produced, has all along been my principle. . . .

The equality alleged [in *Social Statics*] is not among men themselves, but among their claims to equally-lim-ited spheres for the exercise of their faculties: an utterly different proposition. Huxley confused the two and spread the confusion, and I am anxious that it should not be further spread. Pray, if you have occasion to refer to my views, take care to emphasise this distinc-tion.

His interest in affairs of public moment withstood to the last the advance of the infirmities of age.

213

To Frederic Harrison.

5 *March*, 1903.

Doubtless you remember the meeting held many years ago *a propos* of the disestablishment and disendowment of the Church,[1] and doubtless you remember that you were commissioned to draw up the heads of a bill setting forth the aims of those represented by the meeting, among whom, by the way, was Mr. Chamberlain (!).

I presume you have a copy of this draft bill in printed form. The question is again coming to the front, and this meeting of Free Churches at Brighton may be the occasion for bringing it to the front. Would it not be well for you to put before the leaders this same document as indicating what were, and are still, I believe, the aims of those who moved in the matter. . . .

My distinct impression is that all property accruing to the Church after the Reformation was to remain with the Church; but that all property, existing as its property before the Reformation, was to revert to the State and to be used for such secular or other purposes as might be generally or locally decided.

The occasion is a good one for dissipating the injurious error, which is widespread, that those who seek to disestablish desire possession of the whole of the Church property, old and new.

The final occasion on which he was offered an academic title was in the spring of 1903, when the University of London sought to confer on him the honorary Degree of Doctor of Literature. It was intimated to him that the degree was to be conferred on the Prince and Princess of Wales, himself, and on not more than two others.

---

[1] *Autobiography*, ii., 303-305.

THE CLOSE OF LIFE

To Sir A. W. Rücker, Principal of the University of London.

March, 1903.

I greatly regret that acceptance of the honour, which so distinguished a body as the Senate of the University of London proposes to confer upon me, should for any reasons be excluded.

In the first place, my state of health has prevented me from leaving the house since last August. . . .

Even should the Senate, prompted by kind consideration on my behalf, dispense with my presence, there would still remain an insurmountable difficulty. For a third of a century, during which honorary titles, home and foreign, have from time to time been offered to me, I have, in pursuance of the belief that, though apparently beneficial to literature and science, they are in the end injurious, declined the offers. Were I now to accept the distinction which the Senate of the University of London is so good as to hold out to me, these bodies, including sundry British and foreign universities and various continental academies, which have proposed to accord me doctorships and memberships, would be thereby slighted and an act, which would manifestly inflict upon them something approaching to an insult, is one which I naturally cannot bring myself to do.

Of course, my regret that I am thus prevented from accepting the honour offered by the eminent men constituting the Senate is increased by the consciousness that the occasion is quite a special one.

Though unwilling to accept honours for himself, he was always ready to join in proposals to do honour to those who deserved it. When it was proposed to give a reception to Mr. Holyoake on his eighty-sixth birthday, he wrote:

215

To C. Fletcher Smith.

28 March, 1903.

I have not been out of doors since last August, and as Mr. Holyoake knows, it is impossible for me to join in the reception to be given to him on his 86th birthday. I can do nothing more than express my warm feeling of concurrence.

Not dwelling upon his intellectual capacity, which is high, I would emphasise my appreciation of his courage, sincerity, truthfulness, philanthropy, and unwearying perseverance. Such a combination of these qualities it will, I think, be difficult to find.

Though unable to write anything which the Industrial Freedom League might distribute as a leaflet, with a view to combat the growing tendency of municipalities to embark on business undertakings, he wrote to Lord Avebury: " I need hardly say how fully I sympathise with the aims of the Council and how energetically I should have co-operated had it been possible. I shall willingly contribute to the funds, if some fit form is sent to me." The state of his health probably prevented him complying with the request to send to *Le Matin* a message of good will to the French on the eve of the King's visit to Paris; but a similar request, made before M. Loubet's visit to London in July, was responded to:

All advocates of peace (he wrote)—all who believe that future civilisation is bound up with the friendship of nations—will rejoice in the visit to England of a Frenchman who represents France; and I, in common with them, hope that his reception will prove that the general feeling in England expresses something more than the official ceremonies of the occasion.

216

With an effort he roused himself to send a message of encouragement to the Young Scots Society, " which seeks to revive Liberal ideals at a time when Liberal ideals have been forgotten."

Most of his acknowledgments of birthday congratulations this year included the refrain: " I feel now that the prolongation of a feeble old age is not a matter for congratulation—rather for condolence." All through the winter he had hardly ever stirred from his room; and although the return of spring brought back thoughts of the country, once and only once did he express the hope of getting there.

He had a strong prejudice against professional nurses (writes Mr. Troughton), and it was not until it became absolutely necessary that he consented to have one to look after him. Feeble and emaciated as his frame now was, he had lost little of that strength of will which had always been a marked trait with him, and both nurses and doctors found him a by no means easy patient to deal with owing to this. No less emphatic was the assertion of scepticism in regard to the treatment ordered by the doctor. He could not put himself entirely in the hands of another; he wanted to know the reason for this, that, or the other, mode of treatment recommended; the contents and probable effects of the prescribed medicines would be discussed at length, and if the use of them did not conform to his ideas he ignored them.

Marked symptoms of aphasia manifested themselves during the second week of May, along with hallucinations. While he was in this condition Dr. Charlton Bastian, in response to a telegram from Mr. Troughton, came to see him; but, under the impression that the visit

217

was for the purpose of discussing some biological question, he became excited and begged to be left alone. A day or two after, when he began to get better, he had only a vague recollection of the brusque reception he had given to his friend. When his secretary quietly hinted at the purpose of the visit, he was filled with remorse; and dictated an apology " for the rude way in which I met your request for a little conversation." A day or two after he wrote again: " It was a great relief to me to receive your kind note, for I had been dwelling in the fear that you would be offended, and justifiably offended." In a similar vein he apologised on one occasion to his medical attendant: " Please erase from your memory sundry manifestations of my explosiveness and lack of judgment which you saw last night."

His recuperative power was wonderful. Before many days he was again able to undertake correspondence with his more intimate friends. Miss Flora Smith had sent him flowers grown at Ardtornish, with the message: " I thought it might be a pleasure to you to have them from the place where we have with you spent so many happy days." This touched a responsive note. " The scent of flowers coming from Ardtornish hills had a double pleasantness—the general pleasantness of flowers from the hills, and the special pleasantness of flowers from the Ardtornish hills. To me, as to you, they are reminders of long past pleasures, and I am glad to hear that you and your sisters value them in that way, and pleased to think that my presence in those past times was not a disagreeable accompaniment in the thought of these pleasures."

SPENCER'S STUDY AND BEDROOM AT No. 5 PERCIVAL
TERRACE, BRIGHTON.

THE CLOSE OF LIFE

To Sir Joseph Dalton Hooker.

6 *June,* 1903.

It was extremely gratifying to receive through Mr. Scott your kind inquiry. As one's links with life become fewer and fewer each becomes relatively more valuable, and the indication that it still exists excites relatively increasing pleasure.

I am very glad therefore once again to feel the pulse of my still-surviving small circle of friends, and glad especially to feel the pulse of one who had been so good a friend so many years.

I should like to have a few lines giving me indications of your own state, and will excuse you, as you will excuse me, from writing at length.

Sir Joseph Hooker was also extremely gratified to receive this " evidence of abiding fellow-feeling. . . . The dear old X Club is rapidly, with us, I fear, approaching the vanishing point. How curious it seems, that we who were, I think, considerably the oldest members, should be amongst the three survivors."

To Mrs. Sidney Webb.

29 *June,* 1903.

Friends when talking to me about myself have often remarked *à propos* of my state of health, that I have the consolation of remembering all that I have done, and that this must be a great set-off against all that I have to bear. This is a natural mistake, but a profound mistake. Occasionally, past achievements may be said to fill my mind—perhaps once a week, and then perhaps for ten minutes or a quarter of an hour; but they do not form components of consciousness to a greater extent than this. Practically, the bygones are bygones, and the bygones of a large kind do not play much greater parts in memory than those of a smaller kind.

Your wish has recalled a conversation we had some

years ago—I think when you had come down to see me
in Arundel Terrace. Something led us to talk about
meaningless coincidences, which might be thought full of
meaning; and I was prompted to give you examples, two
of them being known to you personally. Further, by
way of making the results very striking, to each successive case as I narrated it you put down what you considered a rational estimate of the probabilities for and
against such a thing occurring to the same person within
say twenty years; and on compounding the numbers the
chances against seemed astounding.

Thoughts of this kind are much more apt to intrude
themselves than are thoughts of the kind you refer to;
and the average colour of the whole consciousness produced is grey.

How pleasant it would be if you were living so close
at hand that you could come in frequently for a few
minutes! But that is one of the things not to be hoped
for.

FROM ALEXANDER BAIN.

8 *June,* 1903.

I have heard with deep regret, of your continued
feeble health and confinement to bed. You have never
been so dependent upon exercise as I am, still you
must feel very weak and depressed. I earnestly hope
you have no actual pain, and can take some interest
in passing events. . . . I send my long-delayed volume
of reprints. . . . Accept my deep sympathy.

TO ALEXANDER BAIN.

13 *June,* 1903.

Very many thanks for your most kind and sympathetic letter, and thanks also for your wishes for my
freedom from pain. Until recently I could have said
yes, but of late spasms have from time to time made
my life difficult to bear.

Knowing that your expressions of fellow-feeling are genuine I shall excuse myself from running further risks by writing at greater length.

This was the last exchange of letters between them. Professor Bain died on 18th September. In intimating this to Spencer, at Mrs. Bain's request, Professor W. L. Davidson added: '' I should like to say from myself that *you* were much in his thoughts of late, and that he frequently expressed his sympathy with you in your illness. His kindness of heart showed itself to the very last in his thoughtfulness for others.''

To WILLIAM L. DAVIDSON.

22 *September*, 1903.

On the loss of a companion one may, of course, fitly condole with Mrs. Bain, but otherwise I do not see that the event is much cause for regret. He had done his work and lived his life, and such portion of it as remained could be little more than continued tolerance. My feeling may be judged when I say that I envy him.

I have on sundry occasions recognised the sympathetic nature on which you remark, and, I think, manifestations of it had become more pronounced in the latter parts of his life.

'' You come to me every day in thought,'' wrote Mr. Carnegie (14 September), '' and the everlasting ' Why ? ' intrudes. . . . Mr. Morley comes in a day or two and you will, as usual, I am sure, be the centre of many talks.''

To ANDREW CARNEGIE.

18 *September*, 1903.

The Why ? and the Why ? and the Why ? are questions which press ever more and more as the years go by. . . .

If means of locomotion sufficed to carry me to Skibo without jolts—if Mr. Spencer's air-ship had been sufficiently perfected, which one may dream of, but nothing more—I should have liked to join John Morley in seeing your feudal stronghold (!) . . .

You have forbidden thanks for grouse: but some words expressing thanks for those which arrived the other day must be added to the above: to which must be joined thanks for the beautiful sea-trout, which I think are more highly coloured in their flesh than any I can remember—more highly coloured than those I have myself habitually caught at Ardtornish.

To the Right Hon. John Morley.

16 *September*, 1903.

When I tell you that a few days ago I consulted with one of my executors respecting details of my funeral, you will see that I contemplate the end of this descent as being not far off—an end to which I look forward with satisfaction. The contemplation of this end prompts me to ask a favour of you.

I have directed that my remains shall be cremated, and I have as you will naturally suppose interdicted any such ceremony as is performed over the bodies or ashes of those who adhere to the current creed.

At the same time, I do not like the thought of entire silence, and should be glad were there given a brief address by a friend. On looking round among my friends you stand out above others as one from whom words would come most fitly; partly, because of our long friendship, partly, because of the kinship of sentiment existing between us, and partly, because of the general likeness of ideas which distinguishes us from the world at large. . . .

Will you kindly undertake this service for me? Should you assent, the consciousness that words of farewell would come from one so wholly appropriate would

222

be a satisfaction to me during the short interval between now and my death.

25 *September.*—Since writing there has occurred to me an obstacle to your assent which may possibly prove fatal. Your next election may be endangered, and if you think so, pray do not run the risk.

FROM THE RIGHT HON. JOHN MORLEY.

26 *September,* 1903.

I need not tell you with what feeling I received your letter. The occasion for it and the purpose of it both alike moved me deeply. That I should comply with your wish, if I survive you, is indeed most certain, and I am grateful to you for mentioning our long friendship and our general community of ideas. I shall always cherish the recollection of your friendship, and I shall never depart from the spirit of your ideas.

Your letter found me at Carnegie's. He desired me, if possible, to ascertain from you one or two objects which you might choose by way of memorial, and he would authorise me when the time comes, to call upon him for the financial means of carrying out whatever among those objects should seem to be most desirable.

I thank you, my dear Spencer, for this high mark of your confidence.

26 *September.*—It is most considerate of you to think of this obstacle. But I do not suppose that my good friends, though staunch presbyterians, could have any notion of curtailing my freedom, and if they had, I should resist it without much fear.

TO THE RIGHT HON. JOHN MORLEY.

27 *September,* 1903.

I thank you most heartily for your assent, and the more so because it is expressed in such a way as to

223

leave me in no doubt respecting the willingness with which it is given. . . . Nothing suggests last words at present. But should there presently come a time when life is obviously ebbing, your face is one of those I should be most anxious to see.

P.S.—If my second letter, which an oversight in the first made needful, should give you the least reason for changing your reply, pray do it. That some speeches of yours in Parliament should be possibly lost is an evil which I recognise as immeasurably greater than the alternative.

P.S. 2—Mr. Carnegie's request I hope to fulfil in a way that will be satisfactory to him.

The hope expressed, that he might be able to fulfil Mr. Carnegie's request to name one or two objects that he might choose by way of memorial, appears not to have been realised, owing, probably, to his rapidly diminishing strength. He was feeling too heavily the burden of years to take up any important matter. He could do little more than wish success to *School*—a magazine which it was proposed to start in January, 1904.

To LAURIE MAGNUS.

12 *October*, 1903.

A periodical which is to adopt the conception of education I have so long entertained, and which is everywhere implied in my writings at large, cannot fail to have my hearty good wishes. The only passage in your programme which calls for comment and suggests a fundamental doubt is that which commits me to the belief that the " training of citizens and the preparation for life " should be undertaken by the State. Now, as from the beginning I have, and do still, maintain that the State has no such functions, and have further maintained that it is not for a government " to mould children into good citizens, using its own discretion in settling what a good citizen is, and how the child may be moulded into one," it appears to me that my approval just given is practically cancelled. Only if the word " State " is omitted from the passage in question, so reducing the proposition to a self-evident one, can I endorse it.

The death of Mr. Lecky severed one more of the few remaining links between him and his old life.

To Mrs. Lecky.

25 *October,* 1903.

The praise of those who are gone very generally contains insincerities, but among the many things which, were I physically able, I might dictate from my sick bed, I can think of none that are not laudatory.

Intellectually clear and judicial, Mr. Lecky was morally sincere in an extreme degree, and his devotion to the setting forth of historic truth has been conspicuous to me as to every one.

The pains incident upon the breaking of a long companionship must necessarily be great. Pray accept my sympathy, now as heretofore.

For some time his more intimate friends had ceased arranging beforehand to come and see him, as the mere anticipation of a visit perturbed him, and he was sure to wish to postpone it. Symptoms similar to those shown in May again made their appearance. By November he was seldom well enough to answer letters, and took little interest in what was going on. In replying to Mr. Shaw Lefevre (now Lord Eversley), who had congratulated him " on the honour conferred on you by the Nobel Trustees," he made no reference to the Nobel Prize. Nor does he appear to have taken any notice of the paragraph in *Der Tag,* of Berlin (November 12), describing

225

him as a candidate for the Nobel Prize for Literature for 1903. *Der Tag,* unfortunately, instead of his portrait gave that of Earl Spencer, with the subscription—" Ein Anwärter für den literarischen Nobelpreis vom Jahre, 1903: Lord Herbert Spencer.'' This was not the first instance of the confusing of Spencer with Earl Spencer by continental writers. In 1885 Earl Spencer apologised for having opened a note from M. Hoguet, addressed " Earl Herbert Spencer, 27 Saint James' Place.'' '' I cannot claim to have any works worthy of the attention of M. Hoguet,'' he wrote, '' though I am proud to bear the same name as one so distinguished in letters as yourself.''

In response to a repeated request he dictated a note on November 20 to M. Coutant of Paris: '' I assent to the addition of my name to the list of those who approve of the aims of the Bibliothèque Pacificiste Internationale.'' After this only one more letter was signed by him, namely, one on the 26th to Mrs. Courtney, who had forwarded a letter addressed to him by Mrs. Steyn, giving an account of the improvement in Mr. Steyn's health and their hope of being able to return to South Africa. '' Even when there,'' Mrs. Steyn wrote, '' we will not forget to think with love and reverence of you as the great Englishman who, in the hour of our deepest suffering, shed so bright a ray on our path and made us again take hope for the future.'' Surely there was a singular fitness in this that the two last letters he signed should have been connected with one of the main purposes of his life—the promotion of peace on earth and goodwill among men.

During the last week of November he took a decided

turn for the worse. He had expressed a wish that Mrs. Sidney Webb should be present when he passed away. She came to see him on the 4th December, but by that time he seemed to have ceased to care to see anybody, only desiring to be left alone. Now and again his indomitable will asserted itself, as when a day or two before he died, after several ineffectual attempts to convey a pill to his mouth, he declined the assistance Miss Killick offered, saying, " I hate to be beaten." On another occasion, when signing a legal document, he remarked to Mr. Troughton, who had moved the paper so as to get the signature at the proper place: " What are you doing? Do you think I am a dying man?" When bidding him good night on the Sunday before he died, Mr. Charles Holme said: " I shall see you to-morrow morning," and was rather surprised by the prompt question: " Why not?"

" All through Monday," Mr. Troughton writes, " he was either unconscious or semi-conscious; and it was during a semi-conscious interval that he motioned me to his bedside, and, holding out his almost fleshless hand, uttered the last words he ever spoke—characteristic in syntactical expression, but apparently meaningless, though it is possible that some definite purpose prompted them. The words were: ' Now I take this step for the benefit of those who are to be my executors; my intention being that after death this my body shall be conveyed by sea to Portsmouth.' " In the evening he became unconscious, remaining so till 4.40 on the morning of Tuesday, 8th December, 1903, when he passed peacefully away. His end was such as his friends desired and he himself wished.

His executors, Mr. Charles Holme and Mr. Frank Lott, found the instructions for the disposal of his body most explicit and detailed. He had forbidden " the now usual display of wreaths and the use of a hearse with open sides for the purpose of display." It was also his wish that those present should not wear mourning. In the event of Mr. Morley not being able to be present, he had left directions that Mr. Leonard Courtney should be invited to take his place. Being at sea on his way to Sicily, Mr. Morley was unable to fulfil his promise to say a few words at the funeral of his friend. Mr. Courtney, who was in Edinburgh engaged in a political campaign, promised to come, if no one else could be found. Lord Avebury found it impossible to come, and Mr. Balfour greatly regretted that official engagements of pressing importance compelled him to decline. Putting aside his own convenience, therefore, Mr. Courtney hastened south.

On the morning of Monday, December 14th, the remains were removed from Percival Terrace, the Mayor of Brighton in his official capacity, and the President of the Brighton and Hove Natural History Society, following the hearse to the railway station. At Victoria station a few friends had assembled. A plain close hearse followed by three carriages constituted the funeral procession through London. As it passed along the streets, few were aware that this was the last journey of one of the greatest thinkers of this or any age. The assemblage at the crematorium at Golder's Green included, in addition to relatives, the members of his household, the executors and two of the trustees, many intimate private friends, distinguished representatives of literature and science, with most of whom Spencer had long been associated as a fellow-worker, and several foreign friends and disciples. A few of his dearest friends were, to their deep regret, unable, owing to the infirmities of age, to pay their last tribute of respect.

The following impressive address was delivered to the assembly of mourners by Mr. Leonard Courtney (now Lord Courtney of Penwith):

I am not worthy to be called to the most honourable duty which has this day fallen upon me. So much I am bound to confess in all simplicity and sincerity at the outset of the few words I may utter. I cannot claim to have been in any fit sense a student of Herbert Spencer's works. I cannot plead for recognition as one of the great company of his disciples. You know, indeed, that Herbert Spencer's first desire was that another man, known and honoured of us all, should speak on this occasion. His consent had been sought and obtained, and his words would have been fitting memorial of the work and worth of the dead. But four years of unremitting and, towards the end, of exhausting toil, have induced John Morley to seek recovery of health and strength by the Mediterranean Sea, and the news of Herbert Spencer's death overtook him as he reached the Sicilian shores of imperishable memories and ever-renewed beauties. His weariness has passed away, his normal vigour is re-established, but it would have been impossible for him to return here to-day had it been right to make the attempt, and it was represented to me that Herbert Spencer had expressed the wish that I should take the place of John Morley if he could not be present himself.

This message was sent to me four days since, when I was in the Northern capital. I was immersed in another sphere of action and occupied with far other thoughts, but to such a call I could not be disobedient, and I am

229

here to-day, craving all forbearance if I fail to satisfy
the unspoken desires which attend this office. I am indeed borne down when I think how vast a concourse
of learners and workers in all lands are, in spirit, if not
in body, attending here to-day to testify with gladness
and gratitude the depth of their debt to the departed.
Yet I must not shrink from adding a few more words
of a personal and private character.

It is many years since I first became acquainted with
Herbert Spencer, and more than a score since our acquaintance became more intimate and my opportunities
of intercourse more frequent and more fruitful by my
entering into a family of which he had been an habitual
guest and honoured friend. Women of that family are
here to-day in whose earliest recollection Mr. Spencer's
personality dwells, who passed from childhood to girlhood, from girlhood to womanhood, under his eye, and
to whom his death is the passing away of the last sur-
vivor of the grown-up people into whose society they
were born. Their memories have in some measure become my own, and upon the advantage thus secured
friendship grew and sympathy increased, a sympathy
in respect to public affairs never so great, so animated,
and so helpful in the years which have quite recently
passed.

The first thought of every one musing over the life of
Spencer must be that of admiration for the vastness of
the work he planned for himself and of gratitude and
even joy that he lived to see his self-ordained task completed. Rarely or never in the history of thought have
we seen so vast a conception carried forward by a single
man into execution. The syllabus which he issued in the
year 1860, inviting support to his undertaking, must
have appeared to many readers a dream that could never
be translated into reality. A thousand chances, apart
from a failure in the pertinacity or resolution of the
planner, might be counted against the fulfilment of his
plans. We know, indeed, that such evil chances soon as-

230

serted themselves. A delicacy of constitution of which, having regard to his long years, Spencer himself was, perhaps, too sensible, threatened to interfere with, if not to arrest altogether, the progress of his work.

The support he received was inadequate to meet the charges of his undertaking, and his means were being consumed at a rate which would soon exhaust them. This second hindrance was more easily set aside than the first. A circular, intimating that the work must be suspended, quickly brought a sufficiency of help. Spencer had already obtained more readers and more disciples than he knew, and friends across the Atlantic united in offering aid substantial enough to remove anxieties. As the result proved, a continually growing sale of his books quickly afforded all needful support, and the special response to his appeal was scarcely necessary.

Indifferent health proved a more lasting difficulty. He was reduced to working very few hours a day, and sometimes to abstaining altogether from work for considerable intervals. The wonder is that with the moderate allotment that was possible so much work was done. Thirty-six years did indeed pass from the first announcement of the undertaking before the final volume was issued. But what a range of inquiry, what an accumulation of illustrations, what a width of generalisation do the volumes of the series not cover.

All history, all science, all the varying forms of thought and belief, all the institutions of all the stages of man's progress were brought together, and out of this innumerable multitude of *data* emerged one coherent, luminous, and vitalising conception of the evolution of the world. It is this harmony issuing out of many apparent discords, this oneness of movement flowing through and absorbing endless eddies and counterstreams and back currents, that constitutes Spencer's greatest glory and caused the multiplying army of readers of Spencer's successive volumes to feel the joy of discovering a great and ennobling vision of progress hitherto unrealised.

If, in later years, some sense of the limitation of the inquiry has supervened, if some feeling has arisen of the insufficiency of the explanations offered, of some steps in the proof, some apprehension of gaps uncovered in the synthesis, there still remains throughout all the varied populations of the civilised world the abiding, undiminished conviction of a great gain realised, of a new plane of thought surmounted and mastered, new footholds of speculation secured which will never be lost in the education of man and the development of society.

Admiration of the range of his inquiry, of the vigour of his analysis, of the scope and comprehension of his great theory, must be our first impression in reviewing Spencer's work, yet must it never be forgotten that his one overmastering and dominant purpose was practical, social, human. Let it be noted that when it seemed too probable that his life would not endure to complete his design in all its parts, he broke off the sociological analysis to reach forward to the right determination of the bases of individual and political ethics. To lay the foundation of these on bed-rocks of truth had always been his ultimate purpose. It was indicated in the first sketch of his proposed labours, and when preparatory clearances threatened to overwhelm him, he left these works to achieve the essential purpose of his plan. The leading principle of his previous inquiries gave him the clue to the solution of this final problem.

The self-adjustment of forces, which he had found explaining all cosmic movements, had a parallel in the self-adjustment of the forces through the working of which has been developed the society of man. In Spencer's vision it seemed inevitable that this should lead him to the highest exaltation of the worth of individual freedom, and to contest with all his energy the interference of the rules of the many with the growth of the one. We may be permitted to cling to the faith that this

232

conception presents a true aspect of ultimate evolution;
and yet it must be admitted that not many of us could
accompany Spencer in all the thoroughness of the immediate application of his principles to society as it is.
If we know but imperfectly what we are, and know not
yet what we shall be, we may still believe in the ultimate
realisation of a perfect order without coercion, and of
the service that shall be perfect freedom; and we may
be bold to insist that meanwhile the presumption is
against interference, the justification of which is a burden to be discharged.

Spencer, indeed, in his late years sadly took note of
movements apparently in contradiction to the leading
principles of his doctrines, and here I may recall a conversation within a week of his death between him and a
friend who had once been wholly with him, but had
latterly leant to Collectivist action. " We have been
separated," said Spencer, " but if we have been moving
along different lines, I know we have both been moving
to the same end." " Yes," she replied—it was a woman
who showed that divergence of opinion could not detach
her from offices of tenderness and of love—" and it may
be that in time some other method of attacking the great
problem will be adopted, which will be neither wholly
yours nor wholly ours." " Yes, it may be," said Spencer, thus revealing in the last week of his life a mind
open to receive new suggestions and to accept new proposals of change.

Standing here by these poor remains so soon to be reduced to " two handfuls of white dust," we are irresist-
ibly drawn on to accompanying Spencer in his last brave
effort to scrutinise the implacable facts of life. The last
chapter of his last book grapples with ultimate questions
and propounds his final judgment on the " Riddle of the
Universe." No record can be more candid, no confession
more striking than that in which he is even appalled
by the thought of space with its infinite extension and
everlasting laws enduring before evolution and creation,

declared things as they are. What is the place of man in this great vision? The brain so full and so powerful has ceased to act. There is no longer any manifestation of consciousness. Can consciousness survive after the organ on which it depended has ceased to be? Is the personality that dwelt in this poor frame to be admitted as in itself indestructible? Or must we acquiesce in its reabsorption in the infinite, the ever-abiding, the ineffable energy of which it was a passing spark? If indestructible in the future, must it not have been as incapable of coming into existence as it is incapable of ceasing to be? Our master knew not. He could not tell.

The last enigma defies our question. The dimensions of the unknown may be reduced through successive ages, but compared with our slender discoveries, estimated at the best, a vastness that remains must ever overawe us. Some fringes of the unknowable may yet prove to be capable of being known, but the great central secret lies beyond our apprehension. Yet two thoughts remain. If the night cometh in which no man can work, we may work while it is day. If we can work, it is somehow within our power to work for what is noble, for what is inspiring, for what is broadening, deepening, and strengthening the life of man. We may devote our lives to the service of supreme goodness. Looking back on the years of Spencer we may say that he thus worked, he thus dedicated himself as truly and as bravely as any man enjoying the solace of a more definite creed. To this spirit, then, whose work survives, whose words yet speak, the wave of whose influence can yet pass from generation to generation, we may say in all the fulness of interpretation which the phrase can bear—"Farewell."

In the afternoon of the same day the ashes were conveyed to Highgate Cemetery and deposited in the sarcophagus which he had kept in readiness for some years.

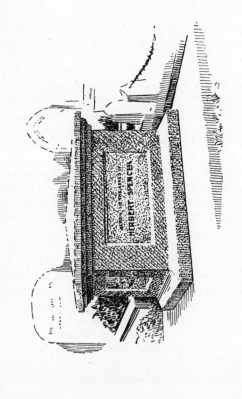

HERBERT SPENCER'S TOMB IN HIGHGATE CEMETERY

The stone, in accordance with his directions, bears only his name, the dates of his birth and death, and his age.

The sense of loss was widespread and profound, as was evident from the letters that came from all parts of the world. Societies at home and abroad vied with one another in their eagerness to pay a tribute to his memory. From Italy condolences were sent by both the Government and the Chamber of Deputies. The Italian Ambassador telegraphed:—

I have been instructed by the Minister of Public Instruction to express the profound regret of the Italian nation for the death of Mr. Herbert Spencer, whose noble life, entirely devoted to the highest aims of philosophy and science, has been an object of deep admiration for all Italian students.

The resolution of the Italian Chamber of Deputies, which was communicated to the Marquess of Lansdowne, Secretary of State for Foreign Affairs, by His Majesty's Ambassador at Rome, and by the Italian Ambassador in London, expressed the condolence of the Chamber with the British Government and the great and friendly nation on the death of Herbert Spencer.

In accordance with an announcement made at the cremation a sum of £1,000 was presented to the University of Oxford, by Mr. Shyamaji Krishnavarma to found a Herbert Spencer Lectureship. Three annual lectures have already been delivered—by Mr. Frederic Harrison in 1905, by the late Hon. Auberon Herbert in 1906, and by Mr. Francis Galton in 1907. A movement was also made for the purpose of raising some fitting memorial, national or international, to be placed, if permission were granted, in Westminster Abbey. The following is the correspondence that took place on the proposal.

I.

To The Very Rev. The Dean of Westminster.

30 May, 1904.

Dear Sir,

We beg to place in your hands herewith a memorial letter addressed to yourself and bearing the signature of those whose names are given in the accompanying list. The original signatures to the form of memorial circulated for this purpose are also enclosed.

In asking you to give consideration to the matter referred to in the memorial, we desire to point out that those who have attached their names have done so in their individual capacities, and not as representatives of any public body or office.

We are, dear Sir,
Yours obediently,
(Signed) R. Meldola,
Geoffrey S. Williams.

II.

To The Very Rev. The Dean of Westminster.

Dear Sir,

A number of the friends, admirers and disciples of the late Mr. Herbert Spencer, being of opinion that some fitting memorial should be raised in this country in recognition of his lifelong devotion to philosophical studies and of his influence upon contemporary thought throughout the world, have come to the conclusion that Westminster Abbey would be an appropriate place for the reception of such a memorial.

In view of the important and stimulating effect of Mr. Spencer's writings in the domains of Philosophy, Science, and Education, we whose signatures are ap-

238

pended feel justified in approaching you with the request
that, in the event of an international fund being raised
for this purpose, you would grant the necessary space in
the Abbey.

We are, Sir,

Yours obediently,

*List of Signatures to the Letter to the Dean of
Westminster.*

His Grace the Duke of DEVONSHIRE, K.G., Chancellor
of the University of Cambridge.

The Rt. Hon. Lord AVEBURY, P.C., D.C.L., LL.D., F.R.S.

The Rt. Hon. Lord HOBHOUSE, P.C., K.C.S.I., C.I.E.

The Rt. Hon. Lord REAY, G.C.S.I., G.C.I.E., LL.D., etc.,
President of the British Academy; President University College, London.

S. ALEXANDER, M.A., Professor of Philosophy, Victoria
University, Manchester.

T. CLIFFORD ALLBUTT, M.D., F.R.S., Regius Professor of
Physic, University of Cambridge.

The Rev. T. G. BONNEY, D.Sc., LL.D., F.R.S., Honorary
Canon of Manchester, Emeritus Professor of Geology, University College, London.

THOMAS BOWMAN, M.A., Warden of Merton College,
Oxford.

E. CAIRD, LL.D., D.C.L., etc., Master of Balliol College,
Oxford.

EDWARD CLODD, Esq.

F. HOWARD COLLINS, Esq.

The Rt. Hon. LEONARD H. COURTNEY, P.C.

A. W. W. DALE, M.A., Vice-Chancellor of the University
of Liverpool.

The Rev. C. H. O. DANIEL, M.A., Provost of Worcester
College, Oxford.

FRANCIS DARWIN, Esq., M.A., M.B., Foreign Secretary of
the Royal Society.

G. H. DARWIN, LL.D., D.Sc., F.R.S., Plumian Professor
of Astronomy, University of Cambridge.

The Rt. Hon. Sir MOUNTSTUART E. GRANT DUFF, G.C.S.I., P.C., F.R.S.

The Rev. A. M. FAIRBAIRN, M.A., D.D., LL.D., Litt.D., etc., Principal of Mansfield College, Oxford.

Sir MICHAEL FOSTER, K.C.B., M.P., V.P.R.S., late Professor of Physiology, University of Cambridge.

The Rev. THOMAS FOWLER, D.D., LL.D., President Corpus Christi College, Oxford; formerly Professor of Logic in the University.

The Rev. J. FRANCK BRIGHT, D.D., Master of University College, Oxford.

FRANCIS GALTON, D.C.L., F.R.S., etc.

The Rev. T. H. GROSE, M.A., Registrar, University of Oxford.

The Rt. Hon. R. B. HALDANE, K.C., M.P., LL.D.

The Rev. D. HAMILTON, D.D., President of Queen's College, Belfast.

C. B. HEBERDEN, M.A., Principal of Brasenose College, Oxford.

ALEX HILL, M.A., M.D., J.P., Master of Downing College, Cambridge.

Sir JOSEPH DALTON HOOKER, G.C.S.I., C.B., D.C.L., LL.D., etc., Past President of the Royal Society.

A. HOPKINSON, K.C., LL.D., Vice-Chancellor of the Victoria University, Manchester.

Sir WILLIAM HUGGINS, K.C.B., O.M., F.R.S., etc., President of the Royal Society.

H. JACKSON, Litt.D., LL.D., Fellow and Prælector in Ancient Philosophy, Trinity College, Cambridge.

The Rev. B. W. JACKSON, D.D., Rector of Exeter College, Oxford.

The Very Rev. J. H. LANG, D.D., Vice-Chancellor and Principal of the University, Aberdeen.

G. D. LIVEING, M.A., D.Sc., F.R.S., Professor of Chemistry, University of Cambridge.

Sir J. NORMAN LOCKYER, K.C.B., F.R.S., etc., President of the British Association.

THE CLOSE OF LIFE

The Rev. J. R. MAGRATH, D.D., Provost of Queen's College, Oxford.

A. MARSHALL, M.A., LL.D., Professor of Political Economy, University of Cambridge.

The Rev. W. W. MERRY, D.D., Rector of Lincoln College, Oxford.

HENRY A. MIERS, D.Sc., F.R.S., Waynflete Professor of Mineralogy, University of Oxford.

The Rt. Rev. J. MITCHINSON, D.D., D.C.L., Master of Pembroke College, Oxford; Canon of Gloucester, formerly Bishop of Barbadoes.

D. B. MONRO, LL.D., etc., Vice-Chancellor, University of Oxford; Provost of Oriel College.

C. LLOYD MORGAN, L.L.D., F.R.S., Principal of University College, Bristol.

JOHN H. MUIRHEAD, M.A., LL.D., Professor of Philosophy, the University, Birmingham.

J. PEILE, Litt.D., Master of Christ's College, Cambridge.

HENRY F. PELHAM, M.A., F.S.A., LL.D., Camden Professor of Ancient History and President of Trinity College, Oxford.

EDWARD B. POULTON, D.Sc., F.R.S., Hope Professor of Zoology, Oxford; President of the Entomological Society, London.

H. R. REICHEL, M.A., LL.D., Principal of University College, Bangor.

J. S. REID, M.A., LL.M., Litt.D., Professor of Ancient History, University of Cambridge.

JOHN RHYS, M.A., Litt.D., Principal of Jesus College, Oxford.

F. F. ROBERTS, M.A., Principal of University College, Aberystwith.

W. R. SORLEY, M.A., LL.D., Knightsbridge, Professor of Moral Philosophy, University of Cambridge.

The Rev. W. A. SPOONER, M.A., Warden of New College, Oxford.

The Rev. J. E. SYMES, M.A., Principal of University College, Nottingham.

Sir WILLIAM TURNER, K.C.B., D.C.L., Vice-Chancellor and Principal of the University, Edinburgh.

JAMES WARD, M.A., D.Sc., LL.D., Professor of Mental Philosophy, University of Cambridge.

W. ALDIS WRIGHT, M.A., LL.D., D.C.L., Vice-Master, Trinity College, Cambridge.

The Rev. P. A. WRIGHT-HENDERSON, M.A., Warden of Wadham College, Oxford.

III.

TO PROFESSOR MELDOLA.

DEANERY, WESTMINSTER.
17 *June,* 1904.

DEAR SIR,

When you first approached me privately with reference to a proposal to commemorate the late Mr. Herbert Spencer in Westminster Abbey, I replied in accordance with precedent that, if a formal request reached me stating the grounds on which the application rested and signed by a few weighty names, it would be my duty to give it grave consideration. I added for your guidance that it would be necessary that I should satisfy myself upon the two following questions:—

(1) Whether Mr. Herbert Spencer's contribution to English thought is of such importance as to merit the assignment to him of one of the very few vacant spaces which are now available in the Abbey for the commemoration of the most distinguished of our countrymen; and

(2) Whether Mr. Herbert Spencer's attitude towards Christianity, as expressed in his writings, may be rightly described as one of suspense rather than hostility, and one which does not make it inappropriate that his memorial should be placed in a Christian church. I said further, that on coming to a decision on these two points I should not be guided entirely by my own judgment, but should seek the aid of persons who would be recognised as experts.

The letter which has now reached me refers to Mr. Herbert Spencer's "lifelong devotion to philosophical studies and his influence upon contemporary thought throughout the whole world," and proceeds to base the request upon the stimulating effect of Mr. Spencer's writings in the domains of Philosophy, Science and Education. With these expressions of appreciation of Mr. Spencer's work I think that there would be a very general agreement, especially in view of the service which he rendered in familiarising the public mind with the general conception of Evolution, and in applying that conception with great courage to various departments of human thought and activity. But I observe that the memorialists do not claim that Mr. Spencer has or will have a high place as a philosophical thinker. When I ask with what important achievement in philosophy or in natural science, or with what permanent contribution to thought his name is destined to be connected, I meet with no satisfactory reply. His philosophical system has called forth the severest criticism, and his views in various branches of knowledge, physical as well as metaphysical, are severely challenged by experts. Eminent he was in his own generation, and stimulating in a high degree. But these characteristics, apart from the enduring quality of work, do not constitute the highest claim to a national homage which is now necessarily restricted to a very few; and I have failed to find evidence that the results which Mr. Spencer has achieved are such as are certain to command recognition in the future.

After what has been said it is unnecessary to enter into the question whether Westminster Abbey as a place of Christian worship could appropriately receive the monument of a thinker who expressly excluded Christianity from his system of thought. It may be right that I should say that this question is answered in the negative by some thoughtful men who differ very widely in religious opinion. At the same time I should wish to recognise the notable softening of his earlier asperity towards religious systems which marks the closing pages of Mr. Spencer's *Autobiography.*

For the reason which I have given above I am compelled to decline the proposal, notwithstanding the distinguished signatures by which it is commended. In doing this I would plead for forbearance on the part of those who will think my decision to be wrong, on the ground that if I have erred it is on the side of caution in the discharge of a great responsibility, and that a mistake of refusal in matters of this kind can be honourably repaired by a future generation.

I beg that you will be good enough to convey this reply to the signatories of the letter.

I remain, your obedient servant,

(*Signed*)   J. ARMITAGE ROBINSON,

Dean of Westminster.

Bearing in mind Spencer's sensitive and high-minded nature and his well-known views on the subject of honours, the present writer would have preferred to pass over in silence the refusal of Dean Robinson to admit any memorial of Spencer into Westminster Abbey—a refusal, be it said, couched in perfectly courteous and dignified terms. But silence might be interpreted as acquiescence in the Dean's judgment upon Spencer's position in the world of thought. On the question whether Spencer had " a high place as a philosophical thinker," it seems enough to say that it may reasonably be assumed that the many very distinguished men of science, philosophy, and letters mentioned above were fully aware of the exceptional nature of their request, and that they deliberately, honestly, and without any mental reservation, subscribed their names to the opinion " that Westminster Abbey would be an appropriate place for

244

the reception " of the memorial. If it was difficult to
understand the Dean's decision at the time, it has been
rendered much more difficult since. In May, 1904, the
Dean refused to a philosopher recognition of " the highest claim to a national homage which is now necessarily
restricted to a very few "; in October, 1905, he conceded
that recognition to an actor. This incident alone would
justify Hegel's famous taunt about the value set upon
philosophy in England.

Whether memorials in Westminster Abbey should be
confined to " those who profess and call themselves
Christians " is a question which it would be out of place
to discuss here; but the readers of this volume will recall
some of the many occasions on which Spencer felt called
upon to suspend his work in order to try to convert
Christians to Christianity.

CHAPTER XXIX

CHARACTERISTICS AND PERSONAL
REMINISCENCES

ONE of the most striking features of Spencer's character was the small weight he attached to authority or, to be more exact, his utter disregard of it. The same trait was possessed by his father, but in a less marked degree; and though his mother displayed the opposite temperament, he himself was inclined to think that a strain of nonconformity had been inherited by him from her recusant ancestry. As he grew up to manhood, the constitutional proneness to set authority at defiance became less an instinctive impulse and more a matter of principle. The tendency for those in power to abuse their position became a settled conviction. Authority had therefore to be jealously watched. When it attempted to restrict his individual liberty, it was firmly resisted, and when it encroached on the liberty of others,

NOTE 1.—This chapter is largely based upon contributions from many of Spencer's personal friends—not always distinguishable in typographical arrangement from the biographer's own narrative. This will explain a certain amount of unavoidable repetition.

NOTE 2.—For published reminiscences of Spencer written by three men who knew him intimately, the reader is referred to the following:—

"Personal Reminiscences" by Grant Allen, written in 1894 and published in the *Forum* for April—June, 1904.

"A Character Study" by William Henry Hudson, *Fortnightly Review* for January, 1904.

"Reminiscences" by James Collier, forming a chapter in Josiah Royce's *Herbert Spencer*. Fox, Duffield and Co., New York, 1904.

their efforts to withstand it claimed his sympathy. Without waiting to acquaint himself with the rights and wrongs of a dispute between those in authority and those subject to it, his first impulse was to take the part of the latter.

In his thinking as well as in his acting, he set authority at naught. Unlike Mr. Gladstone, of whom Mr. Morley says (i., 202) that " in every field of thought and life he started from the principle of authority," Spencer never began by attempting to learn what had already been said. His aversion from reading, which he himself attributed to constitutional idleness, was probably due largely to indifference to other men's opinions. " All my life long I have been a thinker, and not a reader, being able to say with Hobbes that ' if I had read as much as other men I should have known as little.' "

His disregard of authority, human or divine, was disregard of *personal* authority only, and was accompanied by whole-hearted fealty to principles. His profound respect for the *impersonal* authority of principles in human affairs had its complement in a reverence for Divine *impersonal* authority. State ceremonial and ecclesiastical ceremonial were alike distasteful. To pay homage to royal persons while showing little respect for the principles that underlie human society, drew from him the reproof: " It is so disloyal." To bend the knee and utter praise to a Divine person, while ignoring the principles of religion and morality, met with a similar condemnation: " It is so irreligious." One of his most cherished sentiments found expression in what he wrote for the album of autographs and sentiments to be published in Italy at the fourth centenary of the discovery of America: " Be their rank or position what it may, from Emperors and Kings downwards, those who have done nothing for their fellow-men I decline to honour. I honour those only who have benefited mankind, and as one of them I honour Columbus."

Though the moral imperative had not to array itself with the adventitious insignia of personal authority, before it was obeyed, he recognised that personal authority was necessary at a certain stage in the development of the individual and the race. He himself outgrew this stage between his eighteenth and twenty-first year. Referring to the change that took place in his own character during these three years, he says in a memorandum:

This transformation was, I doubt not, due to the falling into conditions more appropriate to my nature. There are those to whom life under authority, with more or less of coercion, is both needful and wholesome, and in whom there is produced by it no distortion of moral attitude. There are others better fitted for self-regulation, less needing control, and to whom control is proportionately repugnant, and in whom by consequence, control is the cause of perpetual chafing and restiveness and a more or less abnormal state. All through my boyhood and up to the time I left home this was the case with me; and as soon as the restraints and the irritation consequent upon them were removed, a more healthful tone of feeling arose, and a beneficial change began, which had, it seems, at the date I name, become very marked. This trait of nature is evidently the same trait which I have just indicated in the description of my religious, or rather irreligious, condition of mind, as also in the tendencies above described to criticise the doings of those in authority, and to originate new plans or invent new appliances. Emotional nature is an all-important factor in the direction taken by intellectual activity, To discover, or to invent, implies a relatively large amount of self-confidence, and therefore a relatively smaller respect for authority; and this relatively small amount of reverence, which runs throughout the conduct towards human beings, is shown also in aversion to that current theory of the universe which makes it the product of a being who demands incessant homage.

The habit of seeking for a cause for every phenomenon was being formed by the time he was thirteen. And as the idea of the universality of natural causation became confirmed, the idea of the supernatural, as ordinarily conceived, became impossible to be entertained. The current theological creed insensibly grew to be alien to his convictions. As his father wrote in 1860: '' It appears to me that the laws of nature are to him what revealed religion is to us, and that any wilful infraction of those laws is to him as much a sin, as to us is disbelief in what is revealed.'' At what time the change took place Spencer could not say, as it had no marked stages. It was unobtrusively going on during the Worcester life. Though in *Facts and Comments* there are indications of a fuller recognition of the reasonableness of religion as a factor in human life, there are no indications of any return to his boyhood's acceptance of a personal Providence intervening in the affairs of the world. His position was frankly agnostic, negation being as unwarranted as affirmation. The mysteries of existence remained mysteries to the last. Though he did not accept the dogmas of any creed, he was, in the truest sense, religious. '' In private life,'' says Mr. Troughton, '' he refrained from obtruding his heterodox views upon

249

others, nor have I ever known him give utterance to any language which could possibly be construed as ' scoffing.' . . . The name of the Founder of Christianity always elicited his profound respect.'' Mr. Troughton recalls more than one occasion on which Spencer strongly condemned language which appeared irreverent.

He had an abundant share of self-confidence. The possible failure of any of his many inventions was seldom taken into account. His doctrines were from the outset deemed secure against attack, notwithstanding repeated experiences of having to modify, or enlarge, or restrict, his previous expositions. More reading and less thinking—more observation and experiment, and less speculation—would have shaken his confidence in some of his conclusions; but would also have caused him to tread with a less firm step the long road he marked out for himself. Self-confidence, however, is natural to all, diffidence comes only with experience of obstacles. Most of us are so familiarised with objections, prohibitions, and troublesome facts, that the idea of another side to what we think, no less than to what we do, is never altogether absent. On Spencer, accustomed to think and act for himself, '' the other side '' did not obtrude. Hence occasional dogmatism; hence also proneness to treat critics and criticisms in a somewhat cavalier fashion.

He was slow to form a friendship; but, once formed, it was not likely to be broken through disregard on his part of even the least of its claims. Several of his closest friendships were with those who had little or no sympathy with his doctrines: as for example, with Mr. Richard Potter, on whose constant affection he had entire dependence. With reference to this Lady Courtney of Penwith writes:—

My mother argued with him a good deal, my father never. It is rather curious that, considering the affection between the two men, and Mr. Spencer's generous appreciation of my father's practical sense and genial and expansive nature, the latter never read Mr. Spencer's books. My father loved an emotion or a sentiment, and understood the concrete; but he had a rooted distrust of abstract ideas, and not much confidence in deductions which depended upon sustained argument; and I can still hear him cheerily ending one of these arguments with: "Won't work, Spencer; won't work, my dear fellow." After I was grown up, I remember vividly an incident illustrating Mr. Spencer's good-humoured acceptance of this attitude of his friend. My mother and I were sitting in the garden at Standish, when Mr. Spencer came up to us with an expression half-annoyed, half-amused, on his face, and said to my mother: " I could almost be angry with your husband, Mrs. Potter, did I not know him so well." " What has he done?" said my mother. Then Mr. Spencer told us how they had been standing together near a large pond we had, of which my father was rather proud, when the latter said: " I wish, Spencer, you would explain the main points of your philosophy to me, just shortly." To which Mr. Spencer replied: " I have been sending you my books these twenty years back; I know you have not read them, and it is a little hard to put them all into ten minutes; however, I will try," and so he began to expound. " Your husband," continued Mr. Spencer, " seemed to be listening intently, as he gazed into the water, and I thought I had at least got my friend to give his mind to my ideas. Suddenly he exclaimed, ' I say, Spencer, are those gudgeon, and rushed round the pond.' "

To go back to my childish memory of Mr. Spencer. He comes back to me as a tall slight man, with a certain air of personal distinction which made even an old coat look well on him. There was a dignity—perhaps also some precision in his manner—which discouraged familiarity, and, except when we were very naughty and in open revolt against our elders, we treated him with great respect. Not that we did not laugh a little over his ways, and even argue with him on subjects of daily life, when we thought we could safely meet him; and we got scolded for it too. I remember when quite a small child, Mr. Spencer coming down to breakfast one morning with his rather long upper lip longer than usual, and saying: " I slept badly, Katie argued with me last night "; and that my remorse was not unmixed with pride that I should so affect a grown up man.

He never liked to feel far removed from opportunities of meeting his friends, though when he knew they were near he could do with little of their company. Few things gave him more satisfaction than to know that the feelings he cherished towards his friends were reciprocated. Lady Courtney gives an instance of this in connection with one of her last visits to him.

I had come armed with all the news I could collect of people he had known, whom I had seen at all recently, and, among others, mentioned the friend whose parents he had so frequently visited in Scotland, and to whose mother he had been much attached. After giving him a greeting from this lady, I said: " She spoke of her mother's affection for you." He started up in bed, coloured up, and said eagerly: " Did she really say that? "; and when I repeated the words as accurately as I could remember them, he lay back looking very pleased and said: " I am very glad to know that. I had a great affection for Mrs. —— [Mrs. Smith], but I never thought she liked me. I fancied she only asked me because her husband did, and because she thought it was a duty to add to the pleasures and health of a man who was doing good work; but I am glad, very glad, she liked me for myself." In spite of his great intellect Mr. Spencer always seemed to me to have a strong element of the feminine in his character: an element which manifested itself in the weaknesses, as well as in the attractive qualities, of his personality.

The Athenæum was greatly prized, among other reasons, because there he could frequently—for many years almost daily—see his friends. The present writer remembers Spencer's unusual elation the morning he received intimation of his election. Readers of the *Autobiography* might be inclined to doubt whether a man of his habits could readily adopt himself to a kind of life so foreign to his experience as that of a London Club, but for thirty-seven years he was an acceptable member of one of those institutions in which absolutely democratic principles have to be reconciled with a nice regard for the feelings and comfort of others. The Club became more of a home to him than his own residence. He tells us that in the beginning of 1868 there occurred " an incident of moment to me, affecting greatly my daily life throughout the future." This was his admission as a member of the Athenæum, under the provisions of a rule whereby the Committee each year elect not more than nine persons of " distinguished eminence in science, literature or the arts, or for public services," and the election must be unanimous. The names of the other eight members elected in the same year were: Mr. W. R. Greg and Professor David Masson, being representative of literature; Mr. (afterwards Sir) Charles Hallé, of music; Mr. W. Holman Hunt, of Art; Mr. (now Sir)

C. R. Markham, Major Sir William Palliser, and Colonel Sir Arthur Phayre, for public services; and Colonel W. J. Smyth, F.R.S., of science. Two of the number, Mr. W. Holman Hunt and Sir C. R. Markham, still survive. Spencer valued the distinction of election to the Athenæum Club by the Committee very highly, and it was the sole recognition of merit which he accepted.

When in London he used to go to the Athenæum almost daily, and occupied himself in looking at the weekly papers, glancing at the magazines, and skimming the new books, to see what was going on. Occasionally he read novels, but only by instalments. Biographies and histories he passed over, but travels had an attraction for him as containing materials for his work. Books dealing with sociology, philosophy, and theology were scanned, both for observing the current of opinion, and also to notice adverse criticism of his views. He was sensitive to anything in the way of misrepresentation and always took action at once, saying he kept in mind the proverb: '' Give a start to a lie and you can never overtake it.'' He used the library for purposes of reference, and never spared time or trouble in verifying facts and statements. An hour or two every afternoon was passed at the billiard table, for which he offered no excuse. He simply liked the game. He was not displeased to have his own dexterity acknowledged, and once modestly boasted that his best break had been one of 47.

In May, 1874, he was chosen a member of the Committee, '' and for a long subsequent time continued to take an active part in the administration of the Club.'' He scarcely missed a meeting, and gave much thought and attention to the smallest details of domestic management, as well as to the more dignified elective duties under the rule above mentioned. He had an extraordinary acquaintance with facts of practical value, and loved to discuss the art of tea-making and kitchen administration on philosophical principles. This does not suggest a very pliable committee-man, but Spencer had more good sense and forbearance in social intercourse than he gave himself credit for. With his usual habit of severe self-judgment he accuses himself of want of tact as a committee-man, and mentions how on one occasion Sir Frederick Elliott, an influential member and ex-Indian official, by means of suavity and cautiousness of expression, carried a motion which Spencer had not been able to accomplish. "Let me add that, though I sometimes failed in my aims from want of tact, I frequently succeeded by persistence." That his services were valued may be seen in the fact that although the usual term of service was three years, and a year must have elapsed before one who had served could become once more eligible, yet he was one of a special committee appointed at the Annual Meeting, and was then elected for a second term. He was thus connected with club business for seven consecutive years. He had long been a member of the London Library Committee. "At this my attendances were far less regular. I suppose in part because the administrative business, neither so extensive nor so complex, attracted me less."

In many respects Spencer was a model club-man. In his relations with his fellow members he invariably showed delicacy and good feeling. It is not enough to say that he was strictly courteous, but he realised that

255

the true spirit of club etiquette is for a man to behave with the studied decorum of one who is living not in his own house, but rather in the house of a friend. In his manners and bearing he showed plenty of that tactful good nature in which he thought himself deficient. He never offended anyone by loud speech, injudicious remarks, or incautious behaviour and was ever most punctilious in adhering to the small unwritten laws upon which so much of the comfort of club life depends.

His craving for companionship and his hospitable impulses were always struggling against the limits which health and work imposed on social intercourse. As he writes in 1870: '' I find more and more that I can manage pretty well when I am master of my circumstances; but when the circumstances master me, I am pretty sure to go to the wall.'' His morbid fear of the results of excitement greatly restricted his personal intercourse with guests, some of whom have been known during a visit of several days duration not to have seen him once. Yet no host could have been more solicitous for the comfort of his guests than he was. When in ordinary health he entered with zest into the amusements of the domestic circle. '' He could thoroughly enjoy a good story,'' says Miss Killick, '' and his powers of relating one were splendid.'' I have heard him repeat a poem of considerable length—' The Northern Lights '—giving it in the Lancashire dialect with great charm. He enjoyed the humour of it so much that the tears streamed down his face.'' His conversation was singularly free from personal gossip, and invariably rose to the general point of view. Seldom adorned by graces of style, it was always fluent, correct, and clear: his deep rich voice adding to the charm. The gift of lucid exposition was shown in his conversation as much as in his writings. Mr. Frank E. Lott mentions a visit in 1871 " to Penrhyn Slate quarries with Sir W. Gull and Sir James Paget, at which Mr. Spencer pointed out the glacial scratches on some of the rounded rocks in the Pass of Llanberis; and his clear and vigorous description of the old glacier coming down from Snowdon, impressed me even more than when, a few years later at the School of Mines, Sir Andrew Ramsay explained the same phenomena in his usual interesting manner."

He cannot be accused of going out of his way to increase his reputation. From his replies to offers of academic and other honours, one may gather that there was at bottom a sense of disappointment that such signs of recognition had not been made earlier in his career, when they might have helped him in his struggle. Had he been less honest and outspoken he would have kept this feeling to himself. Even such notoriety as could not fail to be associated with his name was distasteful, leading him to go out of his way to avoid the manifestations of it, and causing regret, and sometimes offence, to those who wished to show their regard for him. Lady Courtney writes:—

We did not realise Mr. Spencer's reputation till we grew up and came often to London. Probably his fame was not great in general society before that time. It seemed to me to culminate during the seventies and early eighties. I was conscious during those years that you could not mention his name in many companies high or low without exciting a thrill of interest, and even in the most unlikely quarters his name would be known as that of a distinguished man. I remember travelling from Aberdeen to Inverness in a third class carriage (not that this in Scotland was an unlikely quarter), and hearing some Scotch farmers, and a minister from a far away northern village, discussing his books, and finding myself unawares quite a centre of attraction when I remarked that I knew him in the flesh. But he was far from kind to his disciples and admirers, and very disconcerting to those who had contrived to gain a sight or a word for them. He has himself told the story how, when at Cairo, he refused the request of a distinguished personage for a visit. . . . I can add another story of the same period —a Dutch Judge of the Consular Courts was a great Spencerian, and his wife came to my sister and myself, to beg us to bring about a meeting. We thought and thought, and finally hit upon a moonlight ride to the Tombs of the Prophets. Mr. Spencer readily agreed, and the Judge, though he had not ridden for years, and was decidedly stout, eagerly accepted the invitation to join in. We started, and Mr. Spencer's admirer sidled up to him and began with much pomp a carefully prepared sentence. He was hardly under way when up came the Egyptian donkey boys yelling and hitting, and away went the donkeys in various directions, and so the comedy went on all the time. Finally, Mr. Spencer absolutely refused to go to supper with our kind Dutch friends. We went and found all his books spread out on the tables—a pathetic disappointment to the poor gentleman, who was doubtless very stiff the next morning after his unwonted exercise. People talk of Mr. Spencer as having a large measure of egotism, and he certainly did not conceal, as most of us do, what he had of that quality; but a truly vain and self-regarding man would surely not have discouraged admiration and flattery as he did. Not only did he never seek, but most ungraciously refused, worldly honours and advancement all through his long life.

Again and again he complained of his lack of quick perception of the motives and actions of others, leading him to mistaken judgments and wrong courses of conduct. He thought he would be an easy dupe at a spiritualistic *séance*. While deficient in reading the motives of others, he was singularly wanting in ability to hide his own. He doubted his power to say " No "; but few who had to do with him would accept this as a correct delineation. It used to be said of the late Sir Bartle Frere, when Governor of Bombay, that in refusing a request he did so with more than his usual courtesy, leading the applicant to think he had got a half promise. Spencer was not in the habit of toning down the terms of a refusal: his reply being usually more blunt than suave. He thought more of making refusal plain than of how it would be taken: as when requested by an American doctor to bequeath to him " the most perfect and wonderful brain of this century." He did not mince the terms of his refusal. " A bequest such as that which you wish I would not make even to my most intimate friend. You may judge, therefore, how little chance there is that I can be induced to make such a bequest to a stranger." Perhaps it was a certain brusquerie of manner and speech, joined with his unemotional coldness that prevented people, on first acquaintance, feeling quite at ease in his presence. Manner apart, his intellectual and moral superiority could not fail to engender a feeling of remoteness, which, however, disappeared on closer acquaintance.

Though he was not fond of the lower animals, the infliction of suffering on them was intolerable to him. His power of sympathy with human beings was exceptionally strong. Ill-health or distress of any kind, experienced by relatives, friends, acquaintances (even casual acquaintances), or correspondents whom perhaps he had never seen, could not be brought to his notice without exciting his lively interest and leading to measures for alleviation. Hundreds of letters bear eloquent testimony to the practical turn his sympathy took. For verbal expressions of sympathy, his undemonstrative character, and his dislike to exaggeration, unfitted him. As he wrote to a friend who had recently lost her husband: " I always feel so strongly my inability to say anything adequate in the way of consolation that I am habitually debarred from attempting it." To the ailing members of his household he was " kind almost to a fault." Into their personal or family concerns he entered with sympathetic interest: rejoiced when they rejoiced, was grieved when things went wrong with them, warned them against courses which involved risk, pointed out dangers which they were likely to overlook; but never said " I told you so " when his counsel had not been followed, and the bad consequences he had foreseen had to be faced. Above all he was considerate to his domestic servants, there being the fullest recognition of the moral obligations of the employer. In ill-health every care and comfort was bestowed upon them. " On one occasion," writes Miss Killick, " when he was living in the country for a few months, a young woman had been engaged to assist in his household, and, observing her pallor and general lassitude, he gave her strengthening medicine, which, however, proved of small assistance, and she had to discontinue work and return to her home. Mr. Spencer himself drove over one afternoon to see her, and gave her a donation; and on hearing that her bed-room was practically unfurnished sent furniture for it anonymously.'' He could never turn his back upon genuine need, nor refuse to help a worthy person or a worthy cause. Even when a struggling author, he would pinch himself to help a friend. His generosity kept pace with the improvement in his circumstances. To the family of his uncle Henry, to Derby friends and ac-quaintances, to young men preparing for the battle of life, he extended a generous hand. Several who have since taken worthy positions at home and abroad, still remember him with gratitude. Against evil of all kinds, writes Rev. J. W. Chadwick, he '' projected himself with an ardour and vehemence strangely at variance with the idea that a cold, hard, dry intellectuality was exhaustive of the man.''

He often referred to what he called his constitutional idleness, seeming to be rather proud of it than other-wise. If intellectual work consists in acquainting one-self with the opinions of others, the charge may contain an element of truth. But even in that sense, the man who could gather together and assimilate the wealth of facts to be found in his books, cannot have been so want-ing in industry as some of his remarks would make it appear. If there was any defect of verbal memory it was compensated for by the readiness to grasp logical relations, as well as the natural relations of things. His defective memory for words and arbitrary relations, had, in his own opinion, much to do with the development of his mind, favouring as it did internal building up as much as it retarded external building up. The pleasures of thinking were all the greater that he did not coerce

261

the mind. His powers of analysis and synthesis were unsurpassed. He had a rare gift of seizing upon the important aspects of a question, and of keeping the unimportant points in the background. But for this he could not have marshalled his numerous facts so effectively. Complaint is sometimes made of the abstractness of his terms; but such terms were necessitated by the width of his generalisations, only a part of the denotation of which would have been covered by less abstract terms. A more serious complaint was that he not infrequently passed without warning from the general and abstract use of a term or proposition to the special and concrete, or *vice versâ,* drawing conclusions which, though warranted in the one case, were not warranted in the other.

In some ways he gained, and in others lost, by not having had the training given by University life, which as Rev. J. W. Chadwick says, acts as '' a social mill in which men grind each other's angles down. Spencer's never were ground down: they were acute angles always.'' But argumentative and disputatious as he was, he never argued for victory. Always there was a principle to be contended for. Mr. Francis Galton writes:

Mr Herbert Spencer's magnificent intellect was governed by a very peculiar character. It was full of whimsies that unduly affected the opinion of those who did not appreciate its depth and purpose. His disposition was acknowledged by himself to be contentious; I would venture to consider it also as being sometimes a little perverse.

My knowledge of him was chiefly due to our both being in the habit of spending an afternoon hour or so in the then smoking room of the Athenæum Club, which was a very suitable place for quiet conversation. This is quite altered now. He always took interest in my hobbies, and I owe much to his remarks and criticisms, which were not however always accepted. He loved to dogmatise from *a priori* axioms, and to criticise, and I soon found that the way to get the best from him was to be patient and not to oppose. He was very thin skinned under criticism, and shrank from argument; it excited him over much, and was really bad for his health. His common practice when pressed in a difficult position, was to finger his pulse and saying: " I must not talk any more," to abruptly leave the discussion unfinished. Of course, wicked people put a more wicked interpretation on this habit than it should in fairness bear. Anyhow, when Spencer forsook the Club as he did some years ago, to seek greater quiet elsewhere, I was conscious of a void which has never since been filled. . . .

An amusing instance of his strong leaning to *a priori* reasoning rather than to experiment occurred on his coming to a laboratory I had then established for anthropometric purposes. . . . I told Spencer of the difficulty of accounting for the peculiarities in the pattern of finger prints, and that the dissections of embryos had thus far told no more than that they could be referred to folds of membrane in which the sudorific glands were formed, but threw no light on the reason why the pattern should here be a whorl and there a loop, and so on. He said that dissection was not the best way to find out what I wanted to know: I ought to have started from a consideration of the uses of the ridges, and he proceeded to elaborate a line of argument with great fulness in his usual sententious way. It was to the effect that the mouths of the ducts, being delicate and liable to injury from abrasion, required the shield of ridges, and on this basis he reared a wonderfully ingenious and complicated superstructure of imaginary results to which I listened with infinite inward amusement. When he had quite concluded, I replied with mock humility, that his arguments were most beautiful and cogent and fully deserved to be true, but unfortunately the ducts did *not* open out in the shielded valleys, but along the exposed crests of the ridges. He burst into a good humoured laugh, and then told me the story, which also appears in his *Autobiography*, of Huxley's saying, that if Spencer ever wrote a tragedy, its plot would be the slaying of a beautiful deduction by an ugly fact. . . .

The power of Spencer's mind that I most admired, was that of widely founded generalisations. Whenever doubt was hinted as to the sufficiency of his grounds for making them, he was always ready to pour out a string of examples that seemed to have been, if not in his theatre of consciousness when he spoke, at all events in an ante-chamber of it, whence they could be summoned at will. In more than any other person whom I have met, did his generalisations strike me in the light of true " composite " pictures. Whether the examples he gave in justification were selected with a conscious or unconscious bias, or were taken at random, is another matter. Anyhow his wealth of ready illustration was marvellous.

The verdicts on his style have been almost as divergent as those on his doctrines. Occasionally, but rarely, it has been described as obscure—a criticism open to the retort that the obscurity may be due to the inability of the reader to grasp the meaning, no matter how it is expressed. Bearing in mind the highly abstruse nature of his thought, one will have to admit that few writers have so seldom left their readers in doubt. Burdened by wealth of illustration and exemplification, his style is apt to appear wanting in lightness and grace: but occasionally " a grave eloquence lights up his pages." Its massiveness corresponds with the massiveness of his thought. Occasionally it is lightened by singularly felicitous words, or phrases, or passages, which have become part of the English language—thus furnishing additional examples of the survival of the fittest. Though condemned for its " barbarous terminology," it has also been praised for its " wonderful simplicity," its " terseness, lucidity, and precision." The author of the *Philosophy of Style* had, naturally, his own ideas about punctuation, and was often annoyed at the liberties taken by compositors and press readers. " The structure of a writer's sentence is in part the structure of his thought." His faculty of composing, under what would be to many very distracting circumstances, was remarkable: showing his rare power of concentration—of abstracting his thoughts from his surroundings. Whether in a racket court at King's Cross, or in a sports field at Kensal Green, or in a boat on the Serpentine, or under the trees in Kensington Gardens, he was able to carry on a train of abstract thinking, and to dictate to his secretary, as serenely as if he were in the privacy of his study. Unlike his friends, Mr. G. H. Lewes and Professor Huxley, who wrote and re-wrote their compositions,[1] he made comparatively few changes in his manuscript. In revising for future editions, however, he made numerous changes in the expression, but very few in the argument.

One of Mr. Spencer's traits (says Mr. Troughton), was his seeming inability to take in hand two or more things concurrently. If, for instance, some controversy occupied him, permanent work was for the time being put aside altogether. He had a rooted dislike to being hurried. A sequence of this was that he resented being

---

[1] *George Eliot's Life,* ii., 99. *Life of Professor Huxley,* ii., 42, 308.

LIFE AND LETTERS OF HERBERT SPENCER

put under pressure to do any piece of work within a given time. This largely explains his reluctance to engage in controversies, especially newspaper controversies, in which replies and rejoinders had to be made on the instant. The daily increments of work accomplished were very small, but the paucity of the performance never seemed to trouble him, or at all events never stimulated him to quicken the pace.

He was an essentially methodical man. This characteristic manifested itself alike in his personal habits and in the expression of his thoughts. His personal effects were all arranged and distributed on this principle— keys in one pocket, knife in another, and so on. Still more so was this the case with his papers of all kinds. These were all classified and put away in certain receptacles according to a definite plan, so that when required they could be found without any bother. When the time came for using any particular group of materials for the work in hand, that group would be subjected to a sub-classification, and so on, until the materials for a particular section were assembled together. With this orderliness of habit, it was not at all difficult, when circumstances arose which involved a suspension of work, to pick up the thread again when the time came for resuming it.

Some light is thrown upon his general reading by two of his secretaries. Referring to the period about the middle of the eighties, Mr. W. H. Hudson says:—

Once we went through some of the eighteenth century novelists, and he was specially interested in *Humphrey Clinker*. He was also struck by the delicate art of W. D. Howells, though he tired after two or three of his stories. I recall that he thought much of Shakespeare's witty dialogue (as in " Much Ado ") forced and childish. I think of all the novelists I read to him, he most enjoyed Thackeray.

Reading could hardly be called one of his pastimes (says Mr. Troughton, with reference to a later period), unless it was reading the daily and weekly journals, or rather listening to them, for reading them aloud was one of my functions almost from the beginning. Certainly his appetite for the *Times* was invariably keen and he followed the reading of it with close attention, accompanying it with a running commentary on events and opinions recorded, and noting anything especially bearing on his own work. This reading of the paper was the first order of the day, and moreover was always done in a certain sequence—summary first, then the gist of the leading articles, followed by the foreign news, and then the miscellaneous news—this was the order down to the last month of his life, when he usually dropped asleep before it had proceeded far. Then, in addition to the morning paper there was the evening paper, an invariable item in the day's programme, while the various weeklies gave him enough mental food to tide over Sunday. Of the constant succession of books which reached him—mostly of a grave character—a glance usually sufficed, and many of them were put away on the shelves without even that. Fiction he had little taste for, and only at very long intervals read any.

Music was a great pleasure to him (Miss Killick writes), and his taste in the matter of composers good. In early life he enjoyed singing in glees, and in his closing years liked to hear them played on the piano. But in music, as in everything else, he had his own ideas how certain passages should be rendered, and they were as a rule contrary to the prescribed methods.

Spencer " disciplines himself to amusements," wrote Dr. Youmans in 1871. This was quite true. The disciplinary process was also recommended to his friends. " Pray follow my example," he advises Dr. Cazelles, " in taking as much rest and amusement as is needful for your restoration, and be sure that, though at first you may, in consequence of having wedded yourself to work, find amusement dreary and uninteresting, you will in course of time habituate yourself to it, and begin to find life more tolerable.'' While passionately fond of the country and country pleasures, he cared little in boyhood and youth for out-door games. Of skating he was very fond, and Mr. Frank Lott remembers '' the very graceful figure he always made on the ice.'' After the breakdown in 1855 he began the sedulous pursuit of means for restoring his health. At first the quest was mainly not for pleasurable occupations, but for those involving bodily exertion and inducing sleep. After a time pleasurable pursuits were sought. But here also not the pleasure at the time, but the beneficial after-effects were the main considerations. He had few indoor relaxations. Backgammon and whist were played occasionally; but he was not good at the latter, nor did he like playing for money. Miss Charlotte Shickle, who sometimes joined him in a rubber at Queen's Gardens, informed the present writer that it was an understanding that he would pay his losings when he lost, but would not accept winnings when he won. This was his invariable rule.

His ideal of life found no place for asceticism, neither for the asceticism due to religious or moral feeling, nor for that which is dictated by the assumed demands of business. '' Life is not for learning, nor is life for working; but learning and working are for life.'' A strange maxim this to come from one who scorned delights and lived laborious days in order to complete a task he had deliberately imposed on himself. While primarily valuing life and health for the happiness they afforded, he valued them next as the means of accomplishing his work. From worldly ambition, the desire to amass wealth—to " get on " in the ordinary sense—he was singuarly free. He often spoke as if he had a mission—a message to deliver to the world. To this mission everything was subordinated.

His sincerity, truthfulness and honesty, impressed all who knew him. " He was absolutely sincere himself," writes Miss Killick, " and could not tolerate the very smallest deviation from the truth in others. Although at times he might *appear* to condemn unjustly, investigation always showed that some necessary data were unknown to him, and therefore his judgment, while apparently unsound, was in accordance with his knowledge of the facts." Suspicion of the motives of others was characteristic of himself, as well as of his father. Describing his first interview, Mr. Troughton says:

I had been informed that Mr. Spencer was in a precarious state of health, so much so that whoever filled the post could not expect to retain it for more than twelve months at the outside. But really there was nothing in his appearance to suggest any apprehensions of early demise—on the contrary, he struck me as being a man of more than average vigour: his upright bearing as he entered the room, his clear crisp voice, his searching gaze, seemed to betoken a hale, though perhaps not a hearty, physique. My unpunctuality called for serious notice. The time appointed was ten o'clock. Why was I late? The explanation being forthcoming, a multitude of questions followed in quick succession. His inquisitiveness rather took me aback, but what struck me most was the brusque way in which he delivered his questions, and the way in which, when putting them, he concentrated his gaze upon me. Surely this man must have practised a good deal at the bar, I thought. I came to know afterwards that this was only a bit of affectation. Some years later, when about to fill up a vacancy on his domestic staff, he deputed me to interview the applicants: instructing me in detail as to the proper method to pursue in interrogating them. It was just the same as that which he adopted at my first encounter with him. . . .

Numerous as were the instances in which Mr. Spencer appeared to distrust those with whom he had business or professional relations, it would not be fair to say that in more than a very few of them did he harbour any positive suspicion. He was a man who in everything he did, even in trivial matters, was guided by principle, the principle in each case being that which by a process of reasoning he had found to be valid. Because a large proportion of men are either unreliable or dishonest, therefore it must be assumed for the time being, that the man with whom you have dealings belongs to that number. To a certain extent the world at large acts on this assumption, but Mr. Spencer carried it to extreme lengths, and with entire disregard of the law of probability. I more than once told him that in the City, where office boys are more trusted than he trusted men of standing, business would come to a standstill if his principle were carried out to the letter.

He could not readily adapt himself to other people's ways, had very decided views as to how things should be made or done, and was fidgety and irritable when they were not made or done as he thought they should be. Though he was, in consequence, not easy to get on with in the house, yet he lived with the same hostess at Queen's Gardens for about a quarter of a century. While possessing wide knowledge, and a singular power of tracing the working of great cosmic forces, he was as innocent as a child in many of the ways of the world.

270

Master as he himself was in dealing with wide generalities, and in marshalling and co-ordinating the details on which they rested, he overlooked the fact that most people content themselves with passing from detail to detail without a thought of a connecting link between them. They think from hand to mouth, as well as live from hand to mouth. Unable to grasp the principle which gives unity to details, they are liable to be plunged into confusion when told that they should take it as their guide. Allow them to ignore the general rule, all goes well until some unexpected event takes place which a wider outlook might have foreseen. If he himself had had the carrying out of his views on housekeeping, doubtless he would have justified their soundness. But having to depute this to others he would have been well advised had he kept many of his theories to himself. Embued with the notion that convention reigned supreme within the house as without, he continually fought against it. He had his whims and his crotchets—he was exacting in the sense of insisting that duties undertaken should be performed—he was not easily satisfied. But the attractiveness of his personality not only covered a multitude of foibles, but claimed the loyalty of those who lived with him, and who knew the deeply sympathetic nature that lay beneath a certain brusqueness of manner. Of his relations with Spencer, extending from the end of 1888 till the end of 1903, Mr. Troughton writes:

Brusque as Mr. Spencer often was in addressing those about him, he invariably treated me with courtesy. I cannot call to mind a single occasion during the many years I was in daily contact with him when he gave way to temper with me, and I have many remembrances of

271

the kindly feeling he showed towards me. Beneath the asperity of manner which often showed itself, there was a really sympathetic nature ready to manifest itself when circumstances gave the needful stimulus.

Would Spencer have made a successful administrator? If he had taken to teaching, one may say with confidence that as far as high aims, sound methods, and single-minded devotion could command success, he would have made his mark. But it is questionable whether he would have been successful in the administrative side of school-work. His want of tact, bluntness of speech, lack of quick and true perception of character, and impatience with the weaknesses of average human nature, would have stood in the way of smooth working with subordinates, colleagues, educational authorities, and, perhaps most important of all, with parents. Had he adhered to railway engineering, there would doubtless have been some daring feats of constructive skill to be recorded; but whether capital and labour would have co-operated with him is a moot question. Given his highly evolved humanity of the future, he would probably have proved a successful administrator; with humanity as we know it, the issue would have been more than doubtful. Mr. Francis Galton writes:

He was a most impracticable administrator on the only occasion in which I saw him put fairly to the test. We were both members of the Committee of the Athenæum Club, at a long by-gone time, when the dining room management was bad, and there was much discontent. Spencer moved and carried the appointment of a Special House Committee, to consist of only three members. He, of course, was Chairman, another was one of the prominent malcontent members, and he persuaded me to be the third, as having no official duties and therefore presumably a man of leisure. I accepted the nomination with great misgivings, which after events fully justified. A more comically ineffective Committee than ours I never sat upon. Spencer insisted on treating the pettiest questions as matters of serious import, whose principles had to be fully argued and understood before action should be taken, with the consequence that we made no progress. Many funny scenes took place, one was with the butcher, who had supplied tough meat. Spencer enlarged to us on the subject of toughness in the same elaborate and imposing language with which his writings abound, and when the butcher appeared he severely charged him with supplying meat that contained an undue proportion of connective tissue. The butcher was wholly nonplussed, being unable to understand the charge and conscious, as I suspect, of some secret misdoing to which the accusation might refer.

An amusing instance of the failure of some of his theories, when brought to the test of experience, is related by Lady Courtney.

Of course he was an inveterate critic. He says so himself. One form this characteristic took was criticism of our various governesses for their management of us—on one occasion with amusing results. He had complained to my mother that one of these much suffering ladies, and an especially indulgent one, was checking and destroying our natural instincts by her rules and instructions, mainly, I think, because she would not let us take off our jackets and either give them to her to carry or throw them about. Mother and the governess talked it over together, and Mr. Spencer was asked if he would like to take us out himself for the afternoon walk, and readily agreed. So off he started with some half dozen girls, whose ages ranged from six to fourteen, up the hill into the woods. We had heard all about the complaint of our governess, and had had a pretty broad hint that we might behave as we liked. Two of the younger ones began at once to play the fool, and got so excited and outrageous that my eldest sister and I tried to second Mr. Spencer's efforts to control them. In vain and in vain. He eventually stamped his foot and said "When I say no, I mean no!" Finally they managed to lead him into a pit full of dead beech leaves and carried off his hat which had fallen off—" you rude children!" was his exclamation, and all round behind the trees echoed r-r-r-rude children—for he rolled his r's slightly—or at any rate we thought so. He came home a wiser and a sadder man, and told my mother at dinner that two of her children were very headstrong, and would need a good deal of control. . . . I know that he interfered less in future with our governesses.

Mr. Spencer certainly had a keener desire than most men to get other people to adopt and carry out his views, even on quite trifling subjects: such as how to light a fire, or revive it when it was low, the hanging of pictures, the colours in a carpet, or of the flowers on a dinner table, the proper shape of an inkstand, and a thousand other matters; and he allowed what he thought an unreasonable way of doing these things, even when they had nothing to do with himself, to unduly disturb his peace. Indeed, the commonplace person would have said the philosophic temper was curiously absent in this great philosopher—so much so, that as he grew older and more nervous and delicate, his friends almost unconsciously abstained from arguing if they differed from him, unless they could put their point humorously, for a good joke always found Mr. Spencer appreciative. Alluding to this irritability of temperament, I remember Professor Tyndall saying at my father's house in London, Mr. Spencer standing by: "He'd be a much nicer fellow if he had a good swear now and then"— and our hilarity at the very notion of Mr. Spencer swearing.

274

An unsparing critic of others, how did he take criticism of himself? He was too ready to say that he had been " misunderstood " or " misrepresented," and too prone to attribute the one or the other to moral obliquity. But he never deliberately took an unfair advantage of an opponent. Polemical writing was apt to entail " mischievous consequences " on his health. Foreseeing these, he often retired from a contest at an early stage, when the issue was as yet uncertain; thereby causing annoyance to his opponent, besides laying himself open to the suspicion that he had begun to feel a little uncertain of his ground. Between personal and impersonal criticism he drew a sharp line. In the former he seldom indulged, and if in the heat of controversy he was led into the use of personalities, he took care not to perpetuate them. Purely impersonal attacks on his doctrines seldom disturbed his equanimity, though they might lead to sharp thrusts of intellectual polemic. It was different with attacks on his character. To these he was more than usually sensitive.

Spencer's habit (the drawbacks of which he did not seem to realise) of throwing down a book when he disagreed with any of its cardinal propositions, afforded some justification for the suggestion that he was unwilling to deal with arguments and facts opposed to his own views. An accusation of want of candour would have greatly distressed him, conscious as he was of absolute loyalty to his convictions. The fact was that, though his allegiance to the truth never wavered—not a single instance being known of his declining to acknowledge as true what he believed to be true—he sometimes failed to reach it, owing to the engrossment of his mind with the creations of his ever-active constructive imagination precluding the admission of alien ideas. The shortcoming was intellectual, not moral—was due to the limitations of human intelligence, even of the highest. Whatever his moral shortcomings, disloyalty to truth was not one of them. He who could only contemplate " from the heights of thought that far-off life of the race never to be enjoyed by [him], but only by a remote posterity," would have been the last to claim immunity from the infirmities of human nature. But we require to be reminded that the very greatness of the man has helped to bring too much into relief both the shortcomings of his character and the defects of his work. Take him for all in all, he was intellectually one of the grandest and morally one of the noblest men that have ever lived. His life was devoted to a single purpose—the establishing of truth and righteousness as he understood them. The value of a life of self-sacrifice for a lofty ideal is inestimable at all times, and is especially so in the present day of advertisement, push, and getting on in the world. This will endure whatever may be the fate of his philosophical opinions. " In the whole story of the searchers for truth," said the *Times,* just after his death, " there is no instance of devotion to noble aims surpassing his —courage, baffling ill-health, and proof against years of discouragement, unwearied patience, wise economy of powers, and confidence in the future recognition of the value of his work."

CHAPTER XXX

SPENCER'S PLACE IN THE HISTORY OF THOUGHT

By way of criticism on the Synthetic Philosophy much has been written about its *a priori* character. Spencer's habit of setting out from first principles and ever returning to them—his constant endeavour to verify every inductive generalisation by showing it to be deducible from some higher generalisation—has been too readily taken to imply that his philosophy does not rest on the solid ground of nature. Such an opinion is a survival of the Baconian reaction against the *a priori* methods of the schoolmen. It ought not now-a-days to be necessary to repeat the truism that the progress of science depends not on observation and experiment alone nor on theorising and hypothesis alone, but on the co-operation of these methods. Both are essential, and as a matter of fact both are pursued in all departments of knowledge, though not in an equal degree. The nature of the phenomena to be investigated, the stage the enquiry has reached, and the mental endowments of the investigator, each or all of these determine which of the two methods should be chiefly followed. Taking these considerations into account, the scientific enquirer shows his skill in so combining the two complementary methods as to avoid the one and the other of two dangers that lie in the path of the seeker after truth. When theoretical specu-

277

lation predominates there is the risk of losing touch with realities. When it is neglected in favour of observation and experiment there is apt to be aimless groping in the dark. The strict follower of experiment and observation reminds one of the man who had collected an encyclopædic mass of information which he could not use, and of whom an Irish friend remarked: " Yes, he has got all the answers, but he has not got the questions." Unassisted by the guidance of hypothesis, experiment and observation are apt to land the investigator in a labyrinth out of which he has to be assisted by some one possessing the clue. Mr. Darwin, one of the most painstaking of observers and experimentalists, was well aware how indispensable deductive reasoning is in the course of inductive inquiry. " No one," he said, " could be a good observer, unless he was an active theoriser." " Without speculation there is no good and original observation." But the limitations of faculty rarely allow of the same individual possessing superior excellence both as a speculative thinker and as an observer or experimentalist. It has been said by way of disparagement of Spencer, that he was not a specialist, or expert. Had he been so he could not have taken the wide view he did of the whole domain of knowledge. Besides the consideration of constitutional aptitude for the one or the other, there is the further consideration that specialising absorbs a great deal of time. To acquire a minute acquaintance with details is often the labour of a lifetime. The specialist has rarely the time, and still more rarely the aptitude, to follow up wide generalisations. To disparage, therefore, the work of one who takes a wide survey of the field of knowledge, because in matters of detail he is not equal to one who has devoted his life to a very small portion of that field, indicates an entire misapprehension of the limitations of human faculty and of human life. The organiser of knowledge would abdicate his function were he to attempt to emulate the specialist's acquaintance with details. His function is not to accumulate a store of individual facts, but to co-ordinate the facts supplied him, and reduce them to their most general forms. Moreover, as already said, the needs of science are not always the same. Accumulation of data may, at one time, be too far in advance of organisation; just as theorising may, at any other time, be too far ahead of accumulation. The necessity for the guidance of theory was emphasised by Professor Huxley in the testimonial he gave to Spencer in 1860, when the system of philosophy was planned. " Science would stagnate if the co-ordination of its data did not accompany their accumulation." Professor Huxley saw clearly that a man was needed to co-ordinate and systematise the facts and conceptions that had accumulated—to carry an " illuminating conception through all the departments of experience." Spencer came to supply the want by giving to the idea of evolution a development and application hitherto undreamt of.[1] That he was successful in this respect has been freely acknowledged by those best able to judge. " In these days of increasingly straitened speculation it is well," says Professor Lloyd Morgan, " that we should feel the influence of a thinker whose powers of generalisation have seldom been equalled and perhaps never surpassed."

---

[1] See Mr. J. S. Mill's letter, dated 2 December, 1868 (chap. xii., p. 200).

The dread of hypothesis and deductive reasoning was for a time a healthy reaction against the methods of the schoolmen, but it is mischievous instead of salutary when carried to extremes. What Professor Meldola says of Biology is true of other branches of science. " In the case of the purely literary treatment of biological problems by writers who are not experts, the danger of over-weighting the science with hypothesis is much exaggerated. Writers of this class are often capable of taking a wider and more philosophic grasp of a problem than a pure specialist, and ideas of lasting value have sometimes emanated from such sources. . . . The philosophic faculty is quite as powerful an agent in the advancement of science as the gift of acquiring new knowledge by observation and experiment." It is not in the interest of science for those gifted with unusual speculative ability to keep the brake applied on their special endowment so as to secure leisure for observation and experiment, any more than it would be in the interests of science for singularly gifted observers and experimentalists to slight the accumulation of facts in order to soar into the regions of speculation. To restrict the free play of special endowments is the certain road to commonplace results. Each should do what he can do best. He who is endowed with the rare gift of organising knowledge should exercise that gift to the full, and he who has the less rare, but equally valuable, gift of accumulating knowledge should make full use of it. Just as it is bad policy to put checks on experiment and observation; so also is it unwise to clip the wings of speculation. It is far better that a Darwin and a Spencer should each exercise to the full his characteristic intellectual endowment and pursue the scientific method such endowment favours, than that a Darwin should try to be like a Spencer, or a Spencer try to be like a Darwin.

That Spencer came in the fulness of time to render an all-important service to modern thought, and that his mission was successful, are clearly set forth in the following sketch, for which the present writer is indebted to Mr. Hector Macpherson:

It may be fairly claimed for Herbert Spencer that he revived speculative thinking in this country, and inaugurated a new system of philosophy. When Spencer came upon the scene philosophy was at a low ebb. In one of his essays J. S. Mill bears decisive testimony on this head. In his review of Professor Sedgwick's "Discourse on the Studies of Cambridge 1835," reprinted in his *Dissertations,* Mill says: "England once stood at the head of European philosophy. Where stands she now? Consult the general opinion of Europe. The celebrity of England in the present day rests upon her docks, her canals and her railways. In intellect she is distinguished only for a kind of solid good sense, free from extravagance, but also void of lofty aspirations." Mill goes on to complain of the absence of investigation of truth as truth, of thought for the sake of thought. For this state of things there was an obvious reason. Science had eclipsed philosophy in the popular regard. As I have said elsewhere—"The early years of the nineteenth century were years of great fermentation. The practical energies of the nation freed from the great strain of the Continental wars found new outlets in commerce and industry. Scientific study of Nature, no longer tabooed by theology, demonstrated its validity by an imposing record of inventions and discoveries, whose influence on the national prosperity was at once dramatic and all embracing. Science became the idol of the hour. It was inevitable that an attempt would be made to reduce to something like order the ever-increasing mass of facts. Since the days of Bacon thinkers have endeavoured to weave the facts of science into a unified system. Whewell's *History and Philosophy of the Inductive Sciences* was an attempt in this direction. Unfortunately, just when Whewell was engaged upon the task of generalisation and interpretation, epoch-making discoveries were being made, calculated to change the entire foundations of scientific and philosophic thought, for which no place was found in his work; such as the conservation and dissipation of energy, the variation of species, and organic evolution.''

Next came Comte. Valuable as was Comte's contribution to the higher thought of the time, his influence on the philosophic side was rendered sterile by the arbitrary line which he drew between the known and the unknown. Many of the phenomena which science to-day is bringing into the region of knowledge were declared by Comte to belong to the region of the unknowable, to peer into which was a foolish waste of time. He tabooed all enquiries into the nature of gravitation, light, heat, electricity, etc. All enquiries into origins were dismissed as ontological speculations. Hampered by his restricted method, he could get no further than the division of phenomena into six classes—Mathematics, Astronomy, Physics, Chemistry, Biology, and Sociology. He clearly enough showed the relation between the sciences, but his limited conception of philosophy prevented him from tracing them to a common root. Comte left the great problem of the unification of the sciences unsolved; he even declared it insoluble.

The philosophy of J. S. Mill was also inadequate to the task of assimilating and unifying the new facts of science. Mill's empirical theory of knowledge made it impossible for him to trace the bewildering phenomena of the Cosmos to a common root.

Up till the time of Whewell the mechanical conception of Nature held sway—a conception which threw great

obstacles in the way of discovering unity in Nature. If
we treat the Universe as a vast machine we do not readily
discover the idea of unity. Between the various parts
of the machine there may be no necessary unity, which
indeed may exist only in the mind of the constructor.
To the mechanical conception was largely due the waning
influence of philosophy of which Mill complained. The
philosophy of which he was the distinguished representative and exponent was ill-fitted by its fundamental conceptions for grappling effectively with the new views of
Nature which science was disclosing; it could not help in
the endeavour to find necessary unity at the heart of
things. In this sphere Mill was hampered by his theory
of knowledge, which he inherited from Hume. According to this theory, knowledge originates in impressions
made upon the senses, and is limited, of course, by the
external world. Knowledge in this view, in its ultimate analysis and when perfectly organised, will consist
of the classification of facts and the arranging of them
into groups. Are these groups held together by any
necessary law? Can the various branches of knowledge
be traced back to one common root? By the nature of
his philosophy Mill was compelled to answer this question in the negative as follows: " There exists in Nature
a number of permanent causes, which have subsisted ever
since the human race has been in existence, and for an
indefinite and probably an enormous length of time
previous. The sun, the earth, and the planets with their
various constituents—air, water and the distinguishable
substances whether simple or compound of which Nature
is made up—are such permanent causes. Why these particular natural agents existed originally and no others,
or why they are arranged in such a manner throughout
space, is a question we cannot answer: more than this
we can discover nothing regular in the distribution itself. We can reduce it to no uniformity, to no law." In
its final results the Experience philosophy of Mill, like
the Positivism of Comte, lends no encouragement to the

search for unity which the new dynamical theory of Nature was fostering.

Spencer saw clearly that, on the lines of the old Experience philosophy, the problem was insoluble. He saw that if the mind cannot pass beyond particulars, as Mill said, it was hopeless to search for universal laws, hopeless to trace existence in its multifarious aspects to one dynamic process. What Spencer did was to start with two universal intuitions, which cannot be proved, and which must be accepted as necessities of thought—belief in personal identity, and belief in the permanence of the constitution of things which we call Nature. By starting with two intuitive beliefs—subjective existence and objective existence—Spencer escaped the sceptical conclusions of Hume and Mill.

As I have observed in a review of Spencer's philosophy: " Accepting as the data of philosophy, subject and object, self and not-self, Spencer deals with the general forms under which the not-self, the Cosmos, manifests itself to the self, the mind. These general forms under which the not-self, the cosmos, manifests itself to the self, the mind, are space, time, matter, motion, and force. After a careful analysis of these forms by which all thinking is conditioned, he comes to the conclusion that space, time, matter and motion, all necessary data of intelligence, are built up or abstracted from experiences of force. Force persists. When we say that force persists, we are simply saying that the sum total of matter and motion, by which force manifests itself to us, can neither be increased nor diminished. This, like personal identity, is an ultimate fact, an ultimate belief, which we must take with us as the basis of all reasoning; if force came into existence and went out of existence, the Universe would be not a cosmos but a chaos, nay more, reasoning would be impossible. Scientific deductions, as well as abstract reasoning, would be impossible if the forces of Nature did not persist. Viewed thus, the Universe is one fact, the varying phenomena being but so many phases of the redistribution of matter and motion.''

Spencer found in the two great scientific generalisations—the nebular theory and the conservation of energy—precisely the scientific materials which were necessary to the framing of his philosophical system. Here was clear proof that the Universe was not machine-like in construction, but was the outcome of a dynamic process. Starting with the ultimate fact of the redistribution of matter and motion, Spencer proceeds to trace the process by which the Universe evolves from its primitive nebulous form to its latest state of complexity. It is noteworthy that Spencer, in dealing with matter, did not, like so many of his contemporaries, accept the atom as an ultimate. When he wrote, the atom was treated as the foundation stone, so to speak, of the Universe. In his *First Principles,* he showed that matter, under philosophical analysis, resolves itself into a form of energy—a view which the discovery of radium amply confirms.

From the cosmical side, Spencer's great task was to trace the process of evolution. For convenience, phenomena are divisible into sections—astronomic, geologic, biologic, psychologic, sociologic, but the process is one, and the law is one. In those spheres, Spencer has illuminated a whole world of facts, and by his magnificent powers of analysis and generalisation has raised the human mind to higher reaches of thought. It has been finely said that to a thinker capable of comprehending it from a single point of view, the Universe would present a single fact, one all comprehensive truth. Spencer's attempt is the greatest that has yet been made to realise this ideal.

Spencer intended his system to be a philosophy of phenomenal existence, but at the outset he deemed it necessary to deal with ontological problems. By his famous theory of the Unknowable he involved himself in controversies which distracted the public mind and drew attention away from his real aim. He realised that in this he had made a mistake. He was in his later days anxious to make it plain that his system was quite independent of his theory of the Unknowable. His system, he once remarked to me, should be judged on its merits, apart from its metaphysical basis.[1] Spencer's mistake was in prefacing his *First Principles* with a discussion associated with the philosophy of Hamilton and Mansel. The conclusion of his great work was the proper place to treat of its philosophical aspects, when he would have been in a position to deal with ontological problems on modern lines.

Great inconvenience came from the mixing up of the scientific and the metaphysical. For instance, in *First Principles* Spencer proceeds on the assumption that force, which he calls a form of the unknowable, explains all phenomena, living as well as non-living. His attempt to correlate living and non-living forces, and embrace them in a mechanical formula did not latterly satisfy himself. In the sixth edition of his *First Principles,* revised by him in 1900, he no longer believed in the transformation of motion into feeling, but only in a constant ratio between the two. In dealing with life the same change of view is noticeable. In the last edition of the *Principles of Biology* the admission is made that " life in its essence cannot be conceived in physico-chemical terms." The effect of these admissions is to make the " Synthetic Philosophy " dualistic rather than monistic. From a scientific point of view these admissions are of no moment, because, as the psychical only manifests through the physical, it is quite legitimate to use mechanical terminology in dealing with phenomena. Both in biology and psychology the Spencerian formula has been exceedingly fruitful. In regard to the former we have the testimony of a competent authority, Professor Arthur Thomson, the Scottish biologist, who describes the *Principles of Biology* as an epoch-making

[1] See vol. i., chap. xv., p. 268; chap. xviii., p. 336; vol., ii., chap. xxviii., p. 213.

work. " Even as a balance sheet of the facts of life the book is a biological classic; consciously or unconsciously we are all standing on his shoulders." Distinguished scientists on the Continent have given like testimony to Spencer's labours in the region of biology.

In psychology Spencer's work was also epoch-making. His book proved to be the forerunner of a new method in the study of brain and nerve evolution and dissolution. No greater evidence of the value of Spencer's work in this department can be had than the testimony of distinguished medical specialists in brain and nerve disorders. It is claimed for Spencer that in neurology, psychology, and pathology, he has discovered the fundamental principles, and that whatever systems are erected in these sciences must be erected on the foundations he has laid. In Spencer's hands psychology, from being a sterile science confined to academic circles, has been converted into a valuable instrument of scientific research.

To the ethical, sociological, and political sciences, Spencer applied his evolution formula with marked originality. To the utilitarianism of Bentham and Mill he has given something like a scientific foundation, while political philosophy, which before his day was usually associated with forms of government, has now its proper place in sociological evolution. As has been well said: " Spencer, exchanging the point of view from the mechanical to the biological, originated quite a new train of political thinking. An organised society is subject to the law of growth. It has an economic root, and all political structures as well as ethical ideals are determined, not from the outside by legislation, but by the economic conditions at each particular stage. All students of social evolution are his debtors."

What will be the verdict of history upon Herbert Spencer? It will surely be that he belonged to the highly gifted race of thinkers who, by the boldness of their generalisations and their commanding outlook upon life and thought, have opened out to humanity wider intellectual vistas.

The warmth and catholicity of the tributes paid to the remarkable force of Spencer's intellect, the lofty simplicity of his character, the grandeur of his aims, and the heroic devotion which had sustained him throughout a long life, bore eloquent testimony to the extraordinary impression he had made on the men of his day and generation. He had reached the front rank among thinkers. But, it has been asked, will he hold this place in the estimation of future generations? Do these tokens of appreciation warrant the assumption that the impression will be enduring—that there will be a permanent widening and clearing of the intellectual horizon, and such a purifying and strengthening of character as will stand the test of time? This question is more easily put than answered; but an attempt to answer it is desirable, inasmuch as the raising of it, besides carrying with it a suggestion of belittling Spencer and his achievements, implies that an affirmative answer *may* be given to the general question—Is it possible for any one to frame a theory of things that shall be final?

The durability of a thinker's work is seldom discussed with profit: owing partly to the uncertainty attaching to forecasts of events like opinions and impulses, to the formation of which so many subtle elements contribute; and partly to the absence of a clear idea of the question raised. Finality, in the strict sense of the word, may at once be put aside. Scientific theories cannot be final, inasmuch as the revelations of Nature are not final. A theory holds its own so long as, and only so long as, it harmonises better than any other with ascertained facts. In any other sense than this, finality was not claimed by Spencer, nor could it have been claimed by him consistently with his fundamental doctrine. The gradual development of his own conceptions was a striking exemplification of evolution. "It may be," says Rev. J. W. Chadwick, of Brooklyn, "that there are particulars of Spencer's system that will require serious modification. If there are not, it will be an exception to its central law. In Spencer's world there are no finalities, and for him to imagine his own system of philosophy as one would be impossible." Change, he held, is life, absence of change, death. He did not, as was implied by one of the newspaper obituary notices, so far forget himself as to conceive " it possible that he was saying the last word in Philosophy." He would have admitted that many of his generalisations would " have to give way before the tests of future experience and research "; that many of his formulæ were likely to " perish, not by being even refuted, but because they cease to be instructive." A theory, though professing to be the most complete generalisation of the on-goings of the universe as known in the second and third quarters of the last century, does not on that account claim to be installed as the accepted scheme of things for all time, or for even the next generation. To suppose that Spencer, who had traced the genesis and growth of science in the past, assumed that there would be no growth in the future, would be to treat him as one of the most short-sighted, instead of one of the most far-seeing thinkers. Viewed in this light, Spencer's work has nothing to fear from the discoveries, marvellous in number and importance, made in recent years. Even if evolution had now to be consigned to the scrap-heap, where lie so many outworn theories, that would not affect its claim to have been the most complete generalisation of knowledge at the time he wrote. But, though there may be ambiguities of statement, oversights in details, and mistakes in application, there are at present no indications of the doctrine as a whole being superseded. Even the phenomena of radium, revolutionising previous conceptions as to the constitution of matter, do not overthrow the doctrine of evolution. Some there are, indeed, who think with Dr. Saleeby that these phenomena " answer the Spencerian definition of evolution as if it had been framed to explain them.'' Others are of opinion that the formula of evolution will not fit the new discoveries so perfectly as this—that it will require a little letting out here or a little taking in there. When one remembers how the formula evolved in Spencer's mind under the influence of increasing knowledge, one will be prepared for such further modifications as fresh discoveries may necessitate. But whatever discoveries—far surpassing those of radioactivity—lie in the womb of time, they will not affect the contention that Spencer's synthesis of knowledge was the most comprehensive and complete—was final, not as foreclosing his scheme of the Universe against future advances of knowledge, but as the fullest and grandest generalisation of the knowledge of his day. It was a *contribution* towards a settlement, not a closing of the account. In this sense, his permanent place is assured for all time. In the history of the progress of the human mind, the Synthetic Philosophy will be an enduring land-mark. Men's ways of looking at things will never be what they would have been had he not written.

Henceforth it will be " impossible thoroughly to pursue any kind of enquiry without being confronted by his ideas." " No man of the present time," said Rev. J. Minot Savage, of Boston, the Sunday after Spencer's death, " can discuss any one of the great problems of the world . . . without dealing with Herbert Spencer. He has got to agree with him or fight him: he cannot ignore him." What influence more permanent than this could any man have? [1]

In addition to his rare gifts for co-ordinating and systematising the scientific conceptions of his day, Spencer possessed an unrivalled power of stimulating and directing others. To lead men to think for themselves—to suggest paths of inquiry at the end of which may lie a great truth—to direct a searchlight on the road to be traversed —surely these are attributes of the highest power. Sir Andrew Clark was wont to say that when feeling intellectually limp he was in the habit of turning to Spencer's writings, the bracing effect of which he seldom failed to experience. The suggestiveness of his ideas was freely acknowledged in his lifetime. From the American ranch, the Australian bush, and the South African veldt —from those who go down to the sea in ships—from countrymen and from foreigners—from men and women in humble walks of life as well as from those in exalted station—came to him grateful acknowledgments of stimulus and guidance received from his writings. And who can tell the number of those who unconsciously by his thoughts have had their own thoughts made broader and clearer, and their lives turned into the path of new endeavour?

---

[1] Compare Lord Courtney's address, chap. xxviii., p. 231.

We are as yet too near him to form a true estimate of his greatness. This is partly due to the fact that the details of his personality obscure the grandeur of its outlines—that the superficial and immediate effects of his work prevent us from estimating its deep and remote effects. Partly, it is the result of the very success of his teaching, which, having permeated our thought and speech, gives the impression that many of his utterances are platitudes, truisms, common-places. His ideas and his ways of looking at things have become part of the intellectual atmosphere we breathe—have become embedded in the language we speak. The value of his teaching will be rightly appreciated only by future generations. What Professor Theodor Gomperz says of Plato, may be said of Spencer:—

An intellect of the first order, having found and selected the elements of a world-theory, will combine and develop them in such manner as may best accord with its own powerful and strongly marked individuality, and, for this very reason, there will be small prospect of gaining the adherence, within a short interval, of any very extensive section of society. At the same time, such an intellect, out of the abundance of its wealth, will exert an influence upon many later generations, with which it will continually present new points of contact, and thus upon the intellectual life of mankind at large.[1]

To posterity Spencer's reputation as a thinker may with confidence be left.

---

[1] Theodor Gomperz's *Greek Thinkers* (translated by G. G. Berry), ii., 245.

APPENDICES

APPENDICES

NOTE.—*The two following Appendices* [A and B] *being written in the first person, apparently belong to the* Autobiography, *and in a sense do so. The explanation of their appearance here is that the* Autobiography *was finished and stereotyped ten years before the first of them was written, and that now to incorporate them would involve a re-arrangement of the plates, which would be troublesome and costly. Hence I have thought it best to leave them to be used by my biographer. The use of the first person instead of the third will, after this explanation, cause no misapprehension.*

[*March, 1903.*]   H. S.

APPENDIX A

PHYSICAL TRAITS AND SOME SEQUENCES[1]

YEARS ago I met with the remark that biographers do not adequately describe the physical traits of the men whose lives they write. Something is usually said about external appearance; but little or nothing is said about constitution. Both sets of characters should have their places, since both are factors in a man's career. Recognition of this truth has decided me to set down such memoranda concerning my physical nature as seem significant.

Already in the Autobiography I have named the fact that my ultimate height was 5 feet 10 inches: and I think I have remarked that during boyhood I was unusually long-legged. Probably my ability to outrun my school-fellows was due to this trait of structure. . . . On approaching manhood a much greater rate of growth, reaching three inches a year, was, I suppose, due to the more rapid development of the trunk. Eventually the proportions were not far from the normal, though I think the chest was not so large as was needed for a complete organic balance. Like my father and mother, and like all my grandparents, I was '' spare,'' not to say thin. Indeed, the fact that throughout adult life my weight was usually a little over 10 stone implies this thinness, for the normal weight for a man of 5 feet 10 inches is something like a stone greater. I should add that my limbs when fully developed were somewhat slighter than usual, my hands especially being small— too small for a man.

---

[1] Written in the autumn of 1902.

A life's experience has proved my constitutional strength to have been good if not great. There have come round to me reports respecting my feebleness in infancy—feebleness said to have been such that it was doubtful whether I should be reared. I know no warrant for such reports. It is true that my father would not have my brain taxed by early lessons; but beyond this interdict I can remember no evidence. I was allowed to run wild and was freer from children's disorders than is usual.

Something should be said respecting complexion. My hair was brown, leaning rather towards a darker than a lighter shade. A moderate amount of colour in the cheeks was characteristic. I had neither that parchment-complexion which goes along with the strongest constitutions (contrary to common notions) nor that high colour which is popularly thought a sign of abounding health. And here seems the fittest place to remark that during middle and later life I changed very little. In advanced years the usual remark was that I looked ten years younger than I actually was. There were, I think, three causes for this. It was said of me, after the publication of *Social Statics,* that my forehead did not bear any of those lines of thought which were to be expected. The absence of such lines has remained a trait down almost to the present time. As before explained, my thinking has not been forced but spontaneous; and, as a consequence, the face has not been drawn into furrows expressing strenuous mental action. A second cause is, I believe, that as my strong eyes never shrank from any light however bright, there was not induced that wrinkling up of the corners of the eyes which reflex efforts to shut off part of the light cause; and, consequently, there has not been so marked a production of " crow's feet." And then, in the third place, I have retained up to the present time all my teeth. Where the crowns have decayed the roots have been left, and there has not been produced the usual sinking in of the cheeks from lack of the support which the gums normally yield. This has enabled the face to retain its contour in a much greater degree than usual.

Until the time of my nervous breakdown, I had good health. My constitution appears to have been not strong in the sense of possessing overflowing vigour, but strong in the sense of having a good balance. All through life, in late days as in early days, my state of body and mind has been equable. There have never been any bursts of high spirits and times of depression; but there has ever been a flow of energy moderate in amount, but sufficient for the purposes of life.

One consequence has been that I have preserved down to late life a love of amusements of all kinds. I never fell into that state of indifference which characterises many. Concerts and theatres continued to be attractions until my broken health forbade attending them; a good drama being to the last, as at first, one of the greatest pleasures which life yields. Certain sports, too, as salmon and sea-trout fishing, retained their attraction until my strength failed. To friends who have lost liking for other pursuits than work, I have often insisted that it is a mistake, even from a business point of view, to give up amusements; since, when disturbance of health has made a holiday imperative, there remains no means of passing the time with satisfaction. " Be a boy as long as you can," was the maxim which I reiterated. Games, too, I played as long as physical powers allowed. Above all I continued to enjoy the country; my sojourn in which every summer was looked forward to as the great gratification of the year. How fully I entered into its concomitant pleasures may be judged from the fact that I went picnicking when over eighty.

Being moderate in amount, my flow of energy was never such as prompted needless activities. There are men whose fulness of life necessitates some kind of ac-tion—purposeless action, if no other. This was never so with me. Contrariwise, I tended always to be an idler.

Action resulted only under the prompting of a much-desired end, and even then it was with some reluctance that I worked at things needful for achieving the end.

I emphasise this trait since it is so utterly at variance with the trait commonly ascribed to me. On looking at the series of my books, and at the amount of material brought together in them, as well as the thinking shown, it appears to be a necessary implication that I have been a hard worker. The inference is quite wrong, however. In the first place, that which I have done has been done only under pressure of a great object; and even under that pressure it has been done with a very moderate activity. It is true that activity in thinking was constant; and it was partly the pleasure of thinking (which in boyhood took the form of " castle-building," and in later life higher forms) which put a constant check upon action. Probably this trait did much towards shaping my career. Had I been energetic there would not have arisen those quiet contemplations, carried on irregularly and at first without definite aims, which led to the work I have done.

One of the traits of a constitution which, though not vigorous, was organically good, appears to have been a well-finished development of the structures which arise out of the dermal system. I was thirty-two before I had any sign of decay of teeth. I never had a tooth taken out or stopped. Of the eyes, which are also dermal structures, the like may be said. They have all through life remained strong. Down even to my present age (eighty-two) I read without spectacles; sometimes putting on a pair, but finding the inconvenience such that, on the whole, I prefer to do without them. I may add that I have, until quite recently, rejoiced in a strong light. That dislike to a glare which many people betray, even in their early years, I have rarely if ever felt. The like holds with the ears. Those around me say that my hearing is perfect. Is there any significance in this perfection and long endurance of teeth, eyes, and ears, all of

298

them developed from the dermal layer? The implication seems to be that in the process of development there was no failure of nutrition at the periphery.

Part of my motive for setting down the foregoing facts has been that of introducing certain incidents and the effects they probably had on my constitution and career.

First of all there is the achievement in walking when thirteen, as narrated in my *Autobiography* [i., 106]. I have I think expressed the belief that, notwithstanding the passage through this constitutional strain without apparent damage, yet some damage was done. That such a long-continued exertion was possible at that age is strange; and it was, I think, impossible that it could have been gone through without leaving certain imperfect developments of structure.

[After the visit to Switzerland] came the breakdown in health caused by writing the *Principles of Psychology*. If, as above inferred, the vascular system at large, and more especially its central organ, had been injured, it seems an implication that the collapse which occurred under this moderate stress of work would not otherwise have taken place. From that time onwards throughout the rest of my life I have never had a sound night. Always my sleep, very inadequate in quantity, has been a succession of bits: not the broken sleep resulting from an occasional turning over while half awake, but having frequent breaks with no sense of sleepiness, and long intervals with no sleep at all. Always I dropped off without preliminary sense that I was about to do so, and always when I woke I was broad awake. Only during recent years (say after seventy-five) have I approached the normal state, in so far as that is indicated by feeling sleepy before going to sleep and after waking.

I have said that for eighteen months I did nothing. Even reading a column of a newspaper brought on a sensation of fulness in the head; and when, in the winter of 1856-7, I at length undertook to write the article on " Progress: its Law and Cause," the effort entailed was very trying. Still the result was beneficial, and from that time onwards, little by little, I resumed work.

It seems strange that with this nervous disability, accompanied by nights of three, four, or five hours sleep made up of many parts, I should have maintained what seemed to be good health. There was no failure of muscular strength. My usual practice was to run up three flights of stairs two steps at a time, and I remember noting that this habit remained easy to me on my sixtieth birthday. The essential cause was that my digestion remained good. Throughout preceding life I had never been to any extent troubled by dyspepsia, and this eupeptic state continued onwards after my break-down. The first indication of any lack of full digestive power was that, when forty, I found veal at a late dinner was no longer desirable. From that time onwards there has been no kind of food which I have avoided on the ground of indigestibility; my diet even down to this late period including dishes which many people in middle life would shrink from. Of course the ability to obtain a good supply of blood has gone far towards compensating for the evils entailed by bad nights. Repair of the tissues goes on during waking hours as well as during sleep; and sleep serves simply to give opportunity for making up *arrears* of repair and, especially, to give extra opportunity for repair to the heart. Hence it results that a comparatively small amount of sleep with good blood well circulated suffices—suffices better than a long sleep with a slow circulation and poor blood.

A partial ability to continue my work was the consequence. All through the period during which the *Synthetic Philosophy* was in hand, there was never any lack of power to think, and never any reluctance to think. Though my working time was so limited in duration (being checked by the rise of sensations in the head and a

consciousness that mischief would result from perseverance) yet during this abridged period the process of
dictating was in no degree restrained by a sense of
effort or of disinclination; and had I not known that disaster would follow I should have been ready to resume in
the afternoon. The constitution had adjusted itself to
the abnormal conditions, and the functions of all kinds
went on within the prescribed bounds without apparent
strain.

It is a question of some interest whether the state of
things was injurious or otherwise to my work. Of course
had I not lived beyond the usual age, part of it would
have remained undone; but having lived long enough to
complete it (or all but a non-essential part of it), it seems
possible that the slow rate of progress, giving opportunity for more quiet thinking than there would have
been had I worked at the ordinary rate, was beneficial.

Thus far the accounts of my physical nature and of
the incidents which profoundly affected it, have concerned the part of my life which extended to 1882. Then
there came an incident, further illustrating the rash-
ness I have described and leaving no benefit but only
enormous evil. I refer to the initiation of the Anti-
Aggression League, and the effects produced on my
health.

Up to that time I had abided by my resolution not to
enter into any public activity; knowing that my state of
brain was one which forbade any stress. But now the
interest I felt in resisting our filibustering actions was
such as to over-ride my resolution. Not that I thought
of joining in a continued agitation. I thought that after
the League had been set afloat I might retire, and assist
only by name and money.

And now there began to be shown in more manifest
ways the cardiac damage, and damage to the spinal cord,
which had been left by my boyish exploit. I had to
diminish my work, and year by year there came a
diminution of the distance which I could walk without

damage. Every now and then, with my constitutional imprudence, I exceeded the limit of work or exercise, and thereafter made both of them smaller, until, in 1886, came the final breakdown. Thereafter for some years I was obliged to desist from the *Synthetic Philosophy*. . . .

Having returned to a higher level of health I resumed writing the *Philosophy,* of which more than two volumes were still [in 1888] unwritten. Ensuing years witnessed the same general course of life—improvements for a time, relapses consequent on exceeding the amount of exertion bodily or mental which my state allowed, and then long periods during which very little or nothing could be done. The variations were great. From 1890 to 1896 there were times during which I was able to dictate a considerable amount each morning; to walk up and down-stairs; to sit at table to meals (except breakfast, which I had taken in bed since 1886) ; to drive to the Athenæum; and, when up to high-water-mark, to play a game of billiards there. But always after a while some adverse incident—a little too much exertion, or a little too much talk, or a little too much work—brought me down again. And now, since the completion of the *Synthetic Philosophy,* the low level has become settled.

During these later years, when capable of any work, my dictation (according to Mr. Troughton) has amounted sometimes to two periods of ten minutes each during the morning, and sometimes to three. Reading for more than a few minutes at a time is mischievous, and listening to reading has to be restricted to fragments. It has been so even with music. Even so simple a thing as looking at illustrations in monthly magazines is too much for me unless taken in portions. Sometimes things have considerably improved, as at Bepton, in 1900, when I could walk about the garden a little; while at other times, as in the spring of 1901 and again during the present autumn (1902) I have been mainly confined to bed, even the extra effort entailed by reclining on a sofa being too much. To all appearance this state of things will become more pronounced, and infirmities of other kinds, which have during these last years added to my troubles, will make such part of my life as remains still more to be dreaded.

APPENDIX B

NOTE.—When there occurred to me the thought of writing a brief intellectual history of myself I hesitated for some time: doubting whether it would be of any service. Now that it has been completed, however, I am glad that I undertook it. Placing the facts in order of genesis has had the effect of revealing to me some significant connexions of ideas I was previously unconscious of; and I infer that, if to me the narrative has yielded information, it is likely to yield still more to others. As elucidating the natural evolution of a theory, such information may not be without its use.

At the same time some aid may be given to those who have not yet made acquaintance with my books. I would suggest that for such the best course will be to read first a number of the *Essays,* beginning with the more popular; then to read the little book on *Education;* then *The Study of Sociology;* and then the pages which here follow. A sketch plan of an unexplored region is always convenient for guidance, and this " Filiation of Ideas " may serve as a sketch plan of the Synthetic Philosophy.

February, 1899.

THE FILIATION OF IDEAS[1]

A COMPLETE biography should give an account not only of a man's career and conduct but also of his mental development, emotional and intellectual, and of the products of that development. Something is not unfre-

---

[1] The footnotes within square brackets have been inserted mainly to assist reference to the *Life and Letters.*

quently done towards delineating the evolution of character, but not much is done towards intellectual history,
explaining the genesis of ideas and the elaborations of
them. Such a history cannot to much purpose be given
by any one but the man himself, and it has not commonly
happened that the man himself has thought of giving it.

I have already, in the Autobiography, indicated stages
of thought, and shown the origins of certain leading
ideas; but I have done this only in a fragmentary way,
and much of the detail required to make the account
coherent has been unmentioned. Then, beyond the fact
that these indications do not form a continuous whole
there is the fact that they are limited to the first half of
my life. Hence the decision to narrate in full, so far
as is possible, the successive steps, and also to describe
the peculiarities of constitution, culture, and circumstance, which have been influential. One significant result will, I believe, be that of showing how large a part
emotional nature plays in determining the intellectual
activities, and how it enters as an important factor into
the resulting convictions.

The events of childhood and boyhood, narrated elsewhere, indicate to how small an extent authority swayed
me. The disobedience, so perpetually complained of,
was the correlative of irreverence for governing agencies.
This natural trait operated throughout life, tending to
make me pay little attention to the established opinion
on any matter which came up for judgment, and tending
to leave me perfectly free to inquire without restraint.

The nature thus displayed was rather strengthened
than otherwise by my father's habit of speculating about
causes, and appealing to my judgment with the view of
exercising my powers of thinking. By occasional questions of this kind he strengthened that self-asserting
nature of which he had at other times reason to complain, but he did not apparently perceive this. Meanwhile he cultivated a consciousness of Cause—made the

thought of Cause a familiar one. The discovery of cause is through analysis—the pulling to pieces phenomena for the purpose of ascertaining what are the essential connexions among them. Hence one who is in the habit of seeking causes is in the habit of analysing. I have up to this time regarded my father as more synthetic than analytic: being led to do so by his perpetual occupation with synthetic geometry. But now, on reconsidering the facts, I see that he was in large measure analytic. He was a great adept at making solutions of puzzles, verbal or physical; and this evidently implies analysis. Moreover, that analysis of articulations implied by his system of shorthand, exhibited the faculty.

No doubt this habit of mind, inherited from him and fostered by him, flourished the more in the absence of the ordinary appeals to supernatural causes. Though my father retained the leading religious convictions, yet he never appeared to regard any occurrences as other than natural. It should also be remarked that dogmatic teaching played small part in my education. Linguistic culture is based on authority, and as I rebelled against it, the acceptance of things simply on authority was not habitual. On the other hand, the study of Mathematics (conspicuously Geometry and Mechanics), with which my youth was mainly occupied, appeals, at each step in a demonstration, to private judgment, and in a sense recognises the right of private judgment. Many times, too, I assisted in experiments with the air-pump and the electrical machine; so that ideas of physical causation were repeatedly impressed on me. Moreover such small knowledge of natural history as I gained by rearing insects, tended to familiarise me with natural genesis.

I have elsewhere named, as early established, the habit of castle-building, carried to a great extent; and I have expressed the belief that this was a useful exercise of the imagination—not reminiscent imagination, but constructive imagination. Another trait, not thus far named,

306

and which I inherited from my father, was a dominant ideality, showing itself in a love of perfection. In him this love was so strong that it became a hindrance. He could not let a thing alone as being finished. With me the desire to make work better, though pronounced, has not gone to that excess. Still, I have never been able to rest satisfied with anything incomplete. This has been shown in the repeated improvements of expression: correction, again correction, and yet again correction, has been the history of most of my books. The love of completeness has been curiously shown from the beginning by the habit of summarising every chapter. I could not leave a thing with loose ends: the ends must be gathered together and tied up. This trait has been further manifested in the tendency not to rest content with induction, but to continue an inquiry until the generalisation reached was reduced to a deduction. Leaving a truth in an inductive form is, in a sense, leaving its parts with loose ends; and the bringing it to a deductive form is, in a sense, uniting its facts as all parts of one fact.

A general result of these natural traits and this kind of culture was an attitude of detachment. The absence of those studies, linguistic and historical, which form so large a part of the ordinary education, left me free from the bias given by the plexus of traditional ideas and sentiments. This detachment had the same kind of effect as the detachment from surrounding authorities. All influences thus conspired to make me entirely open to receive those impressions and ideas produced by direct converse with things. Elsewhere I have referred to the fact that when thirteen, spite of the high authorities against me, I denied the existence of inertia as a positive force; and have instanced it as showing unusual independence of judgment, at the same time that it implied an unusual intuition of physical truths. These two traits, joined with a constructive imagination unusually active, and a great love of completeness, may be considered as forming my positive mental equipment at the

outset; to which there should be added the negative
equipment, if it may be so called, of absence of culture in
" the humanities."

But I must not forget another trait of nature—a relative liking for thought in contrast with a relative aversion to action. My physical constitution did not yield
such overflow of energy as prompts some natures to
spontaneous activity. In many directions action was entered upon rather reluctantly; while thinking was a
pleasure. Obviously this predominant tendency to contemplation has been a factor in my career.

Letters written home when, at the age of seventeen, I
commenced engineering in London, show an excursiveness characteristic of me. There are, I see, some ideas
respecting the expansion of steam in relation to its heat,
which, quite wrong in their preliminary assumptions,
imply the absurd supposition that the question had not
been fully worked out by those who were competent. I
refer to these as showing both the self-confidence and
the tendency to explore in the field of physics: the idea
of natural causation being dominant. The daily professional culture in surveying and making drawings of machinery, of course conduced to exact thinking; ever im-
pressing on me geometrical truths and the necessities of
relation.

When, after nearly a year, I migrated to the Birmingham and Gloucester Railway, influences of the same class
continued in operation. But I observe here coming out
the trait above named—preference for thinking to acting.
The first original thing I did was devising a new method
of drawing the curves in skew arches; and the prompting
motive was aversion from taking much trouble. Subsequent promptings to invention had the same origin. The
Scale of Equivalents originated from my dislike to the
labour of reducing a set of dimensions taken in inches
and eighths into hundredths of a foot; and though I do
not trace to that cause the invention I called a Velocim-

308

eter, which also is a means of dispensing with calculation, yet the consciousness of such labour, gone through by a coadjutor, directed my thoughts into the channel which led to it. Other devices, dating from that time, illustrated the same excursiveness, self-dependence, and constructive imagination. The latter part of my first engineering period brought me a good deal in contact with men and with business; and, being left in charge of some engineering work and allowed to carry out my own designs, there was a further familiarising with mechanical truths and a further fostering of self-dependence. But here must be noted a significant fact. I became interested in geology, and bought Lyell's *Principles,* etc. The result of reading this was that, rejecting his adverse arguments, I adopted the hypothesis of development, which ever after influenced my thoughts. I was then twenty.

During this time at Worcester politics received no attention from me. But when, after the ending of my engagement on the Birmingham and Gloucester Railway, I returned to Derby, a change took place in this respect; and in June, 1842, my thoughts on political matters resulted in the letters to *The Nonconformist* on " The Proper Sphere of Government "—a somewhat strange subject for a young man of twenty-two to enter upon. The general tenor of these letters betrays the emotional leanings. Individuality was pronounced in all members of the family, and pronounced individuality is necessarily more or less at variance with authority. A self-dependent and self-asserting nature resists all such government as is not expressive of equitable restraint. Our family was essentially a *dissenting* family; and dissent is an expression of antagonism to arbitrary control. Of course a wish to limit State-action is a natural concomitant; and this characterised the letters on " The Proper Sphere of Government." Beyond this constitutional tendency, here first illustrated, there was shown the tendency to regard social phenomena as subordinate to natural law:

the two tendencies being, in an indirect way, correlatives. Already in those early days the culture I have described had fostered the belief that in society as in the world at large, there are uniformities of relation; and national life was vaguely thought of as a life having certain similarities to life at large. Though it had not yet taken shape, there was a dim idea of a social organism.

During the several subsequent years—years of miscellaneous and futile activities mainly spent over inventions, but partly in speculations, political, ethical, linguistic, showing as always the excursive tendency, and during which there was some art-culture—drawing, modelling, and music—there is little to be noted save accentuation of traits already shown. One matter, however, of some significance must be named. From the time when, at about the age of eleven, I heard a series of lectures on phrenology by Spurzheim, who was going through the country diffusing the doctrines of Gall, I had been a believer in phrenology. Though when twenty-one to twenty-four my scepticism had not risen to the height it eventually reached, yet, as might be anticipated, I entertained sundry phrenological heresies, and expressed them in articles published in a quarterly journal called *The Zoist*.[1] Two of these I need not name; the third had results. It appeared in January, 1844, under the title " A New View of the Functions of Imitation and Benevolence." The essential points in the argument were that the function of the organ called Imitation is to produce sympathy and that sympathy is the root of benevolence. Years afterwards I learned that the genesis of benevolence by sympathy had been expounded by Adam Smith; but in 1844 I knew his name only as the writer of *The Wealth of Nations*.

During the second engineering period not much speculative activity went on. There were devices for diminishing monotonous labour and there was the ever-present thought of improvement. From the one cause resulted

---

[1] See vol. i., chap. iv., pp. 51, 58.

SIR CHARLES LYELL.

the little appliance for facilitating the plotting of sections; and from the other the improved levelling-staff and the proposed new type of level. Here, as always, instead of accepting the settled usages, as most do, the fact that they were settled usages had no influence with me.

Though there must have been filiations of the various mechanical ideas which prompted my activities between the time (1846) when my railway career ended and the time (1848) when my literary career began, yet I cannot recall them. There was a little invention, the binding pin, by which I made some money: there was the planing machinery by which I lost it; and there were sundry ideas which did not reach the experimental stage. But new ideas of some kind daily occupied me.

During all this second engineering period there had, I doubt not, been going on some development of the ideas set forth in the letters on " The Proper Sphere of Government." That governmental actions should be definitely restricted was a conclusion which in these letters stood without a satisfactory basis. What ultimate principle is it from which may be inferred the limits of State-action? Analysis was required. The excogitation of this principle and the perception that not only these limits, but also the requirements of equity at large could be deduced from it, prompted the writing of *Social Statics*. This was commenced five years after the letters on " The Proper Sphere of Government " had been written. Let me add that during the interval there had been going on that political activity entailed by membership of the Complete Suffrage Union and advocacy of the doctrine of equal political rights: a kind of activity and a kind of exercised sentiment which kept in mind the principle *Social Statics* elaborated.

Concerning *Social Statics* itself there are various noteworthy things to be said. There is no invoking of authorities. A few references, mostly dissentient, are made to ethical and political writers whose well-known doctrines I had gathered in the course of miscellaneous reading—not from their books; for I never could read books the cardinal principles of which I rejected. The course pursued in this case as in others was to go back to the facts as presented in human conduct and society, and draw inferences direct from them.

In fulfilment of the desire for ideal completeness there was, at the outset, a presentation of the entire field to be covered by a system of ethics. In pursuance of the ordinary conception theologically derived, ethics had been composed of interdicts of many desired actions and inculcations of actions not desired. Ethical teaching had given little or no moral sanction to pleasurable activities. If not tacitly frowned upon, they were certainly not enjoined. But in the programme with which *Social Statics* begins—a programme corresponding with that ultimately adopted in *The Principles of Ethics*—there was a division recognising the ethical sanction of those actions required for the fulfilment of the normal functions of life, and for the obtainment of those pleasures accompanying the normal functions. There was an assertion of the moral claims of the individual to natural satisfactions within specified limits.

And here, in going afresh over the facts, I observe something of which at the time I was not definitely conscious—that the first principle formulated was simply an abstract statement of the conditions under which might equitably be pursued by each that self-satisfaction just insisted upon as ethically warranted. It was an assertion of that liberty, within limits, to pursue the ends of life, which was implied in the assertion that enjoyment of the ends of life is moral. And this leads to a remark of some interest concerning the mode in which this principle was approached. For thirty years I supposed myself the first to enunciate this doctrine of the liberty of each limited only by the like liberties of all— the right of every man to do what he wills so long as he does not trench upon the similar rights of any other man. But after the lapse of that time I learned, from a reference in *Mind*, that Kant had enunciated this principle. After some trouble I found his enunciation; and then it became manifest that Kant had reached the principle from the opposite side. He had specified the *limits* to the free action of the individual, leaving the free action as a thing not itself to be asserted but rather to be tacitly implied in the assertion of limits. I, contrariwise, had primarily asserted the claim of each to free action, and had secondarily asserted the limits arising from the presence of others having similar claim to free action. The two modes of reaching this conclusion are significant of the difference between the social states of Germany and England, and also significant of the individual difference. Kant, native of a country in which subordination to authority had been all along very marked, looked at this matter from the side of restraint—individual action was to be *restrained* within certain limits. And while the limits were made authoritative, there was no corresponding authoritativeness claimed for the right of free action. With me, the converse happened. Being one of a race much more habituated to individual freedom, the primary assertion was that of a claim to free action—not a recognition of subordinations, but the assertion of a *right* subject to certain subordinations. And while this opposite method of conceiving the matter was characteristic of a citizen of a relatively free country, it was more especially characteristic of one in whom the maintenance of individuality had always been so dominant. I emphasise this contrast as clearly showing the extent to which the emotional nature influences the intellectual conclusions.

The next fact to be named is, that there was now displayed the tendency to pass from induction to deduction. The views I had expressed respecting the limitation of State action to certain spheres and exclusion of it from other spheres were lying all abroad: each standing on its own merits as an independent belief. Dissatisfaction with that condition of thought led to the search for an ultimate principle from which the limitations were deducible; and this when found proved to be a principle from which were also deducible the various so-called rights. The whole ethical scheme, in so far as justice is concerned, had been reduced to a completely deductive, and consequently quite coherent, form satisfying the love of ideal completeness.

Another significant fact is, that throughout the whole argument there is tacitly assumed the process of Evolution, in so far as human nature is concerned. There is a perpetual assumption of the moral modifiability of Man, and the progressive adaptation of his character to the social state. It is alleged that his moral evolution depends on the development of sympathy, which is held to be the root of both justice and beneficence. This change of mental nature is ascribed to the exercise of the sympathetic emotions consequent upon a peaceful social life, and, therefore, tacitly implies the inheritance of functionally-produced changes of structure. There is also a passing recognition of Survival of the Fittest. The beneficence of the process by which, among animals and men, the inferior disappear and leave the superior to continue the race, is asserted; but there is no recognition of the consequences seen by Mr. Darwin.

In the last chapter, entitled " General Considerations," the evolutionary conception is distinctly brought out in many ways. Civilisation is described as a continuous moulding of human beings to the social state, and of the social state to the human beings as they become moulded: the two acting and reacting. Along with this there is recognised the analogy between a society formed of individuals and an animal formed of living cells or units; though at that time (1850) the hypothesis that an animal is thus formed was, when here and there hinted, regarded as an absurdity. Along with the conception of this analogy of ultimate components between the social organism and the individual organism, there went another which proved of far greater significance. How I came by the idea that a low type of animal consists of numerous like parts performing like functions, while a high type of animal consists of relatively few unlike parts performing unlike functions, I do not remember. It may have been from Professor Rymer Jones's *Animal Kingdom;* for some of the facts cited are, I think, from that work. But wherever this general truth came from, I immediately recognised the parallelism between it and the truth presented by low and high types of societies. This was the earliest foreshadowing of the general doctrine of Evolution.

For the perception that there is a progress from a uniform to a multiform structure, and that this progress is the same in an individual organism and in a social organism, was a recognition of the progress from the homogeneous to the heterogeneous, though no such words were used. I had at that time no thought of any extension of the idea; but evidently there was the germ which was presently to develop. I should add that the acquaintance which I accidentally made with Coleridge's essay on the Idea of Life, in which he set forth, as though it were his own, the notion of Schelling, that Life is the tendency to individuation, had a considerable effect. In this same chapter it is referred to as illustrated alike in the individuation of a living organism, and also in the individuation of a society as it progresses.

Shortly before, or immediately after, the publication of *Social Statics,* I made the acquaintance of Mr. G. H. Lewes at one of Chapman's *soirées.* We became mutually interested, and walked towards our homes together. I remember the incident because conversation during the walk having turned upon the Development Question, I surprised Mr. Lewes by rejecting the view set forth in the *Vestiges of the Natural History of Creation,* which he supposed to be the only view, and asserting the view that functional adaptation is the sole cause

315

of development. I name the fact as showing what my belief was at the close of 1850 or beginning of 1851.

Nothing noteworthy in the development of ideas occurred during that period of mental inertia which followed the publication of *Social Statics*. I think it probable, however, that further materials for thought were afforded by the lectures of Professor Owen on Comparative Osteology, given at the College of Surgeons, which I attended. Along with a mass of details, there were presented to me certain general facts which were suggestive. An hypothesis sets up a process of organisation in thoughts previously lying unorganised. The effect is analogous to that which results when a sperm-cell is added to a germ-cell. In the facts as exhibited throughout Professor Owen's lectures, there were many illustrations of the truth that the skeletons of low types of animals are relatively uniform in their structures— showing what he then and at other times used to call " vegetative repetition." I could not accept his Platonic notion of an ideal vertebra, of which he considered each actual vertebra an embodiment; but his facts illustrated progress from the uniform to the multiform in the course of osteological organisation. I do not remember that I thought anything to that effect, but here were materials for further development of the conception illustrated at the close of *Social Statics*.

The acquaintance made with Mr. G. H. Lewes was followed by two country excursions which we made together in the autumn of 1851—the first up the Thames Valley from Maidenhead as far as Abingdon, and the other in Kent, in the neighbourhood of Maidstone. They were accompanied by a great deal of philosophic talk. One effect, as indicated in *George Eliot's Life,* was to give him an active scientific interest. Another effect was that a leaf I gathered suggested to me certain facts of plant-structure: recognition of the Law of Organic Symmetry being the ultimate consequence.[1] During the second ex-

---

[1] See vol. i., chap. vi., p. 82.

cursion I made acquaintance with a little book just published by Milne-Edwards, which we looked into on board the steamer carrying us to Gravesend. It set forth the luminous idea of '' the physiological division of labour.'' Though the conception was not new to me, for it was illustrated at the close of *Social Statics,* yet this phrase, expressing an analogy between individual organisations and social organisations in so vivid a manner, gave greater distinctness to pre-existing thoughts. The reading of Lewes's *Biographical History of Philosophy,* which resulted from my acquaintance with him, did not, so far as I remember, give origin to any special ideas; but it gave me an interest in philosophical and pyschological inquiries greater than had before existed. Presentation of the doctrines of various schools throughout the past served, not so much as a means of acquiring their thoughts as a means of stimulating my own thoughts, and this effect began presently to show itself.

During the first months of 1852 the essay on the '' Theory of Population '' occupied me. Chapman, then proprietor of the *Westminster Review,* to whom I had on some occasion expressed my view respecting the decrease of fertility which goes along with higher development, had been anxious to have an article on the subject. I at first declined for the assigned reason that I proposed to write a book about the matter. Subsequently circumstances decided me to accede to Chapman's proposal, and the article was written for the April number. Here again was illustrated the truth that a germinal idea thrown among unorganised materials sets up organisation. The notion had been present with me, certainly from 1846-7, and how much earlier I do not know.[1] But now the working hypothesis soon caused such knowledge as I had to take shape, and gave the power of rapidly assimilating other knowledge. Support was found in the doctrine of individuation above named; for a thesis running throughout the essay is that individuation and

---

[1] See vol. i., chap. vi., p. 84.

reproduction are antagonistic—a formula which, expressed in physical terms, as I should in later days have expressed it, is equivalent to—Integration and Disintegration are antagonistic. A collateral effect of the reading of Coleridge's essay on the Idea of Life was that of making one seek a better definition of Life than " the tendency to Individuation." Hence resulted the definition given in that essay—the coordination of actions. Though a better one, this formula was incomplete because it limited the conception to actions going on within the organism, without reference to those external actions which they are adjusted to.

As narrated elsewhere, this essay on " The Theory of Population " led to my friendship with Huxley.[1] I name the fact here because within a few weeks of its commencement there was an incident which fixes the date of one of my beliefs. I had suggested an introduction to Lewes, and had taken Huxley to Bedford Place, Kensington, where Lewes then resided. On our way back the discussion turned on the Development question, and he ridiculed the notion of a *chain* of beings. I said that I no more accepted that symbol than he did, and that a tree was the true symbol. How long I had thought this I do not know; but the incident shows that before that time there had arisen a belief which we shall presently see pervaded other speculations. It is observable that this conception of divergent and redivergent branches implies the conception of increasing multiformity or heterogeneity—one thing giving origin to many things: the thoughts are manifestly akin.

Persuaded by Lewes, who was at that time literary editor of the *Leader* (a paper which died a few years afterwards), I wrote for it a series of short essays under the title of " The Haythorne Papers "—a name given as a bracket holding them together. They show the usual excursiveness, and a tendency everywhere to analyse and to generalise. The second of them, entitled

---

[1] See vol. i., chap. vi., p. 85.

" The Development Hypothesis," was of fundamental significance.[1] It shows that in 1852 the belief in organic evolution had taken deep root, and had drawn to itself a large amount of evidence—evidence not derived from numerous special instances but derived from the general aspects of organic nature, and from the necessity of accepting the hypothesis of Evolution when the hypothesis of Special Creation has been rejected. The Special Creation belief had dropped out of my mind many years before, and I could not remain in a suspended state: acceptance of the only conceivable alternative was peremptory. This distinct and public enunciation of the belief was but a giving definite form to thoughts which had been gradually growing, as was shown in *Social Statics*.

From this time onwards the evolutionary interpretation of things in general became habitual, and manifested itself in curious ways. One would not have expected to find it in an essay on " The Philosophy of Style "; but at the close of that essay, written in 1852, the truth that progress in style is from uniformity to multiformity—from a more homogeneous to a more heterogeneous form —finds expression: showing that in mental products, too, the distinctive nature of high structure was beginning to be recognised. The progress of thought in another direction was shown in an essay on " The Universal Postulate."[2] I had been reading Mill's *Logic*. In it occur his strictures on Whewell; and while agreeing as to the unsoundness of Whewell's doctrine, I did not agree in the reason for rejecting it. Hence the essay. This involved the first expression of metaphysical convictions; for the outcome of the argument was a defence of realism and an assertion of the impossibility of establishing any belief at variance with it. Up to this time, thinking with me had been mainly concrete in character, but now it assumed an abstract character; and thereafter the abstract and the concrete went hand in hand, as the

---

[1] See vol. i., chap. vi., p. 85.   [2] See vol. i., chap. vi., pp. 87, 90, 95.

inductive and the deductive were already doing. This essay on " The Universal Postulate " ended in a controversy with Mill, which, taking its first shape in the next edition of his *Logic,* went on at intervals in an amicable manner for some years and eventually led to our friendship.

In an essay on " Manners and Fashion " developmental ideas again displayed themselves. The origin of institutions by a process of evolution was taken for granted; and there was delineated the rise of the different kinds of government by divergence from one original kind, which united the ceremonial, the political, and the ecclesiastical. There was also this same idea running throughout the account of the genesis of the different forms of manners from simple original forms—a multiplication of kinds from one kind.

A like trend of thought was shown in " The Art of Education," published in the *North British Review* (since deceased), and now embodied in my little book on *Education.* Various evolutionary corollaries were drawn from the proposition that the unfolding of a child's mind repeats the unfolding of the mind in the human race. It was urged that education must proceed " from the simple to the complex," since the mind, " like all things that develop, progresses from the homogeneous to the heterogeneous." It was contended that the development of mind " is an advance from the indefinite to the definite," and that teaching must follow that course. A further corollary was that as " humanity had progressed solely by self-instruction," " self-development should be encouraged to the uttermost in the child."

About this time, 1854, Miss Martineau's abridged translation of Comte's works was published. I had already gathered a notion of his system from Lewes, who was a disciple and had written in the *Leader* some papers giving an abstract of it; and a more specific knowledge of Comte's cardinal ideas had been gained in 1852, from reading the introduction at the instigation of George Eliot, and with her aid. She, too, was anxious that I should accept Positivist doctrines. But the reading of the Introduction, while it left me undecided respecting the doctrine of the Three Stages, was followed by immediate rejection of the Classification of the Sciences. Now that the translation was published, I looked further into the Positive Philosophy, with the result that I engaged to write a review of it for the *British Quarterly*. Being an impatient reader, especially when reading views from which I dissent, I did not go far. But the part I read, and which prompted me to write a criticism, had a very important effect. I have said elsewhere that I owe much to Comte—not in the sense assumed by his disciples, but in an opposite sense. I owe to him the benefits of an antagonism which cleared and developed my own views, while assigning reasons for dissenting from his. Rejection of his ideas concerning the development of the sciences, led to those ideas of my own which are set forth in " The Genesis of Science "; and these had significant relations to the psychological ideas soon afterwards elaborated. The rise of certain fundamental perceptions and fundamental acts of reasoning was ascribed to gradual organisation of experiences. There was a development of the idea of likeness, and out of this the idea of equality and inequality. From the likenesses and unlikenesses of things, a transition to the likenesses and unlikenesses of relations, was alleged; and this, leading to recognition of the equality of relations, was represented as the basis of reasoning. Then it was shown that throughout this development divergence and re-divergence go on, causing multiplication and heterogeneity of sciences: the symbol of a tree being here again used. And it was further pointed out that along with differentiation of the sciences there goes increasing interdependence, that is to say, integration. Thus, while there were several traits foreshadowing a psychological theory, there were other traits foreshadowing a general evolutionary conception, in so far as it concerns intelligence and its products.[1]

In what year I decided to write a book on the *Principles of Psychology* I do not remember.[2] But in 1853, there was reached one of its leading views, consequent on the perception that the definition of life as " the co-ordination of actions," required to be supplemented by recognition of the relations borne by such co-ordinated actions to connected actions in the environment. There at once followed the idea that the growth of a correspondence between inner and outer actions had to be traced up from the beginning; so as to show the way in which Mind gradually evolves out of Life. This was, I think, the thought which originated the book and gave its most distinctive character; but evidently, the tendency to regard all things as evolved, which had been growing more pronounced, gave another special interest to the undertaking. The evolutional view of human nature had been assumed all through *Social Statics,* and in the essay on " The Development Hypothesis " belief in evolution had been distinctly avowed as holding of the organic creation. The progress of organisms and of societies from the uniform to the multiform had been recognised, and the thought of increasing mutual dependence of parts had been accentuated by meeting with Milne-Edwards's phrase " the physiological division of labour." Then came the congruous formula of Von Baer—of development from the homogeneous to the heterogeneous. At the same time had arisen the correlative conception of divergence and redivergence, and consequent increasing multiformity, as occurring in organisms, in governmental organisations, and in the genesis of the sciences. Advance from the indefinite to the definite, as displayed in the individual mind and in the mind of humanity, had also been recognised. Thus various ideas, forming components of a theory of evolution, were lying ready for organisation. And after publication

---

[1] See vol. i., chap. vii., pp. 93, 96.   [2] See vol. i., chap. vi., p. 87.

of the essay on " The Genesis of Science," in which the evolutional view of mental progress was so pronounced and coherent, the *Principles of Psychology,* which for a year or more previously had been taking shape, was commenced.[1]

Under the promptings above described, the part entitled " General Synthesis " was the one to which I first devoted myself; and it was the writing of this that led to a wider and more coherent conception of evolution. Among the component chapters are some entitled " The Correspondence as direct and Homogeneous," " The Correspondence as direct but Heterogeneous," " The Integration of Correspondences." Here, then, in another sphere had arisen the recognition of progress from the homogeneous to the heterogeneous; and it was the joining of this with the various previous recognitions which led to the question—Is not change from homogeneity to heterogeneity universal? The question needed only to be asked to be answered affirmatively. In pursuance of that tendency which I have before described as characteristic, there forthwith arose a desire to find for this induction a deductive interpretation. This universal proclivity must have a universal cause. What is that cause? And the answer soon reached was that it is the multiplication of effects. It was at Tréport in August, 1854, that this generalisation, inductive and deductive, was reached;[2] and I immediately decided that as soon as the *Principles of Psychology* was completed I would write an essay under the title " The Cause of all Progress." Whether I then wrote to Chapman proposing such an article for the *Westminster Review,* or whether I made the proposal when I saw him in London later in the year, I cannot remember. I think the last is the more probable. Certainly, however, before the close of the year an agreement was made for such an article: the title, however, being negatived by Chapman as appearing

[1] See vol. i., chap. vii., pp. 93, 96.
[2] See vol. i., chap. vii., p. 98.

too ambitious, and " Progress: its Law and Cause " being substituted.

Of course the evolution of mind thus traced up throughout the Animal Kingdom as a part of the progressive correspondence between inner and outer actions, could be made clear only by various sequent interpretations. Hence resulted the chapters on " The Nature of Intelligence " and " The Law of Intelligence." After these more abstract conceptions came the more concrete conceptions of Reflex Action, Instinct and Reason as conforming to the general view. Finally, on rising up to human faculties, regarded as organised results of this intercourse between the organism and the environment, there was reached the conclusion that the so-called forms of thought are the outcome of the process of perpetually adjusting inner relations to outer relations; fixed relations in the environment producing fixed relations in the mind. And so came a reconciliation of the *a priori* view with the experiential view. The whole theory of mental development as thus presented, assumed that the correspondence between inner and outer came to be gradually established because the effects registered in the nervous systems of one generation were more or less transmitted as modifications of the nervous systems in the next generation. Though, nowadays, I see that the natural selection of variations in the nervous system has been a factor, and, *in the earliest stages,* perhaps the most important factor, yet I still hold, as I then held, that the inheritance of functionally-wrought modifications is the chief and almost exclusive factor in the genesis of all the more complex instincts and all the higher mental powers. But the evolutionary view of mind, though manifested throughout the whole argument of these chapters, was not put into the foreground; partly, I suppose, because the evolutionary view of Life in general was at that time almost universally rejected and mostly ridiculed.

The thesis elaborated in the division entitled " Special Analysis " was suggested by the conclusions reached in the essay on " The Genesis of Science," respecting the development of the ideas of equality of things and equality of relations. It needs but to read that essay to see that this conception of growing intellectual perceptions arose in the course of a search for the initial ideas of science; and, on comparison, it will be manifest that the successive chapters of this " Special Analysis " are but an elaboration of that initial thought. Here the remarkable fact to be noted is that there has, unintentionally as I believe, resulted a complete correspondence between the General Synthesis and the Special Analysis—between the putting together and the taking to pieces; for the adjustment of inner relations to outer relations, posited in the one case, is, in the other case, the root down to which the mental structure is traced. Concerning the conclusions which make up the " Special Analysis " one only calls for separate mention—the paradoxical one that Logic, hitherto regarded as a subjective science, is in reality an objective science. Authority and long usage may give such strength to a belief that no disproof changes it. I have furnished a triple demonstration of the objective nature of Logic, but the old idea persists without even a sign of change.

As stated in the preface to the volume when published in July, 1855, there was omitted a final part which would have been called, as in after years it was called, " Physical Synthesis." In this I had intended to show the way in which these evolutionary mental processes are to be interpreted as resulting from the passage of nervous discharges along lines of least resistance, which became lines of less and less resistance in proportion as they were oftener and more strongly traversed.

Concerning the ideas of this work it remains only to add that in the " General Analysis " was set forth the logical justification of that Realism without which the evolutionary view, in common with scientific views at large, becomes inconceivable. It was an elaboration of the Universal Postulate and its corollaries: the general thesis being that Idealism takes for granted at every step of its argument the validity of that test-proof which it ends by tacitly denying.

After the interval of incapacity for work extending from July, 1855, to January, 1857; I at length prepared the long-contemplated essay on " Progress: its Law and Cause." [1]   This was published in April, 1857; and in it the general conception which had been reached in August, 1854, was set forth in detail.   Here may fitly be remarked a disproof of the statement not uncommonly made that my thinking has been *a priori*.   Besides many other evidences, the genesis of this essay is a clear demonstration to the contrary.   Progress from homogeneity to heterogeneity was observed now in one class of phenomena and now in another, until the instances had become many and varied.   Only then came the generalisation that this transformation is universal; and only then did there commence a search for the ultimate truth from which the induction might be deduced.   But in some men—and especially so was it in Huxley—the hatred of deductive reasoning is such that the mere fact that an induction can be interpreted deductively arouses doubt.   The rhythm of action and reaction necessarily carries opinion to extremes; and the reaction against *a priori* reasoning in Biology and Geology, had gone to the extreme of repudiating all reasoning but the *a posteriori*.

The origin of the next step I cannot remember.   Whether it was that on contemplating the multiplication of effects there arose the question—How does there arise the first effect?—I do not know.   But a short time after the publication of the above-named essay, came perception of the truth that a state of homogeneity is an unstable state.   In an article originally called by me " Transcendental Physiology," but entitled by the editor " The Ultimate Laws of Physiology," a statement of this gen-

---

[1] See vol. i., chap. vii., p. 108.

eral truth was published in the *National Review* for
October, 1857.[1] This generalisation was not like the
other inductively reached, but was, I think, deductive
from the outset: resulted from the prosecution of analysis. But though not forced upon me by observation
it was, in the essay named, exemplified by facts of various orders: the deduction was here verified by induction. At the same time was set forth the process of integration as part of the process of evolution, both organic and social. But, as in the *Principles of Psychology* so here, it made its appearance as a subordinate or
secondary process—was not recognised as a primary
process. The development of thought in this direction
was delayed until some seven years had passed.

During the same summer, while rambling in Scotland,
there was written another essay, evolutionary in substance though not professedly forming a part of the doctrine—the essay on " The Origin and Function of
Music." How there had arisen the belief that music
results from development and idealisation of those
cadences of the voice which indicate emotion, I cannot
remember. But it shows again the ever-present belief
in natural genesis—the growth of the complex out of the
simple. There had probably suggested itself the question—Where does music come from? and in default of
the theory of supernatural endowment, the origin set
forth seemed the only possible one.

The drift of thought thus so variously displayed, was
now made still more decided by re-reading my essays
while preparing them for publication in a volume: and
thereupon followed the final result.[2] During a walk one
fine Sunday morning (or perhaps it may have been New
Year's Day) in the Christmas of 1857-8 I happened to
stand by the side of a pool along which a gentle breeze
was bringing small waves to the shore at my feet. While
watching these undulations I was led to think of other

[1] See vol. i., chap. vii., p. 108.   [2] See vol. i., chap. viii., p. 110.

undulations—other rhythms; and probably, as my manner was, remembered extreme cases—the undulations of the ether, and the rises and falls in the prices of money, shares, and commodities. In the course of the walk arose the inquiry—Is not the rhythm of motion universal? and the answer soon reached was—Yes. Presently —either forthwith or in the course of the next few days —came a much more important result. This generalisation concerning the rhythm of motion recalled the generalisation which was to have been set forth in the unwritten part of the *Principles of Psychology*—the generalisation that motion universally takes place along the line of least resistance. Moreover there had become familiar to me the doctrine of the Conservation of Force, as it was then called—in those days a novelty; and with this was joined in my mind Sir William Groves's doctrine of the correlation of the physical forces. Of course these universal principles ranged themselves alongside the two universal principles I had been recently illustrating—the instability of the homogeneous and the multiplication of effects. As, during the preceding year, I had been showing how throughout all orders of phenomena, from nebular genesis to the genesis of language, science, art, there ever goes on a change of the simple into the complex, of the uniform into the multiform, there naturally arose the thought—these various universal truths are manifestly aspects of one universal transformation. Surely, then, the proper course is thus to exhibit them—to treat astronomy, geology, biology, psychology, sociology and social products, in successive order from the evolution point of view. Evidently these universal laws of force to which conforms this unceasing redistribution of matter and motion, constitute the *nexus* of these concrete sciences—express a community of nature which binds them together as parts of a whole. And then came the idea of trying thus to present them. Some such thoughts they were which gave rise to my project, and which, a few days later, led to the writing

328

out of the original programme, still extant. This I sent
to my father on the 9th January, 1858.[1]

During the subsequent two years, partly occupied with
vain endeavours to find some way of executing my
project, there appears to have taken place some elaboration of this programme; but, so far as I remember, no
important addition was made to its leading ideas; unless
it be the conclusion that these laws of transformation,
and the ultimate physical laws whence they result, are
all corollaries from the Persistence of Force. This may,
however, have been a later conclusion, but, whenever
arrived at, it implied the analytic habit; since it gave an
answer to the questions—Why is the homogeneous unstable? Why do effects multiply? Why is motion
rhythmical? There was no rest till there was reached
this final truth not to be transcended—a truth equivalent
to the truth that existence can neither arise out of nothing nor lapse into nothing.

The evolutionary belief implied interest in all orders
of phenomena throughout which, according to its thesis,
it should be displayed. Hence physical astronomy became interesting. During many preceding years the
Nebular Hypothesis had been apparently discredited by
the revelations of Lord Rosse's telescope: the resolution
of various apparent nebulæ into clusters of stars, was
supposed to have given the *Coup de grâce* to the theories
of Kant and Laplace; or, at any rate, it was concluded

---

[1] In reply to questions from Professor A. S. Packard, of Brown
University, Providence, Spencer wrote (15 August, 1902): "I
believe you are right in crediting me with the introduction of
the word 'evolution.' I did not, however, introduce it in the
place of 'epigenesis,' or any word of specially biological application, but as a word fit for expressing the process of evolution
throughout its entire range, inorganic and organic.

"I believe the introduction of it was between 1857, when
'Progress: its Law and Cause' (was issued), and the time when
the scheme for the Synthetic Philosophy was drawn up; and
the adoption of it arose from the perception that 'progress' has
an anthropocentric meaning, and that there needed a word free
from that."

that all such support as appeared to be furnished by the present existence of nebulous matter was dissipated. It was supposed that these luminous patches which powerful telescopes proved to consist of enormous numbers of stars, were remote sidereal systems similar to our own. Of course under these circumstances I was prompted to look into the evidence, and was soon convinced that the reasoning assigned for this conclusion was vicious. This led to the essay on '' Recent Astronomy and the Nebular Hypothesis,'' published in the *Westminster Review* for July, 1858. It contained proofs that the current conclusion was untrue, and that these clusters of stars form parts of our own sidereal system. This has since become an accepted doctrine. The invalidity of the reason for rejecting the nebular hypothesis at large having been shown, there followed an exposition of the reasons for believing in the nebular genesis of the solar system. Additional reasons of significance were assigned. One of them was that according to the ratio between centrifugal force and gravity in each planet is the greater or smaller number of satellites it possesses. Another was that to variations in this ratio, unlike in each planet, are ascribable the different specific gravities of the planets. With acceptance of the hypothesis of Olbers respecting the missing planet, went the conclusion that the celestial bodies are neither solid nor liquid all through; but that the interior of each consists of gases reduced by pressure to the density of liquids. It had been shown that gases may be compressed to that degree of density without liquefying; and since then the experiments of Prof. Andrews, proving that there is a critical temperature above which no pressure, producing however great a density, will cause liquefaction, has made this view more tenable than it at first appeared. In recent years it has been enunciated afresh in Germany by Dr. August Ritter in 1882. Of course the conclusion that from the bursting of a planet thus constituted, resulted the asteroids, has gained an ever-increasing support from the ever-increasing number of them discovered; for it is manifest that of the multitudinous fragments the larger would be relatively few, and that with successive decreases of size would go increases of numbers: an inference corresponding with the facts. An explanation of comets and meteor-showers was also afforded. It should be added that I ventured to dissent from the theory of the Sun held by Sir John Herschel, that the photosphere incloses a dark body, rendered visible through breaches in the photosphere known as spots. In pursuance of the view that the Sun is the product of a still-concentrating nebula, the temperature of which is too high to permit solidification, it was contended that the photosphere consists of metallic vapours ever rising and precipitating: a view soon afterwards verified by the discoveries of Kirchhoff and Bunsen. An extreme illustration of that disregard for authority characterising me was thus shown; for the then current view respecting the nebulæ, and the view respecting the constitution of the Sun, had the highest warrant. I must however, in candour, add that the essay contained some serious mistakes—one especially concerning the distribution of comets from which I thought evidence was derivable.[1]

The ever-present interest in the idea of evolution as extending to all orders of phenomena, prompted other audacities displayed at this time. One of them was a criticism upon Prof. Owen's *Archetype and Homologies of the Vertebrate Skeleton*. It was published in the *British and Foreign Medico-Chirurgical Review* for October, 1858, and afterwards appended to the second volume of the *Biology*.[2] Of course his theory, which was a modern application of the Platonic theory of Ideas, conflicted with the evolutionary view of the organic world. The purpose of the essay was two-fold— to show the inconsistencies of his reasoning, and to show

[1] *Supra*, chap. xxvi., pp. 155-156.
[2] See vol. i., chap. viii., p. 113.

how, by mechanical actions and reactions between organism and environment, the segmentation of the vertebral column might be produced.

In the same manner was to be accounted for, and I may add excused, the audacity shown in an article written in 1858 on "Illogical Geology," in which certain views of Lyell, Murchison, and Hugh Miller were adversely criticised.[1] The pushing of evolutionary inquiries in all directions necessarily brought me face to face with geological facts, and theories, and with the palæontological evidence accompanying them. The notion, still at that time generally accepted among geologists, that during past eras there had occasionally occurred a sweeping away of the old organic types and the creation of a new set, was of course utterly repugnant to me, and it became needful to examine the reasonings which led to such a conception. It was shown that geological evidence does not warrant it.

This same period (1858-60) gave birth to several other essays pervaded by the same general thoughts. One of them, on "The Law of Organic Symmetry," was published in the *Medico-Chirurgical Review* for January, 1859.[2] As already said, this arose from an observation I made during my excursion with Lewes in 1851. I do not remember that the general formula of Evolution was referred to (I have not got the essay at hand), but the interpretation was evolutionary. The transitions from spherical and radial symmetry to bilateral symmetry, and in some cases to asymmetry, were shown to illustrate the general proposition that the forms of parts are determined by their relations to surrounding actions: growths being equal where the incident forces are equal and unequal where the incident forces are unequal. I should remark, however, that the interpretation was incomplete in so far that it recognised inorganic forces only—heat, light, gravitation, etc.—and did not recog-

---

[1] See vol. i., chap. viii., p. 123; *Supra,* chap. xxvi., pp. 155-156.
[2] See vol. i., chap. viii., p. 113.

nise any organic agency, such as the influence of insects in developing the forms of flowers.

A criticism of Prof. Bain's work on *The Emotions and the Will* was written at this time, and naturally from the evolution point of view. Especially is this seen in a proposed classification of mental states, which is said to be justified " whether we trace mental progression through the grades of the animal kingdom, through the grades of mankind, or through the stages of individual growth." [1]

Then came the essay on " The Social Organism," [2] in which is observable the growth between 1850 and 1860: the first being the date at which, in *Social Statics*, there had occurred the primary recognition of the analogy between an individual organism and a social organism. In this essay, as in its germ ten years before, the fundamental parallelism recognised is in that mutual dependence of parts which both display; and all the phenomena of organisation, individual or social, are regarded as having this as their cause. Any one who refers to *Social Statics* (pp. 452—456, original edition; pp. 264—267, revised edition) will see that this was the root-idea and that this dominates the developed idea. He will also see how entirely without kinship it is to the fanciful notions of Plato and of Hobbes. But in the essay on " The Social Organism " the general conception indicated in *Social Statics*, while developed in detail, has also become affiliated on the general doctrine of Evolution. In the first place, the mutual dependence of parts is shown to involve an increasing integration, and in the second place, numerous illustrations which society furnishes are summed up by the statement that " not only is all progress from the homogeneous to the heterogeneous, but, at the same time, it is from the indefinite to the definite."

And now came the actual start.[3] Ideas which had be-

---

[1] See vol. i., chap. viii., p. 125.   [2] See vol. i., chap. viii., p. 124.
[3] See vol. i., chap. ix., p. 131.

come fairly definite and coherent were now to be made quite definite while being elaborated in *First Principles*.

As shown by the original programme, I had from the outset seen the need for specifying my position in respect to metaphysico-theological beliefs. If all things were to be interpreted in terms of the redistribution of matter and motion, I must guard myself against ascription of the materialism apparently implied. Along with such an interpretation must go the admission, or rather the assertion, that our ideas of matter and motion are but symbols of that which transcends the possibilities of knowledge: and that hence, any explanation of the *order* of the changes which the Cosmos exhibits, still leaves unexplained the *nature* and *origin* of them.

Hence came to be thought out and written the preliminary division of *First Principles*—" The Unknowable." An absurd misconception resulted. While this was simply an introduction intended to exclude misinterpretations, it was, by the few who paid any attention to the book, regarded as its substance. Having inspected the portico, they turned their backs on the building! The general doctrine of a universal transformation, conforming everywhere to the same laws, was passed by as not calling for exposition or comment; or, if recognised at all, was supposed to be a sequence of Darwin's doctrine of " natural selection "! The thought of the muddle-headed public seems to have been:—Both are evolutionary; one was published later than the other; therefore the second is a development of the first.[1]

The second division of *First Principles*, constituting its essential part, is mainly, as above implied, an elaboration of the ideas already specified. It contains, however, three further ideas of cardinal importance. One is the process of " Segregation " which, though indirectly implied in some of the essays, had not before taken shape as a necessary part of Evolution. A second concerned

[1] See vol. i., chaps. xv., p. 268, xviii., p. 336; *Supra*, xxviii., p. 211; xxx., p. 286.

the final stage. I have a dim recollection that, referring to the general process of transformation set forth in " Progress: its Law and Cause," which had been the topic of conversation (during an afternoon call at Huxley's), Tyndall put to me the question—" But how does it all end?" or some question to that effect.[1] I cannot now remember whether the answer was given forthwith or whether it came only after reflection; but my impression is that up to that time I had not considered what was the outcome of this unceasing change to a state ever more heterogeneous and ever more definite. It needed only to ask the question, however, to bring the inevitable answer, and the chapter on " Equilibration " was the result. And then, in pursuance of the same line of thought, embodying itself in the question—" What happens after equilibration is completed? " there came the reply, " Dissolution." This was at once recognised as complementary to Evolution, and similarly universal.

I may add that the expositions contained in the successive chapters of the second division of *First Principles*, were easier to write than at first appears. Having in each case got hold of the clue, it was not difficult to follow it out among all orders of phenomena. Bearing the generalisation in mind, it needed only to turn from this side to that side, and from one class of facts to another, to find everywhere exemplifications.

In the first paragraph of the *Principles of Biology* may be perceived the effect of bringing a general view to the study of a special subject. The characterisation of organic matter is obviously determined by the doctrine contained in *First Principles*. It is pointed out that its elements present two marked contrasts—carbon extremely fixed, hydrogen very volatile; oxygen extremely active, nitrogen very inactive. That is, the components are specially heterogeneous; and the heterogeneity of the compound is increased by the presence of phosphorus

---

[1] See vol. i., chap. ix., p. 135.

and sulphur. To this peculiar composition is ascribed that great instability which fits organic matter for those easy and perpetual changes implied by life; while in the fact that three of its chief components, being gaseous, severally contain in their combined state immense amounts of molecular motion, is seen that constitution which makes it a source of visible activities. It is clear that, in the absence of the leading truths set forth in *First Principles,* organic matter would not have been thus conceived.

There is also exemplified, before the close of the chapter, the effect of bringing together the leading conceptions of different sciences. Complete knowledge of one science is by many urged as an educational ideal, rather than a general knowledge of several. But in each science progress depends on ideas which the other sciences furnish. Prof. Graham's all-important investigations respecting the colloid and crystalloid forms of matter, well exemplified the need for transcending the limits of pure chemistry for the further advance of chemistry. The contrasts he draws between colloids and crystalloids—between the instability of the one and the stability of the other, between the consequent *energia* of the former and the quiescence of the latter, have important implications of many kinds, especially biological. But, not being guided by the relevant biological ideas, there is a corollary which he did not reach. Had he looked at the vital changes from the physiological point of view, and observed that while the wasted tissues are continually being rebuilt the waste-matters have continually to be carried away; he would have seen that it is because the tissues are formed of colloids while the waste-matters are crystalloids that the vital processes are possible. From the small molecular mobility of the large colloid molecules and the great molecular mobility of the small crystalloid molecules, it results that these last can rapidly diffuse through the first and escape into the channels which carry them out of the body.

Concerning interpretations contained in the immediately following chapters, it will suffice to say that they are dominated by the thought of interpreting vital activities in terms of latent motion taken in and visible motion given out—molecular motion in food and molar motion expended through muscles. And here came recognition of the part played by nitrogen. From the feebleness of its affinities for other elements it results that, easily liberated from its combinations with them, it becomes a constant cause of molecular disturbance and vital motions. This interpretation was suggested by remembrance of the various cases in which nitrogenous substances, both inorganic and organic, are made to serve artificially as agents initiating changes—explosions, fermentations, etc.

The succeeding division of the work, " The Inductions of Biology," of course consists mainly of expositions of those general truths currently accepted at the time the work was written. Presentation of these in a relatively-coherent form was the natural result of an endeavour to affiliate them on the general principle of Evolution. In each chapter there are indicated the relations borne to first principles by the truths set forth. There may be noted, however, sundry special inferences reached through the systematic mode of contemplating the facts. Everywhere arose the inquiry—What are the physical terms involved? with the result that conclusions—true or untrue as it may turn out—were set down which would not have been reached had not this question been asked.

The chapter on " Growth " furnishes a good example, and furnishes, too, another illustration of the way in which, to interpret the truths of a special science the truths of more general sciences have to be brought in aid. The amounts and limits of growth exhibited by the different classes of organisms, plant and animal, are inexplicable by one who limits himself to biology alone. Mathematics and physics have to be invoked—certain relations between masses and surfaces, certain relations between proportional sizes and proportional strains, certain relations between the genesis of energy and the tenacity of the parts which expend energy. And here let me exemplify the way in which an interest in scientific inquiries at large, may bring in, from a remote subject, the solutions of certain problems. Some time between the issue of the first edition in 1864 and the recent edition in 1898, I met with a report of Mr. Froude's experiments made to determine the resistance to vessels moving through the water. The surprising result was that the chief resistance is not due to continued displacement but to '' skin friction.'' When revising the chapter on '' Growth '' a significant corollary hence resulted. It became clear that by growth an aquatic animal gains in relative speed: since the increase of energy going along with increase of mass is not met by a proportionate increase of resistance: the skin-friction increases at a slower rate than the increase of energy. Hence great aquatic animals can come into existence. The catching of more prey needful for larger growth would not be possible in the absence of this relation between energy and resistance.

The aid which one science furnishes towards solution of the problems presented by another, is again exemplified in the chapter on '' Adaptation.'' The processes of modification constituting adaptation of organic structures, are rendered quite comprehensible by reference to the analogous social processes.

The cardinal idea which runs through the chapters on '' Genesis,'' '' Heredity,'' and '' Variation,'' is, as shown in § 66, an example of reasoning *a priori*—an exceptional example, for, as I have shown, *a posteriori* conclusions have habitually preceded the *a priori* verifications. The argument is that the specific traits of organisms cannot be conveyed by the morphological units or cells, nor can they be conveyed by the molecules of protein substances into which these are chemically resolvable: these being common to all organisms. There appears therefore no alternative but to assume some intermediate units conveying the specific characters—physiological units as I called them, or, as I would now call them, constitutional units. That the structure of each organism results from the organic polarities of these seems implied by the facts that a scale from a Begonia leaf, or a fragment of a Polyp's body, begins to assume the typical structure of the species; and yet it seems inconceivable that the complex structures of organisms of advanced types can be thus produced. A more feasible conception was suggested in the final edition of the work; and here again sociological facts aided interpretation of biological facts. For evidence was given that beyond the tendency of a whole aggregate of units of a particular kind to assume the structure peculiar to that kind, whether a society or an animal, there is an ability of the units in each locality to form themselves into a structure appropriate to that locality, quite independently of the influence of the whole aggregate. Recent experimental evidence (1896-7) here came in verification.

Passing over minor ideas in Part III., the first to be named is, that the process of natural selection becomes incapable of producing specific adaptations as fast as there arise complex animals in which many organs co-operate to achieve a single end. The great Irish elk with its enormous horns is instanced; and the argument is that growth of such horns is useless for offence and defence without an accompanying adjustment of numerous bones and muscles concerned in wielding them; that appropriate variations cannot be assumed to take place simultaneously in all the co-operating parts; and that without simultaneous variations in them, increase in the size of the horns must be injurious. After this, the thing of chief importance in this division is the interpretation of the two essential factors of organic evolution—Adaptation and Natural Selection—in physical terms. And here I come upon a fact which obliges me to qualify the description of my method of thinking, namely, allowing

339

some germ of thought accidentally occurring, to grow by accretions until it became a fully-developed hypothesis. I was now met by a problem which demanded solution. Adaptation is not a process known to physical science; and the hypothesis of Natural Selection is in both of its terms foreign to that class of ideas which physics formulates. How, then, are adaptation and natural selection to be conceived as caused by that universal play of forces which universal evolution postulates? At first the interpretation seemed hopeless; but when the life of an organism was regarded as a combination of functions forming a moving equilibrium in presence of outer actions, an interpretation presented itself. All the phenomena fell into place as attendant on the maintenance of moving equilibria and the overthrow of them. It was in thus studying the facts that the expression " survival of the fittest " emerged; for this is, as the context shows, as direct a statement as ordinary language permits of the physical actions and reactions concerned. Here again general truths served as interpreters of special ones.

Some months before completion of the first volume of the *Principles of Biology,* there occurred a digression which had important results. More than once after writing the " Genesis of Science," in which M. Comte's classification of the sciences was rejected, I had endeavoured to make a valid classification, and had failed. Only now, early in 1864, did I hit upon the right mode of regarding the facts: recognising that the primary basis of a classification is a division into Abstract, Abstract-Concrete, and Concrete, dealing respectively with the forms, the factors, and the products.[1] The conclusions arrived at seemed important enough to justify suspension of other work for the purpose of publishing a brochure setting them forth in detail. Incidentally there came a result of greater importance. While trying to arrange the concrete sciences, and asking what most general truth

---

[1] See vol. i., chap. x., p. 147.

there is which must take precedence of all those truths presented by astronomy, geology, biology, etc., I saw that it must be a truth concerning the unceasing redistribution of matter and motion which all concrete things exhibit. This truth was that integration of matter and dissipation of contained motion are concomitant changes, and that the converse concomitant changes are increase of contained motion and dissipation of matter: the first resulting in Evolution and the last in Dissolution. In this way I was suddenly made aware that in setting forth the process of Evolution in *First Principles*, I had followed a wrong order; since I had represented the increase of heterogeneity as the primary process, and integration as a secondary process. Forthwith I decided to reorganise *First Principles* as soon as the *Principles of Biology* was completed. And here I note the second case in which the writings of M. Comte had an all-important influence; but, as in the preceding case, an influence opposite in kind to that supposed. Had I not made acquaintance with his views concerning the development of the sciences; had I not been thus led to reject his classification; had I not been, consequently, prompted to seek another classification; I should probably never have reached the above conception, and the doctrine set forth in *First Principles* would have retained that very imperfect form originally given to it.

For completion of the narrative, I must add that about this time was written an essay on "The Constitution of the Sun," containing, among other things, the hypothesis that solar spots result from the condensation of metallic vapours in the rarefied interiors of cyclones; and must add that about the same time was written an essay under the title "What is Electricity?" I name these merely to show the excursiveness still displayed.[1]

Returning to the *Principles of Biology*, the first remark to be made is that the interpretation of the special

---

[1] Vol. i., chap. x., p. 153; *Supra*, chap. xxvi., pp. 159-164.

by the aid of the general, is shown throughout Vol. II. in a conspicuous manner; for in this there begins the deductive explanation of biological phenomena at large in terms of the formula of Evolution.

" Morphological Development " sets out by regarding the facts plants and animals display as primarily phenomena of integration. There is growth by simple accumulation of primary aggregates (cells or protoplasts); there is growth by union of groups of these into secondary aggregates; and then again by union of groups of groups into tertiary aggregates. The rise of the two largest divisions of the plant world is dealt with from this point of view. From the needs of the interpretation there resulted a speculation respecting the origin of Endogens and Exogens (Monocotyledons and Dicotyledons). For in tracing out the origin of plant aggregates of the third order, produced by integration of those of the second order (each in its separate form a thallus or frond), there arose the question—By what different methods of integration did there arise these two different types of vegetal organisation? The interpretation implies a rejection of Schleiden's doctrine, which regards the shoot or axial organ as primary, and the leaf or foliar organ as secondary; for it implies that the foliar organ is the homologue of a primitive separate frond or thallus, which of course came first in order of evolution. I may add that though in most cases the materials for my arguments were ready to hand in works on Biology, it was in some cases otherwise; and here is an instance. Observations pursued for some years brought abundant support to the inference that axial organs may, under conditions of excessive nutrition, develop out of foliar organs. " The Morphological Composition of Animals " was dealt with in like manner. Cells, aggregates of cells, and unions of these aggregates into still higher ones, were the stages: the various types of *Protozoa* falling within the first group, *Porifera* and simple Coelenterates coming within the second group,

342

and the compound coelenterate animals, fixed and moving, as well as *Tunicata,* coming within the third group. How far this compounding of groups proceeds in the animal kingdom was a question which arose. The conclusion drawn was that while the *Vertebrata* are aggregates of the second order, annulose creatures (Arthropods and Annelids) are aggregates of the third order: each segment being the homologue of what was originally an independent organism. This speculation was, I supposed, peculiar to myself; but I recently found that it had two years earlier been propounded by M. Lacaze Duthiers. There are many reasons for and against it, but true or untrue, it is manifestly a sequence of the mode of regarding organic progress as exhibiting integration.

In conformity with the general order of evolution, as set forth in *First Principles,* there came next the production of structural differences: advance in integration being accompanied by advance in heterogeneity. And here arose the occasion for carrying out in new directions the speculation initiated in 1851, and subsequently set forth in " The Law of Organic Symmetry." The general thesis that the parts of an organism become unlike in form in proportion to their exposure to unlike conditions, was illustrated throughout: first in the shapes of plants as wholes, then in the shapes of branches, then in the shapes of leaves, then in the shapes of flowers, and finally in the shapes of vegetal cells. There followed a like series of interpretations of animal forms—general, and then more and more special. In this exposition was incorporated that theory of vertebrate structure indicated in 1858, as an alternative to the theory of Professor Owen—the theory, namely, that vertebræ have arisen from the mechanical actions and reactions to which the original undivided axis was exposed by lateral undulations; these becoming as the vertebrate animal developed, more and more energetic, at the same time that the axis became by its reactions more and more indurated at the points of muscular insertion; segmentation being a necessary compromise between flexibility and stability.

In the next division, "Physiological Development," there is again shown the way in which the interpretations in general and in detail are dominated by the general formula of Evolution: more markedly shown, because, while Morphology had been studied from the evolution point of view, Physiology had been scarcely at all thus studied. As currently understood, Physiology was concerned only with the single and combined functions of organs, and scarcely at all considered the question how functions have arisen. Thus a new field had to be explored, and the exploration was guided by the conceptions set forth in *First Principles*. The general question was " how heterogeneities of action have progressed along with heterogeneities of structure "; and it was held that to the various problems presented the " answers must be given in terms of incident forces."

Here the hypothesis of Evolution raised a new set of questions, and the raising of them almost of itself prompted the answers. " Intercourse between each part and the particular conditions to which it is exposed " was shown " to be the origin of physiological development." Throughout successive chapters, proof was given that physiological differentiations exemplify " the inevitable lapse of the more homogeneous into the less homogeneous "; and evidence that the changes result from " the necessary exposure of their component parts to actions unlike in kind or quantity " was furnished by the order in which the differences appear. It was contended, further, that " Physiological development has all along been aided by the multiplication of effects ": the differentiated parts acting and reacting on one another with increasing complexity. Then came the inquiry— How does there arise that mutual dependence of parts which is the necessary concomitant of the physiological division of labour? Physiological integration accompanies physiological differentiation, and the question was —" What causes the integration to advance *pari passu* with the differentiation? " a question to the solution of which the analogy between the individual organism and the social organism was once more brought in aid. Then, lastly, came to be treated the phenomena of physiological equilibration, as it establishes itself more and more completely in proportion as organic evolution becomes higher: the result of the play of organic forces being such as continually to re-establish a disturbed balance between outer and inner actions, and to establish a new balance where outer actions of a permanent kind arise.

I indicate these chief heads of the argument simply to show how the filiation of ideas was here determined by the need for presenting the facts of physiological development in terms of evolution at large. General truths again served as keys to the more special truths, and caused these to fall into coherent order.

Something must be said respecting an inquiry which arose while writing this division. The genesis of the circulation in plants was one of the topics to be dealt with; and I found very little information ready to my hand. Either I must treat the topic in a cursory manner or must investigate it for myself, and this last alternative I chose. In pursuance of the idea dominant throughout, that the differentiations of parts are due to differences in the incident forces, I inferred that, initiated by slight differences of pressure in certain directions, the produced currents themselves gradually formed channels and so prepared the way for the differentiated structures. The current doctrine was that circulation is through the wood; but there seemed to have been ignored the question— What happens in plants having no woody tissue, and in those young plants and young parts of plants in which woody tissue has not yet been formed? Examination proved that in such places the spiral, fenestrated, or annular vessels are the sap-carriers, and that these fall out of use as fast as the woody tissue arises. The investigation led to the discovery of absorbent organs in certain leaves and roots which had not been seen because the sections of the leaves had not been made in such a manner as to disclose them. By compulsion I was in this case led into experimental research; and I do not remember any other case in which an experimental research was undertaken.[1]

The remaining part of the *Principles of Biology,* entitled " Laws of Multiplication," need not detain us. It is an amplified and elaborated statement of the hypothesis which was set forth pretty fully in " The Theory of Population deduced from the General Law of Animal Fertility," published in 1852. In this Part VI. of the *Biology* many additional illustrations, sundry developments, and various qualifications, are set forth. These supplementary ideas it is needless here to specify.

I am often astonished at the large results which grow from small causes. When drawing up the programme of the " System of Philosophy," as it was at first called, and laying out the plan of each work, it occurred to me that, before beginning deductive interpretations in pursuance of the doctrine of Evolution, it would be needful to set down the truths which had been, or which might be, reached by simple induction. And then it occurred to me that, before this statement of inductions, it would be needful in each case to specify the data. This conception determined in large part the arrangement followed. In each science the first and second divisions set forth respectively the data and the inductions, on which the evolutionary interpretations might stand.

This method of procedure had the effect of drawing my attention to truths, some already current and some not current, which would have been passed over unspecified or unrecognised, had it not been for the necessity of filling up these divisions of the skeleton plan. Especially was this cause influential in giving to the *Principles of Psychology* an extended development.

---

[1] See vol. i., chap. x., pp. 162, 163.

What were the data? What were the inductions? were questions to be answered; and search for answers led to some significant results.

The science of Life at large had to supply the data to the science of Mental Life. Setting out from the biological view, it was needful to regard the nervous system as the initiator of motion, and to trace up its development in relation to the quantity of the motion and the heterogeneity of the motion. It was also needful to formulate such truths of structure as are common to all types of nervous systems. Beginning with the simplest structure, in which there is seen nothing more than an afferent nerve, a ganglion, and an efferent nerve, it was contended that the nervous arc formed by the fibre carrying a stimulus, the ganglion corpuscles to which it went, and the fibre running to a part to be excited, constituted the unit of composition out of which nervous systems are built—a unit of composition with which, in developing types, there is joined a fibre passing from the primary simple ganglion to a higher and more complex one. The thesis was that, throughout their extremely varied types, nervous systems are formed by compounding and re-compounding this unit in multitudinous ways.

Not particularising others of the Data set down, and passing at once to the Inductions, the first to be named concerns the substance of mind. After showing that of this in its ultimate nature we can know nothing, it was contended that of its proximate nature we may know something. Setting out from our knowledge of the sensation of sound, which is made up of minute nervous shocks rapidly recurring, there was ventured the hypothesis that sensations of all kinds, and by implication higher feelings of all kinds, result from the compounding and re-compounding in infinitely varied ways of minute nervous shocks, akin in their ultimate natures.[1]

---

[1] The instalment of the *Principles of Psychology* containing this view was issued in Oct., 1868. M. Taine, in Vol. I. of *De l'Intelligence*, propounded a like view in 1870.

So that possibly there is an ultimate element of mind which, like some ultimate element of matter, is, by entering into more and more complex aggregates and unions of aggregates, capable of generating the multitudinous kinds of consciousness, as the supposed ultimate element of matter, by its endless ways and degrees of compounding, produces the various substances we know. There is thus hypothetically illustrated in another sphere the general doctrine of Evolution, since the supposed process implies increasing integration and increasing heterogeneity.

The question next to be dealt with was—What are the general truths respecting our mental states which admit of being set down as simple inductions, based upon introspection, and not involving any hypothesis respecting origin. Writers on Psychology have mostly had in view not structural traits but functional traits. We see this in the grouping by Aquinas into Memory, Reason, Conscience; by Reid into Memory, Conception, Judgment, Reasoning; by Dugald Stewart into Attention, Conception, Abstraction, Memory, Imagination, Reasoning. These various heads in the main connote kinds and degrees of action. It seemed to me that the first thing must be to contemplate the aggregate of mental states, and group them according to their characters and behaviours. Examination proved that there are marked structural distinctions in consciousness, and that these are related to structural distinctions in the nervous system. The broadest classification is into feelings and relations between feelings, of which the first are mental states existing for appreciable times, while the last exist but momentarily; and it was inferred that while the feelings are correlated with changes in the nerve-cells, the relations are correlated with discharges along nerve-fibres. Examination proved that feelings themselves are first of all divisible into centrally-initiated or emotions, and peripherally-initiated or sensations. Among the peripherally-initiated, the broadest division is into those initiated on the outer surface and those initiated in the interior; and it was of course recognised that all these kinds have their vivid or original forms and their faint or revived forms. These groups of feelings differ greatly in definiteness—that is, in the distinctness with which they are mutually limited: the feelings derived from the highest senses being mutually limited in the sharpest way, and the mutual limitation becoming vague in proportion as the feelings are internally generated, and have not sense-organs divided into numerous sensitive elements. Sharpness of mutual limitation was discovered to be connected with ability to cohere—readiness to be associated: where there is vague mutual limitation there is incoherence. Another result reached was that feelings which are definitely limited by others and which, as a concomitant, readily cohere, are also feelings which can be called into consciousness with facility; while feelings of the lower kinds, as those initiated internally, can be revived with difficulty and, consequently, take but small parts in intellectual operations. Once more it was found that these truths which hold of feelings hold also of the relations among them. Here as elsewhere it was found that progress in mental organisation, as in nervous organisation, is presentable in terms of Evolution; for in rising to the higher types of mental states characterised by definiteness, coherence, and revivability, we progress in integration and heterogeneity.

Concerning the parts entitled " General Synthesis " and " Special Synthesis," it is unnecessary to say much here, since they repeat with small alterations, mainly verbal, the corresponding parts in the first edition. The only significant fact is that to § 189 I have added a note saying that " Had Mr. Darwin's *Origin of Species* been published before I wrote this paragraph, I should, no doubt, have so qualified my words as to recognise ' selection,' natural or artificial, as a factor." At the time the first edition was written the only factor I recognised was the inheritance of functionally-produced changes; but

Mr. Darwin's work made it clear to me that there is another factor of importance in mental evolution as in bodily evolution. While holding that throughout all higher stages of mental development the supreme factor has been the effect of habit, I believe that in producing the lowest instincts natural selection has been the chief, if not the sole, factor. This modification of belief, however, affects but slightly the argument running through these two parts.

Part V. is the one referred to in the preface to the first edition as, for the time being, omitted. It sets forth and elaborates the idea, reached some time before the programme of the Synthetic Philosophy was drawn up, that the structures of nervous systems are to be interpreted as consequent upon the general law that motion follows the line of least resistance. The first chapter describes the genesis of nerves in pursuance of this hypothesis, and subsequent chapters carry it out in the description of simple and compound nervous systems.

Concerning the filiation of ideas exemplified in Parts VI. and VII. of the *Principles of Psychology,* there is not much to say here. The first of them reappears with no considerable change; and the second of them, though greatly developed, is chiefly an elaboration of the argument set forth in Part I. of the first edition—an elaboration which, though it contains many ideas not contained in the first, does not call for detailed notice.

In Part IX., "Corollaries," there is yielded another exception to what I supposed to be the uniform process with me—gradual development of a thought from a germ; for here I had forthwith to solve the questions put before me as best I might. After dealing with general psychology it became requisite to enter upon the special psychology of Man in preparation for Sociology. Certain traits of human nature are presupposed by the ability to live in the associated state, and there came the questions—What are these? and, How are they evolved? One only of the leading ideas in this part need

350

here be named as illustrating the course of filiation. Before there can be social co-operation there must be established in Men a liking, such as we see in gregarious animals, for living more or less in presence of one another. And there must be developed in them, as in gregarious creatures, but in a far higher degree, the faculty of sympathy—the aptitude for participating in the feelings exhibited by others. Development of the required type of emotional nature was shown to be a part of the general process of mental evolution. The discipline of social life, beginning in feeble ways, itself little by little developed the capacities for carrying on social co-operation: there was gradual evolution here as everywhere else.

The filiation of ideas as exhibited in the *Principles of Sociology,* cannot be understood without knowledge of certain acts and incidents which occurred while the work on the *Principles of Psychology* was in course of execution. Recognising how large an undertaking the *Principles of Sociology* would be, how vast the required assemblage of materials, and how impossible it would be for me to gather them, I decided as far back as 1867 to obtain help. I had to study the leading types of societies, from the savage to the most civilised; and I required something like a comprehensive account of the institutions of each. The only course was that of engaging one or more assistants who should, under guidance, collect facts for me. My first step was to scheme an arrangement in which they should be so presented that while their relations of co-existence and succession were easily recognised, they should be so presented that those of each kind could be readily found when required. In the tables drawn up the primary division of social phenomena is into Structural and Functional, and the main divisions under these are Regulative and Operative. A glance will show that ranged under these main and subordinate groups, the heterogeneous masses of facts societies exhibit, disorderly as they at first seem, are made intelligible, and the comparing and generalising of them easy. Sundry modifications of beliefs at once resulted from thus facilitating induction.

The work on *The Study of Sociology* formed no part of the programme of the Synthetic Philosophy.[1] But, rather fortunately, it was written before the *Principles of Sociology* was commenced; and, while serving to prepare the public, was also a good discipline for me. The cultured classes and their leaders—Carlyle, Froude, Kingsley, etc.—were in utter darkness about the matter. They alleged the impossibility of a " science of history," and were without any conception that there had been going on the evolution of social structures, not made or dreamed of by kings and statesmen, or recognised by historians. Two chapters " Is there a Social Science?" and " The Nature of the Social Science," explained that there is a distinction between history and the science of sociology like that between a man's biography and the structure of his body.

Evidence was given at this time of continued natural growth from a germ dating far back. In the comparison between a society and an organism, made in *Social Statics,* where the mutual dependence of parts common to both and the progress in both from a primitive state of no dependence to a state of great dependence, were pointed out, there was no recognition of any fundamental division in the classes of parts or classes of functions. But " The Social Organism," published ten years later, exhibited the analogy between the expending organs of the two and between the sustaining organs of the two. And now this conception had become more definite. In an essay on " Specialised Administration " published in December, 1871, it was shown that the militant structures and the industrial structures, while growing more distinguished as expending structures and sustaining

---

[1] See vol. i., chap. xiii., p. 211.

structures, grow more distinguished also by the different forms of government proper to them: the one being under a despotic central control needful to produce efficient joint action, and the other being controlled by the mutual influences of the co-operating parts and not, in respect of their functions, subject to central direction. At the same time it was shown that individual organisms of high types furnish a parallel to this contrast in the contrast between the cerebro-spinal nervous system and the visceral nervous system. And here, more than before, was emphasised the truth that from the beginning war has been the cause of the development of centralised governmental structures, which become coercive in proportion as war is the dominant social activity; while growth of that decentralised co-operation characterising sustaining structures, becomes more marked as war ceases to be chronic: a corollary being that social types are essentially distinguished by the proportion between the militant structures and the industrial structures, and undergo metamorphoses according to the growth or decline of either order of activity.

One more essay, published in 1870, on " The Origin of Animal-Worship," must be named as containing another idea destined to undergo much development in the *Principles of Sociology*, the first instalment of which was issued in June, 1874. In the third paragraph (Essays, i. 309) it is said that " The rudimentary form of all religion is the propitiation of dead ancestors, who are supposed to be still existing, and to be capable of working good or evil to their descendants ";[1] and that to prepare

---

[1] After the publication of the first volume of the *Principles of Sociology*, a controversy arose between Mr. (now Prof.) E. B. Tylor and myself concerning our respective views. Though his view, as set forth before 1870, was that animism is primary and the ghost-theory secondary, while my view was that the ghost-theory is primary and animism secondary, yet he had the impression that I had derived my view from him. In the course of the controversy, when referring back to things I had written, I overlooked these sentences just quoted, which (setting

for " sociology, I have, for some years past, directed much attention to the modes of thought current in the simpler human societies." [1]

Growing complexity of subject-matter implies growing complexity of causation; and with recognition of additional factors comes proof of the inadequacy of factors previously recognised. This is manifest when tracing the filiation of ideas throughout the *Principles of Sociology*. The modifications resulted from evidence contained in the *Descriptive Sociology* and added to from various other sources. Simple induction now played a leading part.

Already in *Social Statics* there were recognitions of the truth that the fitnesses of institutions are relative to the natures of citizens. More definitely the *Study of Sociology* again displayed this conviction. In youth my constitutional repugnance to coercion, and consequent hatred of despotic forms of rule, had involved a belief like that expressed in the American Declaration of Independence, and like that which swayed the French at the time of the Revolution—the belief that free forms of government would ensure social welfare. A concomitant was a great abhorrence of slavery, and a conviction that it has always been an unmitigated evil. Ecclesiasticism, too, excited in me profound aversion. Along with this went an unhesitating assumption that all superstitions are as mischievous as they are erroneous. These and allied pre-judgments were destroyed or greatly modified by contemplation of the facts. So that many ideas now set forth were not affiliated upon preceding ones, but generated *de novo:* some independent of, and some at variance with, preceding ones.

As in the works on Biology and on Psychology, fulfilment of the original programme, which in each case set

---

aside any difference of view between us) conclusively dispose of his supposition.

[1] See vol i., chaps. xii., p. 195; xiv., p. 252; *Supra*, xxvii., p. 193.

out with Data and Inductions, was largely influential in producing certain of these changes. Especially did search for the data compel attention to those traits of human beings which are factors in social co-operation. Throughout many chapters the affiliation of every kind of superstition upon the universal belief in the doubles of the dead, was traced; and it became manifest that all religious ceremonies originate from endeavours to please or pacify the ghost. The multitudinous facts showing this conspired also to show that belief in the continued or rather the increased, power of the dead ruler came to supplement the power of the living ruler; so that strengthening of natural control by supposed supernatural control became a means of maintaining social unions which could not else have been maintained. This was an all-important idea not affiliated upon preceding ideas. Nor could there be affiliated on preceding ideas the convictions produced by the logic of facts, that kingship and slavery are institutions naturally arising in the course of social evolution, and necessary to be passed through on the way to higher social forms. So, too, it had tó be reluctantly admitted that war, everywhere and always hateful, has nevertheless been a factor in civilisation, by bringing about the consolidation of groups— simple into compound, doubly-compound, and trebly-compound—until great nations are formed. As, throughout the organic world, evolution has been achieved by the merciless discipline of Nature, " red in tooth and claw "; so, in the social world, a discipline scarcely less bloody has been the agency by which societies have been massed together and social structures developed: an admission which may go along with the belief that there is coming a stage in which survival of the fittest among societies, hitherto effected by sanguinary conflicts, will be effected by peaceful conflicts.

To these indications of the re-moulded conceptions pervading the *Principles of Sociology*, have now to be added the ideas characterising the successive parts.

In " The Inductions of Sociology," the analogy between social organisms and individual organisms was elaborated: various minor ideas being brought to enforce the general idea. Here, as before, the assigned warrant for the comparison is the incontestable truth that in both there is co-operation of parts with consequent mutual dependence of parts; and that by these the life of the whole, individual or social, is constituted and maintained. Among further developments of the conception the first was a perception of the fact that whereas in individual organisms the co-operation is among parts which are in physical contact, in societies the co-operation is among parts which are in various degrees separated. At the same time it is shown that the co-operation, effected in living bodies by molecular waves propagated through the tissues, is, in societies, effected by " signs of feelings and thoughts conveyed from person to person." A concomitant difference is named. Whereas the animal organism has one sentient centre, for the benefit of which, in superior types, all other component parts exist, in the social organism there are as many sentient centres as there are persons; and, consequently, the units can no longer be regarded as existing for the benefit of the aggregate. Recognition of this essential difference explains the apparent anomaly that while societies highly organised for corporate action, and in that respect analogous to superior types of animals, are to be regarded as the highest *so long as militancy is great,* and the preservation of the society as a whole is the dominant end; under peaceful conditions, when corporate action is no longer needed for offence and defence, the highest types of society are those in which the coercive governmental organisation has dwindled, and corporate action, with its correlative structures, gives place to individual action, having directive structures of a relatively non-coercive kind.[1]

---

[1] Some fifty years ago M. Milne-Edwards pointed out the analogy between the division of labour in a society and the physio-

The ideas contained in Part III., " Domestic Institutions," mostly show little evidence of descent from preceding ideas. The first significant one is contained in a chapter on " The Diverse Interests of the Species, the Parents, and the Offspring "; in which it is shown that along with a certain community of interest there go certain antagonisms. In low types the sacrifices of individual life and well-being to the maintenance of the species, are great; and the sacrifices of parents to offspring and of offspring from inefficiency of parents, are also great; but as evolution progresses, all such sacrifices gradually become less. The next conclusion suggested by the evidence is that the sexual relations which arise, are, in a measure, appropriate to the respective social stages reached: polygamy having a natural relation to a chronic warfare which entails much male mortality. A further conclusion which the facts establish is that the *status* of women is low in proportion as militancy is high, and gradually improves (as does that of children also) in proportion as industrialism develops. Of chief

---

logical division of labour in an animal, and regarded the growing complexity of structure as a concomitant in the one case as in the other. If any one had thereafter asserted that he based the science of Biology on the science of Sociology, the assertion would have been regarded as extremely absurd. But the absurdity would have been no greater than is that fallen into by some American sociologists—Prof. Giddings and Mr. Lester Ward among them—who assert that I base Sociology upon Biology because I have exhibited this same analogy under its converse aspect; and who continue to 'do this though I have pointed out that the analogy does not in either case furnish a foundation, but merely yields mutual illumination. (See *Essays*, vol. iii., p. 323 *et seq.*) Those not biassed by the desire to make their own views appear unlike views previously enunciated, will see that if Sociology was by me based on Biology, biological interpretations would be manifest in all parts of the *Principles of Sociology* succeeding the part in which the above analogy is set forth. But they are not. The interpretations running through Parts III., IV., V., VI., VII., and VIII., though they are congruous with this analogy, are not guided by it, but have quite other guidance. They are based on the general law of Evolution, which is from time to time referred to as illustrated in the particular group of phenomena under consideration.

importance, however, is the doctrine that a radical distinction must be maintained between the ethics of family life and the ethics of social life. The ethics of family life, as concerning offspring, are that benefits received must be great in proportion as merit is small; whereas, on passing into social life, the individual must become subject to the law that benefits shall be proportioned to merits. And it is contended that the effects are immediately fatal in the first case and remotely fatal in the last if a converse *régime* is in force.

The next division exemplifies not the filiation of ideas but the entire overturn of an earlier idea by a later. Dominant as political government is in the thoughts of all, it is naturally assumed to be the primary form of government; and this had been assumed by me, as by everybody. But the facts which the *Descriptive Sociology* put before me, proved that of the several kinds of control exercised over men the ceremonial control is the first. After recognition of this unexpected priority, the cardinal truth recognised was that ceremonies at large originate in the relation between conqueror and conquered: beginning with mutilations and trophies, and running out into all forms of propitiatory actions and speeches—obeisances, modes of address, presents, visits, titles, badges and costumes, etc. The development of these exhibits very clearly the evolution from a simple germ to a complex aggregate, characterised by increasing heterogeneity and definiteness. A guiding truth finally emphasised was, that not only does ceremony begin with the behaviour of the conquered man to the conqueror, but that throughout all its developments it maintains its relation to militancy; being peremptory and definite in proportion as militancy is great, and diminishing in its authority and precision as industrialism qualifies militancy. This connexion is one aspect of the truth that militancy implies the principle of *status*, which involves ceremonial observances, while industrialism, implying contract, does not involve ceremonial observances.

After premising that political institutions must be regarded as relative to the circumstances and natures of the peoples living under them, there is drawn a fundamental contrast between the two kinds of co-operation which societies exhibit. There is conscious co-operation in the actions of a society as a whole against other societies, and unconscious co-operation in the actions of citizens severally satisfying their own wants by subserving the wants of others, but who do this without concert: no arrangement for undertaking different kinds of production having been made or even thought of. Efforts for self-preservation by the aggregate originate the first form of organisation; while efforts for self-preservation by the units originate the last form of organisation; the first being coercive and the last non-coercive. Here, while setting down these leading truths, there is disclosed to me one which I had not observed—one which, like so many others, is seen in the analogy between individual organisation and social organisation. For the contrast between the conscious co-operation of the structures which carry on the external actions of a society, and the unconscious co-operation of the industrial structures which carry on sustentation, is paralleled by the contrast between the conscious co-operation of the senses, limbs, and cerebro-spinal nervous system of a vertebrate animal, and the unconscious co-operation of its visceral organs and the nervous system of organic life which controls them.

The general truth referred to before, and again implied in the statements just made, is that political organisation is initiated by war and develops with the continuance of war. The primitive chief is the leading warrior. During long stages the military chief and the civil chief are the same, and even in the later stages in which the king becomes mainly the civil chief, he remains nominally the military chief. By implication the political organisation is at first identical with the army organisation. Chiefs and sub-chiefs, kings and feudal lords, are in peace central and local rulers; and the civil discipline among them and their subordinates is simply the military discipline: the servile or non-fighting portion of the population being the commissariat.

One final truth—an all-important truth—has to be named and emphasised. This is that the fighting structures and the industrial structures, though in a sense co-operative, are in another sense antagonistic; and that the type of the society is determined by the predominance of the one or the other. The militant type, in proportion as it is pronounced, entails compulsory co-operation, the *régime* of *status,* and the entire subjection of the individual; while the industrial type is characterised by voluntary co-operation, the *régime* of contract, and the independence of the individual: all the habits, sentiments, and ideas which prevail being in either case accompaniments of the type.

In Part VII. it is shown that just as political institutions are initiated by the emergence of a leading warrior who, first chief in war, presently becomes chief in peace; so ecclesiastical institutions have their beginning in the emergence of a special ancestor-worship from the pervading ancestor-worship carried on by all families. The propitiation of the deceased chief rises into predominance; the son who rules in his place, and succeeding rulers, being the primitive priests. Thus arising, the cults of heroes, conquerors, kings, generate a polytheism with its various priesthoods; and, by implication, a developed ecclesiastical system arises when victories produce composite societies and supreme rulers. Thus differentiated from political institutions, ecclesiastical institutions are partly co-operative and partly competitive: co-operative in so far that they join in enforcing the laws derived from the past, and competitive in so far that there grows up a struggle for supremacy: the ecclesiastical power, in virtue of its assumed divine authority, often becoming predominant. Differentiating as the ecclesiastical structure thus does from the political structure, it long participates in political functions. Its priests take part in war, and act as judges and local rulers during peace. But the differentiation becomes almost complete as social evolution progresses. And while ecclesiastical structures separate from political structures, there is shown within them progressing integration and progressing heterogeneity.

The futility of historical studies as ordinarily pursued, indicated already, is again shown on turning to the evolution of "Professional Institutions." Even before the collection and classification of the facts presented by inferior societies had gone far enough to make possible a complete tabulation, it became manifest that all the professions are differentiated from the priesthood. But so little recognised was this truth that the tabular representation, implying derivation of the one from the other, created surprise among highly educated critics.

Some significant evolutionary facts are exhibited in "Industrial Institutions." The division of labour displays unfamiliar features when developmentally considered. Out of the primitive homogeneous stage there arise by degrees the three distinguishable processes, Production, Distribution, and Exchange; and it is pointed out that in each of these divisions there arises a secondary division into the essential and the auxiliary—the actual processes and the aiding processes. The increasing interdependence of all these processes is shown to constitute an industrial integration. On passing from the division of labour to the regulation of labour, we come upon the truth, inferable *a priori* and established *a posteriori,* that the regulation of labour has a common origin with political regulation, and gradually differentiates from it. The first stage succeeding that in which each male member of a tribe, while warrior and hunter, makes for himself all such things as women cannot make, is the stage in which conquered men are made slaves; and the directive power exercised over the slave is, like the political directive power, purely coercive. Social life and domestic life alike exhibit the relation of ruler and subject; since this form of regulation for slaves is also the form of regulation for children. As the paternal passes into the patriarchal, the control of industry continues to be similar in nature to governmental control. The like holds in large measure when communes arise; and though under gild-regulation there is independent industrial action, it is subject to the coercive, quasi-political action of the gild. Only by degrees does the industrial regulation, based on contract, separate itself from the original form of industrial regulation, based on *status:* the law of evolution is again illustrated. Passing over corollaries, it will suffice to name the generalisation finally reached, that the essential differences in industrial regulation, as in political regulation, are implied by the question—To what extent does a man own himself, and to what extent is he owned by others? In actively militant states, like Sparta, he is the slave of the society, compelled to devote his activities and his life to its preservation: each is owned by the rest. But as fast as industrialism qualifies militancy, he acquires increasing possession of himself; until, in a society like our own, he is coerced scarcely more than is implied by paying taxes and, possibly, in case of war, going as a conscript. Still, however, he remains in considerable measure subject to the coercion of his industrial combinations—gilds or trade-unions. He is but partially master of himself, since he can use his abilities for self-maintenance only under such conditions as they prescribe. Complete possession of himself can be had by each citizen only in a perfectly peaceful state, and in the absence of all restraints on his power to make contracts.

In the *Principles of Ethics,* the title of the second chapter "The Evolution of Conduct," implies a point of view differing widely from the ordinary point of view. The idea that Ethics is to be conceived as a certain aspect of evolving conduct, was utterly alien to current ethical ideas, at the same time that it was congruous with the ideas contained in the preceding works. The tap-root of the system goes back to *Social Statics,* in which some root-fibres went into Biology, Psychology, and, largely, into Sociology. These fibres had now developed into branch roots, as is shown by the titles of successive chapters—" The Physical View," " The Biological View," " The Psychological View," " The Sociological View." Ethics was thus conceived as treating of conduct in relation to physical activities, vital processes, and mental functions, as well as in relation to the wants and actions of surrounding men. Hence not only duty to others, but also duty to self, had to be recognised and emphasised.

After these and other Data came the question—What are the Inductions? Under this head had to be ranged the various kinds of conduct, and the various ideas of right and wrong, found in human societies of all kinds and in all stages of progress. The first general conclusion drawn from this Comparative Ethics was that there is, in each case, an adaptation between the ideas of right and wrong and the kind of life which inherited nature and environing conditions produce; and the second conclusion was that there exists no such thing as a moral sense common to all mankind, but that the moral sense in each society, and in each stage, adjusts itself to the conditions.

Part III., dealing with " The Ethics of Individual Life," recognised, in pursuance of the general conception, the moral sanction of all those individual activities implied in the healthful and pleasurable pursuit of personal ends, bodily and mental. The conclusions drawn, though checked by Biology and Psychology, were in the main empirical; for there are no adequate data on which to base a definite code of private conduct. Personal nature must largely determine the special activities and special limits to them, though vital laws must regulate these. But there is named, though not adequately emphasised, a general consideration furnishing much guidance; namely, that to achieve the fullest life and greatest happiness, a due proportion must be maintained among the activities of the various faculties: excess in one and deficiency in another being, by implication, negatived. Doubtless, in our social life the sub-division of occupations necessitates great disproportion; but consciousness of the normal proportion serves to restrain.

In " The Ethics of Social Life—Justice," there is at length a return to the topic with which the whole series of my writings commenced. In " The Proper Sphere of Government," and then in *Social Statics*, endeavours were made to reach definite ideas concerning the just regulation of private conduct and the just relations of individuals to the social aggregate, represented by its government. And now, after all the explorations made in an interval of forty years, this topic came up once more to be dealt with in the light of the results which had then been reached. No essential changes of the views set forth in *Social Statics* proved needful; but there came to be recognised a deeper origin for its fundamental principle. The assertion of the liberty of each limited only by the like liberties of all, was shown to imply the doctrine that each ought to receive the benefits and bear the evils entailed by his actions, carried on within these limits; and Biology had shown that this principle follows from the ultimate truth that each creature must thrive or dwindle, live or die, according as it fulfils well or ill the conditions of its existence—a principle which, in the case of social beings, implies that the activities of each must be kept within the bounds imposed by the like activities of others. So that, while among inferior creatures survival of the fittest is the outcome of aggressive competition, among men as socially combined it must be the outcome of non-aggressive competition: maintenance of the implied limits, and insurance of the benefits gained within the limits, being what we call justice.

And thus, this ultimate principle of social conduct was affiliated upon the general process of organic evolution.

" Negative beneficence " was recognised as a needful supplement to Justice. While society in its corporate capacity is bound to enforce Justice to the uttermost, there falls on each individual, acting independently, the obligation to refrain from doing some things which the law of equal freedom warrants him in doing. This special obligation follows from the general obligation of each to discharge his debt to the society which has fostered him: doing this by aiding in its improvement— by cultivating a sympathy such as will not tolerate the taking of every advantage strict justice accords. But it was held that this qualification of the dictates of justice by those of negative beneficence must be left to the private judgment of each.

In the final division " Positive Beneficence," not passive altruism was enjoined, but active altruism. In the chapter on " The Evolution of Conduct," it was shown that the highest life, and consequently the highest happiness, can be reached only when " all the members of a society give mutual help in the achievement of ends "; and, by implication, can be reached only when they give mutual help in the avoidance of evils. In this final division it was contended that, while there is an indirect obligation on each to maintain and improve that social state which gives him the facilities of living he enjoys, he gains by cultivating the feelings which cause fulfilment of this obligation; since the sympathy which prompts alleviation of others' pains is the same sympathy which makes possible the participation in others' pleasures, and therefore exalts personal happiness.

March, 1899.

APPENDIX C

LIST OF HERBERT SPENCER'S WRITINGS

The Synthetic Philosophy

First Principles. First edition, 1862; second edition, 1867; third edition, 1875; fourth edition, 1880; fifth edition, 1884; sixth edition, and finally revised, 1900. Reprinted with an additional appendix and a new index, 1904.

Principles of Biology. Vol. i., 1864; vol. ii., 1867; revised and enlarged edition, vol. i., 1898; vol. ii., 1899.

Principles of Psychology. First edition, 1855; second edition, vol. i., 1870; vol. ii., 1872; third edition, 1880; fourth edition, 1899.

Principles of Sociology. Vol. i., first edition, 1876; second edition, 1877; third and enlarged edition, 1885. Vol. ii., Part IV., 1879; Part V., 1882. Vol. iii., Part VI., 1885; Parts VII. and VIII., 1896.

Principles of Ethics. Vol. i., Part I., 1879; Parts II. and III., 1892. Vol. ii., Part IV., 1891; Parts V. and VI., 1893.

Other Works

Social Statics. First edition, 1855; abridged and revised edition, 1892.

Education. First edition, 1861; cheap edition, 1878; sixpenny edition, published by the Rationalist Press Association, 1903. Reprinted, 1905.

The Study of Sociology. International Scientific Series, first edition, 1873; second to seventh editions, 1873-78; library edition, 1880.

The Man versus *the State.* First edition, 1884; reprinted with abridged and revised edition of Social Statics, 1892.

Essays. First Series, 1857. Second Series, 1863. Third Series, 1874. Revised edition in three volumes, 1890.

Various Fragments. First edition, 1897; enlarged edition, 1900.

Facts and Comments. 1902.

Descriptive Sociology:—

    English. 1873.

    Ancient American Races. 1874.

    Lowest Races, Negrito Races, and Malayo-Polynesian Races. 1874.

    African Races. 1875.

    Asiatic Races. 1876.

    American Races. 1878.

    Hebrews and Phœnicians. 1880.

    French. 1881.

    Autobiography. In two volumes, 1904.

ESSAYS, ARTICLES, AND LETTERS PUBLISHED IN MAGAZINES
AND NEWSPAPERS

1836.

" Crystallization." *Bath and West of England Magazine* for January.

" The Poor Laws." *Bath and West of England Magazine* for March.

1839.

" Skew Arches." *Civil Engineer and Architect's Journal* for May. (*Autobiography,* i., 517.)

1840.

" A Geometrical Theorem." *Civil Engineer and Architect's Journal* for July. (*Autobiography,* i., 520.)

1841.

" A New Form of Viaduct." *Civil Engineer and Architect's Journal* for July.

" The Transverse Strain of Beams." *Civil Engineer and Architect's Journal* for September.

" Scale of Equivalents." Written for the *Civil Engineer and Architect's Journal*, but not published. (*Autobiography*, i., 525.)

1842.

" Architectural Precedent." *Civil Engineer and Architect's Journal* for January.

Letter on above. *Civil Engineer and Architect's Journal* for March.

" Velocimeter." *Civil Engineer and Architect's Journal* for July. (*Autobiography*, i., 522.)

Letters " On the Proper Sphere of Government." *Nonconformist*, 15, 22 June; 13, 27 July; 10 August; 7, 21 September; 19, 26 October; 23 November; 14 December.

1843.

" Effervescence—Rebecca and her Daughters." *Nonconformist*, 28 June.

" Mr. Hume and National Education." *Nonconformist*, 2 August.

" The Non-Intrusion Riots." *Nonconformist*, 11 October.

Letter about the Derby flood of April, 1842. *Architect, Engineer, and Surveyor* for October.

1844.

" Imitation and Benevolence." *Zoist* for January.

" Remarks on the Theory of Reciprocal Dependence in the Animal and Vegetable Creations, as regards its bearing on Palæontology." *Philosophical Magazine* for February. (*Autobiography*, i., 533.)

LIST OF HERBERT SPENCER'S WRITINGS

" Situation of the Organ of Amativeness." *Zoist* for July.

" The Organ of Wonder." *Zoist* for October.

Various Articles. Birmingham *Pilot,* September to December.

1846.

" Justice before Generosity." *Nonconformist,* 30 December.

1847.

" The Form of the Earth no proof of Original Fluidity." *Philosophical Magazine* for March. (*Autobiography,* i., 546.)

1848.

Article on " Political Smashers." *Standard of Freedom,* June or July.

1851.

" A Solution of the Water Question." *Economist,* 20 December. (*Various Fragments,* p. 229.)

1852.

" Use and Beauty." *Leader,* 3 January. (*Essays,* ii., 370.)

" The Development Hypothesis." *Leader,* 20 March. (*Essays,* i., 1.)

" A Theory of Population." *Westminster Review* for April. (*Principles of Biology,* i., 577.)

" The Bookselling Question." *Times,* 5 April. (*Various Fragments,* p. 1.)

" A Theory of Tears and Laughter." *Leader,* 11 October.

" The Sources of Architectural Types." *Leader,* 23 October. (*Essays,* ii., 375.)

" The Philosophy of Style." *Westminster Review* for October. (*Essays,* ii., 333.)

" Gracefulness." *Leader,* 25 December. (*Essays,* ii., 381.)

1853.

" The Value of Physiology." *National Temperance Chronicle* for February.

" The Valuation of Evidence." *Leader,* 25 June. (*Essays,* ii., 161.)

" Over-Legislation." *Westminster Review* for July. (*Essays,* iii., 229.)

" The Universal Postulate." *Westminster Review* for October.

" The Use of Anthropomorphism." *Leader,* 5 November.

1854.

" Manners and Fashion." *Westminster Review* for April. (*Essays,* iii., 1.)

" Personal Beauty." *Leader,* 15 April and 13 May. (*Essays,* ii., 387.)

" The Art of Education." *North British Review* for May. (*Education,* chap. ii.)

" The Genesis of Science." *British Quarterly Review* for July. (*Essays* ii., 1.)

" Railway Morals and Railway Policy." *Edinburgh Review* for October. (*Essays,* iii., 52.)

1855.

" An Element in Method." A chapter in *Principles of Psychology.* (*Various Fragments,* p. 3.)

1856.

Letter to Editor on charge of Atheism. *Nonconformist,* 23 January.

1857.

" Progress: its Law and Cause." *Westminster Review* for April. (*Essays,* i., 8.)

LIST OF HERBERT SPENCER'S WRITINGS

" The Ultimate Laws of Physiology." *National Review* for October. (*Essays*, i., 63.)

" The Origin and Function of Music." *Fraser's Magazine* for October. (*Essays*, ii., 400.)

" Representative Government: What is it good for? " *Westminster Review* for October. (*Essays*, iii., 283.)

1858.

" State Tamperings with Money and Banks." *Westminster Review* for January. (*Essays*, iii., 326.)

" Moral Discipline of Children." *British Quarterly Review* for April. (*Education*, chap. iii.)

" Recent Astronomy and the Nebular Hypothesis." *Westminster Review* for July. (*Essays*, i., 108.)

" A Criticism of Professor Owen's Theory of the Vertebrate Skeleton." *British and Foreign Medico-Chirurgical Review* for October. (*Principles of Biology*, second edition, ii., 548.)

1859.

" The Laws of Organic Form." *British and Foreign Medico-Chirurgical Review* for January.

" The Morals of Trade." *Westminster Review* for April. (*Essays*, iii., 113.)

" Physical Training." *British Quarterly Review* for April. (*Education*, chap. iv.)

'" What Knowledge is of most Worth." *Westminster Review* for July. (*Education*, chap. i.)

" Illogical Geology." *Universal Review* for July. (*Essays*, i., 192.)

Letter on Mr. J. P. Hennessey's paper read at the meeting of the British Association. (*Athenæum*, 22 October.)

1860.

" Bain on the Emotions and the Will." *British and Foreign Medico-Chirurgical Review* for January. (*Essays*, i., 241.)

" The Social Organism." *Westminster Review* for January. (*Essays*, i., 265.)

" The Physiology of Laughter." *Macmillan's Magazine* for March. (*Essays*, ii., 452.)

" Parliamentary Reform: the Dangers and the Safeguards." *Westminster Review* for April. (*Essays*, iii., 358.)

" Prison Ethics." *British Quarterly Review* for July. (*Essays*, iii., 152.)

1862.

" Theological Criticism." *Athenæum*, 8 and 22 November.

" On Laws in General and the Order of their Discovery." Part of the first edition of *First Principles*. (*Essays*, ii., 145.)

1864.

" The Classification of the Sciences." Published as a brochure in April. (*Essays*, ii., 74.)

" Reasons for Dissenting from the Philosophy of M. Comte." Appendix to the foregoing. (*Essays*, ii., 118.)

" What is Electricity? " *Reader*, 19 November. (*Essays*, ii., 168.)

1865.

" The Constitution of the Sun." *Reader*, 25 February. (*Essays*, i., 182.)

" The Collective Wisdom." *Reader*, 15 April. (*Essays*, iii., 387.)

" Political Fetichism." *Reader*, 10 June. (*Essays*, iii., 393.)

" Mill *versus* Hamilton—The Test of Truth." *Fortnightly Review* for July. (*Essays*, ii., 188.)

1866.

" On Circulation and the Formation of Wood in Plants." *Transactions of the Linnæan Society*, vol. xxv. (*Principles of Biology*, ii., 567.)

1870.

" The Origin of Animal Worship." *Fortnightly Review* for May. (*Essays*, i., 308.)

1871.

" A New Fishing Rod." *Field*, 14 January. (*Autobiography*, ii., 504.)
" Morals and Moral Sentiments." *Fortnightly Review* for April. (*Essays*, i., 331.)
" Mental Evolution." *Contemporary Review* for June.
" Specialised Administration." *Fortnightly Review* for December. (*Essays*, iii., 401.)

1872.

" Survival of the Fittest." *Nature*, 1 February.
" Mr. Martineau on Evolution." *Contemporary Review* for June. (*Essays*, i., 371.)

1873.

" Replies to Criticisms." *Fortnightly Review* for November and December. (*Essays*, ii., 218.)
" Obituary Notice of J. S. Mill." *Examiner*, 17 May. (*Autobiography*, ii., 506.)

1874.

Correspondence relating to Physical Axioms. *Nature*, March to June. (*Essays*, ii., 298-314.)

1875.

" Professor Cairnes's Criticisms." *Fortnightly Review* for February. (*Various Fragments*, p. 14.)

1876.

" The Comparative Psychology of Man." *Mind* for January. (*Essays*, i., 351.)

1877.

" Views concerning Copyright." Evidence given before the Royal Commission. (*Various Fragments*, p. 18.)

" A Rejoinder to Mr. McLennan." *Fortnightly Review* for June. (*Various Fragments*, p. 63.)

" Mr. Tylor's Review of the Principles of Sociology." *Mind* for July.

1878.

Letter on the toast of " The Fraternity of the two Nations " proposed at a dinner in Paris. *Standard*, 30 May.

" Consciousness under Chloroform." *Mind* for October. (*Principles of Psychology*, i., 636.)

1879.

Letter to M. Alglave about the " Lois Ferry." *Revue Scientifique* for July.

1880.

Letter on the feeling in England about the time of the outbreak of the Civil War in the United States— written in 1869, but not then published. *New York Tribune*, 28 June. (*Autobiography*, ii., 497.)

" Professor Tait on the Formula of Evolution."

Nature, 2 and 16 December. (*Various Fragments,* p. 75.)

Letter disclaiming having had to do with "George Eliot's" education. *Standard,* 26 December.

1881.

"Replies to Criticisms on the Data of Ethics." *Mind* for January.

"Views concerning Copyright." Speech delivered at a meeting of the National Association for the Promotion of Social Science, held in May. (*Various Fragments,* p. 57.)

"Professor Green's Explanations." *Contemporary Review* for February. (*Essays,* ii., 321.)

1882.

Letter on "The Anti-Aggression League." *Nonconformist and Independent,* 2 March.

"Professor Goldwin Smith as a Critic." *Contemporary Review* for March.

Pecuniary liberality of Mr. J. S. Mill. *Daily News,* 27 March.

"Concerning the Misstatements of the Rev. T. Mozley." *Athenæum,* 22 July. (*Autobiography,* i., 549.)

"Ability *versus* Information." (*Various Fragments,* p. 91.)

"Book Distribution." (*Various Fragments,* p. 93.)

1883.

Letter on the *Edinburgh Review* and on the Land Question. *St. James' Gazette,* 14 February.

"The Americans." *Contemporary Review* for January. (*Essays,* iii., 471.)

1884.

Political Articles. *Contemporary Review* for February, April, May, June and July.

Letter on a misquotation in the Duke of Argyll's *Unity of Nature*. *Athenæum*, 16 February.

" Mental Evolution in Animals." *Athenæum*, 5 April.

" Retrogressive Religion." *Nineteenth Century* for July.

Letter repudiating the opinion attributed to him that we should be all the better in the absence of education. *Standard*, 8 August.

" Mr. Herbert Spencer and the Comtists." *Times*, 9 September.

" Mr. Herbert Spencer and Comte." *Times*, 15 September.

" Last Words about Agnosticism and the Religion of Humanity." *Nineteenth Century* for November.

1885.

" A Rejoinder to M. de Laveleye." *Contemporary Review* for April. (*Various Fragments*, p. 98.)

Letters on the Spencer-Harrison Book. *Times*, 1, 3, 4 and 6 June. *Standard*, 10 and 13 June.

" Government by Minority." *Times*, 21 December. (*Various Fragments*, p. 110.)

1886.

" The Factors of Organic Evolution." *Nineteenth Century* for April and May. (*Essays*, i., 389.)

1888.

" A Counter Criticism." *Nineteenth Century* for February. (*Essays*, i., 467.)

Letter with Reference to his Opinions on Painting. *Architect*, 24 February.

" The Ethics of Kant." *Fortnightly Review* for July. (*Essays*, iii., 192.)

LIST OF HERBERT SPENCER'S WRITINGS

1889.

Rev. J. Wilson's Statements about articles on "Sociology" in the Birmingham *Pilot*. *Pall Mall Gazette*, 12 April.

Letters on the Land Question. *Times*, 7, 11, 15, 19, 27 November.

1890.

"Absolute Political Ethics." *Nineteenth Century* for January. (*Essays*, iii., 217.)

"Reasoned Savagery so-called." *Daily Telegraph*, 7 February.

"The Inheritance of Acquired Characters." *Nature*, 6 March.

"Panmixia." *Nature*, 3 April.

"Our Space Consciousness." *Mind* for July. (*Principles of Psychology*, ii., 717.)

"The Moral Motive." *Guardian*, 6 August. (*Principles of Ethics*, ii., 446.)

"The Origin of Music." *Mind* for October.

1891.

"From Freedom to Bondage." Introduction to *A Plea for Liberty*. (*Essays*, iii., 445.)

"The Society for Prevention of Cruelty to Children." *Pall Mall Gazette*, 16 and 28 May.

"The Origin of Music." A discussion. *Mind* for October.

1892.

Letter to *Figaro* about his unfamiliarity with M. Renan. *Pall Mall Gazette*, 20 October.

Letter on the sales of his books. *Daily Chronicle*, 3 December.

1893.

"Social Evolution and Social Duty." (*Various Fragments*, p. 119.)

" The Inadequacy of Natural Selection." *Contemporary Review* for February and March. (*Principles of Biology*, i., 602.)

" Professor Weismann's Theories." *Contemporary Review* for May. (*Principles of Biology*, i., 633.)

" A Rejoinder to Professor Weismann." *Contemporary Review* for December. (*Principles of Biology*, i., 650.)

" Evolutionary Ethics." *Athenæum*, 5 August. (*Various Fragments*, p. 111.)

1894.

" Obituary Notice of Professor Tyndall." *Fortnightly Review* for February.

" Parliamentary Georgites." *Times*, 20 February. (*Various Fragments*, p. 122.)

Letters relating to the Land Question Controversy. *Daily Chronicle*, August to September.

" Weismannism Once More." *Contemporary Review* for October. (*Principles of Biology*, i., 671.)

" A Record of Legislation." *Times*, 24 November. (*Various Fragments*, p. 125.)

" The Booksellers' Trade Union." *Times*, 26 October. (*Various Fragments*, p. 161.)

" The Book Trade." *Times*, 30 October and 6 November. (*Various Fragments*, pp. 163, 167.)

" The Bookselling Question." *Times*, 21 November. (*Various Fragments*, p. 169.)

" Publishers, Booksellers, and the Public." *Times*, 24 October. (*Various Fragments*, p. 156.)—*Athenæum*, 24 November. (*Various Fragments*, p. 171.) —29 December. (*Various Fragments*, p. 174.)— *The Author*, December. (*Various Fragments*, p. 177.)

" Origin of Classes among the ' Parasol ' Ants." *Nature*, 6 December. (*Principles of Biology*, i., 687.)

1895.

" Herbert Spencer on the Land Question." (*Various Fragments,* p. 196.)

" The Antiquity of the Medical Profession." *Nature,* 27 June.

" Mr. Balfour's Dialectics." *Fortnightly Review* for June.

" The Nomenclature of Colours." *Nature,* 29 August.

Note on the Ethical Motive. *Nineteenth Century Review* for September.

" American Publishers." *Times,* 21 September. (*Various Fragments,* p. 236.)

" Heredity Once More." *Contemporary Review* for October.

Letter on Canadian Copyright. *Times,* 21 October.

" Lord Salisbury on Evolution." *Nineteenth Century Review* for November.

" The Board of Trade and Railway Station Boards." *Times,* 2 December. (*Various Fragments,* p. 235.)

On Mr. Howard Collins' letter suggesting a portrait. *Times,* 14 December.

1896.

" Dr. Bridges's Criticisms." *Positivist Review* for January.

" Anglo-American Arbitration." Letter read at a meeting in Queen's Hall, 3 March. (*Various Fragments,* p. 128.)

" Against the Metric System." *Times,* 4, 7, 9, 25 April. (*Various Fragments,* p. 130.)

Letter on Mr. Bramwell Booth's charges of Inconsistency. *Times,* 17 December.

1897.

Clearing himself of seeming implication of " positive or negative defect of quotation." *Fortnightly Review* for January.

" The Duke of Argyll's Criticisms." *Nineteenth Century* for May.

1898.

Letters on " Primitive Religious Ideas." *Literature*, 5 and 19 February. *Spectator*, 23 July.

" A State Burden on Authors." *Times*, 9 and 16 February. (*Various Fragments*, p. 220.)

Letter on " Mr. Mallock's Representation of his Views." *Literature*, 2 April.

The *Times* Art Critic on the Herkomer portrait. *Times*, 5 May.

" Cell Life and Cell Multiplication." *Natural Science* for May.

" Stereo-Chemistry and Vitalism." *Nature*, 20 October.

" Asymmetry and Vitalism." *Nature*, 10 November.

" What is Social Evolution? " *Nineteenth Century* for September. (*Various Fragments*, p. 181.)

1899.

" The Duke of Argyll and Mr. Herbert Spencer." *Nature*, 12 January.

" Prof. Meldola's Explanation." *Nature*, 26 January.

Mr. Crozier's Charge of Materialism. *Literature*, 21 January and 11 February.

" Publishing on Commission." *Literature*, 4 February. (*Various Fragments*, p. 217.)

" The Metric System Again." *Times*, 28 March, 4, 8, 13 April. (*Various Fragments*, p. 205.)

" Professor Ward on ' Naturalism and Agnosticism.' " *Fortnightly Review* for December.

Letter on a misrepresentation of Spencer's Ethics. *Spectator*, 16 December.

Letter to Mr. Leonard Courtney on the South African War. (*Various Fragments*, p. 223.)

1900.

On the South African War. *Speaker,* 13 January; *Morning Leader,* 5 February. (*Various Fragments,* p. 224.)

" Professor Ward's Rejoinder." *Fortnightly Review* for April.

" An Inhumanity." *Times,* 25 July. (*Various Fragments,* p. 225.)

" Genesis of the Vertebrate Column." *Nature,* 25 October.

1901.

Letter on Space Consciousness, with reference to Dr. Tolver Preston's statement. *Mind* for January.

1902.

" The Spread of Small Pox." Signed " Observer," *Daily News,* 18 January.

" Ethical Lectureships." *Ethics,* 1 March.

The Education Bill. *Daily News,* 8 April.

Sir Michael Foster as M.P. for London University. *Times,* 28 May.

APPENDIX D

ACADEMIC AND OTHER HONOURS [1]

1871.

University of St. Andrews. Lord Rector.
University of St. Andrews. Doctor of Laws.
St. Andrews Medical Graduates' Association. Honorary Member.

1874.

Royal Society. Fellow.
University of Edinburgh. Lord Rector.

1875.

University of Aberdeen. Lord Rector.

1876.

Reale Accademia dei Lincei, Rome. Member.
London Dialectical Society. President.

1880.

Royal Academy of Sciences, Turin. Correspondent.

1882.

Royal Society of Naples. Correspondent.

---

[1] With a few exceptions these proffered honours were declined. In cases where a mark of honour had been conferred before obtaining his consent, he made no use of the distinction.

ACADEMIC AND OTHER HONOURS

1883.

Institut de France. Correspondent.
Institucion Libre de Enseñanza, Madrid. Honorary
Professor.
American Philosophical Society, Philadelphia. Fellow.
Twilight Club, New York. Member.
Birmingham Natural History and Microscopical Society.
Vice-President.

1885.

Society of Physiological Psychology, Paris. Correspondent.

1888.

University of Bologna. Doctor of Philosophy and
Letters.
Neurological Society of London. Honorary Member.

1889.

Royal Danish Academy. Member.

1891.

Royal Academy of Belgium. Associate.

1892.

Scientific Society of Athens. Member.

1895.

Royal Order " Pour le Mérite."
Imperial Academy of Vienna. Member.
Royal Lombardian Institute, Milan. Member.

1896.

University of Buda Pesth. Doctor.
Associazione Educativa Spenceriana, Rome. Honorary
President.

1897.

Psychological Society of Moscow. Member.
University of Cambridge. Doctor of Science.
University of Edinburgh. Doctor of Laws.
International Peace Association — Lombard Union.
Honorary President.

1901.

British Academy of Letters.

1903.

University of London. Doctor of Literature.

APPENDIX E

THE NEBULAR HYPOTHESIS

To the Editor of *The Fortnightly Review*.[1]

SIR,—Often in the heat of controversy things are said which, whether true or not, should be left unsaid. Somewhat irritated by Professor Ward's expression " A fugitive essay," I named some facts in a way suggesting interpretations which I overlooked. Only when I saw the note after publication did I perceive the construction that would be put upon it. What mental lapse caused so great an oversight I cannot understand; but a shattered nervous system entails countless evils—failure of judgment being one.

Though the note cannot now be cancelled, it is not too late to correct one of its expressions. It is between forty and fifty years since the period referred to, and I was incautious enough to speak from memory. I said that the belief that the nebulæ are remote galaxies was current among astronomers. I should have said *some* astronomers. As will be seen on turning to the essay, I quoted a relevant passage from Humboldt's *Cosmos*. As he was in touch with Continental astronomers, and was in fact presenting the current astronomical conclusions, his representation of nebulæ as remote galaxies was manifestly held by at least some of them. Doubtless it was the wide circulation of *Cosmos* during the fifties (I quoted from the seventh edition) which dif-

---

[1] See Chap. xxvi., p. 185, note. It was arranged that this letter should be put in type, but that it should not be published in the *Fortnightly* if Professor Ward did not make a move. The occasion for its appearance in the *Review* not having arisen, it is now published for the first time.

fused this belief, and caused its acceptance as one which astronomers had established. Hence it happened that in 1857-8 any one who still adhered to " the Nebular Hypothesis " was smiled at. It was this which prompted the essay in question, and gave its original title " *Recent Astronomy and* the Nebular Hypothesis "; its primary purpose being to show the illegitimacy of the inferences drawn from Lord Rosse's disclosures. This should not, indeed, have needed showing. As far back as 1849, Sir John Herschel, in a description of the nebulæ, had put together facts which, when duly considered, sufficed to show the fallacy of the current belief. But he made no reference to this belief; and though its untruth was readily to be inferred, the inference was not generally drawn. In the essay just named I quoted this passage from Sir John Herschel, appending the remark that it furnished " another *reductio ad absurdum* " of the belief. Let me add that the question at issue was not one of mathematics, nor of mathematical physics, nor of physical astronomy. It was simply a question of general reasoning.

There is an error in the closing part of my last letter which I must rectify. I had referred to a passage from Sir John Herschel's *Outlines* expressing the belief that in clusters of stars having partially opposing impulses there must occur collisions; but that after such collisions there must ultimately arise a circulation of a permanent character. Since globular clusters, like others, are formed of stars which, so far as appears, have opposing impulses, I assumed that all of these were included in the statement. I had before me at the time the second volume of Dr. Isaac Roberts's *Photographs of Stars, Star-Clusters, and Nebulae,* in which, at pp. 1730-8, it is shown, both by the photographs and the descriptions, that those called globular clusters are in course of concentration—that is, are not in moving equilibrium (globular is a misleading word, since it connotes a definite limit, which nowhere exists) ; and I was the more led thus to regard them by Sir John Herschel's own statement respecting diffused and globular clusters, that " it is impossible to say where one species ends and the other begins " (*Outlines,* p. 639). Hence, it never occurred to me that he assumed some of the globular clusters to be already in a state of moving equilibrium; nor do I understand now for what reason (save the theological one named) he thus assumed them. This, however, is beside the question, which is whether he did so assume them; and here closer study of his words obliges me to admit that I was wrong.

This admission, however, does not in the least touch the main issue. In opposition to a view I had expressed, Professor Ward said that " the little that is known concerning the distribution and motion of our Sidereal System points clearly to the existence of stable arrangements comparable to that of the Solar System, but of greater complexity "; and he asserts that, in the passage I have quoted, " this view is maintained " by Sir John Herschel. My reply was that the passage makes no reference to our Sidereal System, either directly or by implication, but only to extremely minute components of it—telescopic star-clusters. And now to this negative proof of misrepresentation I have to add positive proof; for on pp. 630-1, Sir John Herschel discusses the speculations that had been ventured respecting the rotation of our Sidereal System, and after rejecting the only definite one named, that of Mädler, expresses his own neutrality, and thinks that an opinion can be formed only after some thirty or forty years of a special class of observations.

HERBERT SPENCER.

Brighton,
April 18*th,* 1900.

INDEX

389

INDEX

America: Spencer's literary relations, i. 128, 133, 138, 143 *seq.*, 211, 217, 286; ii. 88, 135; first subscribers to Synthetic Philosophy, i. 131; Civil War, i. 138, 191, 276; practical sympathy with Spencer, i. 167, 217, 290; ii. 231; Spencer's proposed dedication of philosophy to friends in, i. 193; International Scientific Series, i. 209; political machinery, i. 211; attitude towards Spencer, i. 268, 303, 338; ii. 105; Spencer's visit, i. 271, 289, 299; ii. 39; copyright question, i. 278, 354, 363 *seq.*; political state, i. 279; Twilight Club, i. 307; Japanese relations, ii. 15; Chinese Immigration, ii. 17; Henry George's attack on Spencer, ii. 37; testimonial, ii. 39; admiration of "smart" men, ii. 78; "dreadful catastrophe" impending, *ib.*; Spencer's pamphlet on metric system, ii. 94; arbitration, ii. 94; war with Spain, ii. 135; doctor asks for bequest of Spencer's brain, ii. 259; Declaraton of Independence, ii. 354

Amphimixis, Weismann's theory, ii. 56

Amusements, recommended by Spencer to his friends, ii. 297

Anarchist, use of term by an individualist, ii. 77

Ancestor Worship, ecclesiastical institutions derived from, ii. 360

Andrews, Prof., physicist, **ii.** 165, 320

Animism, controversy with E. B. Tylor concerning, ii. 63 *seq.*, 134, 193

Anti-Aggression League, i. 295 *seq.;* ii. 95, 136, 301

Anti-Gambling League, ii. 23, 66

Antiquity, veneration for, i. 44, 59

Anti-Vaccination League, ii. 152

Ants, differentiation of classes, ii. 132

Appleton, D., & Co.: Spencer's American publishers, i. 144, 290, 347 *seq.;* ii. 44

Appleton, W. H., i. 269, 278; ii. 186

A priori method in Spencer's philosophy, ii. 277 *seq.*

Arbitration, Anglo-American, ii. 95

Architect, The, i. 377; ii. 376

Architect, Engineer and Surveyor, ii. 368; "Architectural Precedent," paper by Spencer on, i. 44, 378; ii. 368

Architecture, often spoiled by excess, ii. 137

Ardtornish (formerly Achranich), Argyllshire, Spencer's visits to, i. 106, 123, 131, 134, 143, 152, 161, 180, 227, 239, 253 *seq.*, 266, 288, 315, 412 *seq.;* ii. 222; a last reminder of, **ii. 218** (illustration opp. page i. 412)

Arena, ii. 3

Argoed The, Monmouthshire, i. 383, 385

Argyll, [Eighth] Duke of, ii. 97; letter to, ii. 49

INDEX

Aristotle, Spencer's knowledge of his writings, ii. 147

Arnold, Matthew, i. 278; ii. 199, 205

Arnold, Dr. [Thomas], i. 397

Arnott's smoke - consuming grate, i. 107

Art: French architectures and furniture, i. 99; Spencer's scheme for classifying artistic characters of paintings, ii. 88 *seq.*; Ruskin's views, ii. 127; need for restraint, ii. 137

"Art of Education," ii. 320, 370

Artisans (*see* Working Classes)

Assouan, i. 273

Astronomy: in scheme for Synthetic Philosophy, ii. 91, 156; Spencer's writings concerning, ii. 156 *seq.*, 329; genesis of asteroids, ii. 330 *seq.*

Atheism, repudiated by Spencer, i. 105 (*v.* ll. 249, 370)

Athenæum, The, (Club): i. 188, 286, 319, 390, 398; ii. 129, 302; Spencer's election, ii. 253 *seq.*; Spencer's attachment to, ii. 253 *seq.*; his qualities as a club-man, ii. 254 *seq.*; Galton's smoke-room talks with Spencer, ii. 262; Spencer's impracticable administration, ii. 272 *seq.*

Athenæum (periodical), i. 105, 137 *seq.*, 267; ii. 36, 371, 375, 378

Athleticism, ii. 24

Australia: Press attitude to "Religious Retrospect, etc.," i. 339; Spencerian Society in Melbourne, ii. 209

Author, The, ii. 378

Authority: women always supporters of, i. 182; honorary titles strengthen, i. 314 (*see also* Herbert Spencer, Characteristics)

Autobiography of Spencer: in relation to this work, vii. *seq.*, initiation, i. 234; lacuna, i. 273; writing of, i. 317; contemplated publication of part during life, i. 343; coincidences, ii. 130. (Frequent other references throughout this work)

Avebury, Lord (*see* Lubbock)

Avenue Road, No. 64, St. John's Wood, Spencer's ménage at, ii. 22 *seq.*, 26 *seq.*, 75, 95, 128 *seq.*

BABBAGE, CHARLES, i. 148

Bacon, Francis: Spencer's knowledge of his writings, ll. 140, application of say ing by, ii. 148

Baden-Powell, Sir G. S., ii. 99, 157

Baer, K. von: formula of development, ii. 322

Baillière, French publisher, i. 257, 262, 274

Bain, Prof. Alexander: i. 106, 150 *seq.*, 286, 345; ii. 99; *Emotions and the Will*, i. 124, 240; ii. 333; Mill on his psychological work, i. 150; Spencer's regard for, i. 151 *seq.*; ii. 201, 220, 221; founder of *Mind*, i. 229; false report of death, i. 251; *Mental and Moral Science*, i. 259; review of "Data of Ethics," i. 267; opinion of Spencer's last

391

INDEX

ethical teacher, ii. 147; commencement of life on the earth, ii. 182; filiation of Spencer's ideas in, ii. 315 *seq.*, 322 *seq.*, 326, 331, 335 *seq.; a priori* reasoning, ii. 326; first use of word "evolution," ii. 331 *note;* alleged basis for Sociology, ii. 357 *note*

Birks, Canon, i. 249

Birmingham: Complete Suffrage Conference, i. 47; *Pilot* newspaper, i. 61, 384

Birmingham and Gloucester Railway(afterwards merged in Midland Railway): Spencer's appointment on, i. 29; ii. 308

Birmingham Natural History and Microscopical Society, i. 307, 333

Bitter Cry of the Outcasts of London, i. 325

Black, William, i. 286, 291

Black and White, ii. 194

Blunt, ——, i. 362

Blunt, Wilfred Scawen, writes *Satan Absolved* at Spencer's instigation, ii. 138 *seq.* Letters to, ii. 136 *seq.*, 192

Boehm, Sir Edgar, R.A.: his bust of Spencer, i. 326

Boers: policy towards outlanders, ii. 151; relief fund, ii. 210

Bologna, Italy, i. 272

Bologna, University of, degree conferred on Spencer, i. 389

Bonney, Canon T. G., ii. 239

Booksellers' discounts and net prices, i. 88, 220; ii. 70, 369, 378

Booth, W. Bramwell, attack on Spencer, ii. 111

Bosanquet, Bernard, ii. 99

Botha, General Louis, letters to, on management of Boer Relief Fund, ii. 210

Boughton Monchelsea, ii. 129

Bourne, H. R. Fox: letter to, on the Kanaka Question in Queensland, ii. 21

Bournemouth, i. 373

Bowditch, J. I., i. 131

Bowen, Sir Charles, i. 357

Bowen, F., i. 131

Bowman, Thomas, Warden of Merton, ii. 239

Boys, Prof. C. V., ii. 99

Bradbrook [Sir], E. W., ii. 99

Bradlaugh, Charles, i. 295

Brant-Sero, Mr. (Iroquois), proposes translation of *Education* into Mohawk, ii. 194

Bray, Mrs., letter to, ii. 208

Brett, John, A.R.A., i. 377

Brettell, Settlement of Immigrants so named, at Stourbridge, i. 1

Brettell, Jane (*see* Holmes)

Brettell, Jeremiah, i. 2

Brettell, John, i. 2

Brettell, Joseph, of Wordsley, Spencer's descent from, i. 2

Brettell, Joseph, Wesleyan Minister, i. 2

Bridge, James, Spencer's secretary, i. 296

Bright, Rt. Hon. John, M. P., i. 71, 276. Letters to, i. 294, 297

Bright, Rev. Dr. J. Franck, ii. 240

Brighton, Sussex: i. 98, 107, 130, 256, 286, 296, 319; 368; ii. 58; Spencer's residence at, ii. 130, 197; Free

393

INDEX

s-ent

Carnarvon, Earl of, ii. 86

Carnegie, Andrew: ii. 9; gift of piano to Spencer, i. 407, 414; views concerning wealth, *ib.;* asks Spencer to sit for his portrait, ii. 104, 112; thoughts of Spencer in his illness, ii. 221; request for memento, ii. 223 *seq.* Letters to, i. 407; ii. 104 *seq.*, 148, 212, 221

Carpenter, W. B., *Principles of Physiology*, i. 80

Carr's Dynamometer, i. 34

Carus, Prof. Victor: ii. 66; translator, ii. 150; pays Spencer the highest compliment he ever received, ii. 150

Cary, Henry C., i. 131

Cause: relativity of idea, ii. 124; investigation of, an analytic process, ii. 305

Cazelles, Dr. E.: French translator of Spencer's works, i. 169, 202, 295; ii. 75; Introduction to Evolution Philosophy, i. 202 *seq.*, 225 *seq.;* relinquishes translation for political reasons, ii. 120; Spencer recommends amusements to, ii. 267. Letters to, i. 203 *seq.;* ii. 120 *seq.*, 166

Cecil, Lord Arthur, i. 266

Cecil, Lord Lionel, i. 266

"Ceremonial Institutions" (a division of Spencer's *Principles of Sociology*), i. 254, 257, 267, 272, 317; ii. 354

Chadwick, Rev. J. W., Brooklyn: on Spencer's characteristics, ii. 261 *seq.;* on Spencer's philosophy, ii. 289 *seq.*

Chamberlain, Rt. Hon. Joseph: ii. 210; Canadian copyright, ii. 89; presence at disestablishment meeting recalled, ii. 214

Chambers, Robert: i. 86; on Spencer's population theory, i. 83; on programme of Synthetic Philosophy, i. 126

Chapin, E. H., i. 131

Chapman, Dr. John, i. 69, 75, 83, 111, 114; ii. 317, 323

Character, in relation to politics, ii. 7, 149 (*v.* ii. 314, 363)

Chemistry, evolution of elements, ii. 168, 184

Chesson, F. W., i. 292

Children: Spencer's advice to a mother, i. 382; ii. 9 *seq.;* prevention of cruelty to, i. 405 *seq.* (*See also* Education)

China: relations with foreigners, ii. 11; *Descriptive Sociology*, ii. 196 *note;* translation of Spencer's work, ii. 207 *note*

Christian Examiner, i. 168, 170

Christianity: attitude of clergy to Spencer, i. 269, 336, 339; ii. 23; objection to Spencer's *Study of Sociology* at Yale, i. 276; profession and practice contrasted, i. 293, 411; ii. 122, 139, 153; dissociation of religion and ethics, ii. 19; eternal torment, ii. 60; relapse of those who abandon, ii. 212; Spencer's attitude, in connection with proposed memorial in

395

losophy, ii. 282 *seq.;* what Spencer owed to him, ii. 320, 340

Congregational Board of Education, i. 78

Congreve, Richard, letter from, on Harrison-Spencer controversy, i. 341

Consciousness, evolution of, exemplified, i. 238 *seq.*

" Consciousness under Chloroform," i. 255, 259; ii. 374

Conservation of Energy: Spencer's criticism of term, i. 232

Conservative Party, Spencer's attitude, ii. 3

" Constitution of the Sun," ii. 165, 341, 372

Contemporary Review, i. 196 *seq.,* 211 *seq.,* 249, 282 *seq.,* 289, 301, 317 *seq.,* 327; ii. 49, 140, 373 *seq.*

Conway, Moncure: i. 192; proposal for " supreme court of civilisation," ii. 135. Letters to, ii. 61, 135 *seq.,* 191

Cooper, J. Astley, letter to, ii. 24

Co-operation, ii. 65

Copyright: international, i. 210, 278, 354, 355, 363; Royal Commission, i. 251; ii. 195, 374; Canada, ii. 89 *seq.* Letter to A. J. Balfour suggesting legislative action, ii. 195

Cornhill Magazine, ii. 164

Corn-Law Repeal: effect on pauperism, i. 212

Correspondents, examples of requests received by Spencer from, ii. 188 *seq.*

" Cosmic Philosophy," Spencer's objection to title, i. 208

" County Council Tyranny," ii. 4

Courtney, Leonard (now Lord C. of Penwith): ii. 97; address at Spencer's funeral, ii. 228 *seq.,* 291. Letter to, on relations with his constituents, ii. 153 *seq.*

Courtney, Mrs. Leonard (now Lady C. of Penwith, *née* Kate Potter): i. 272; acts as " grundyometer," ii. 2 *seq.;* visit to Spencer in his illness, ii. 148; his last letter, ii. 226; reminiscences of Spencer, ii. 251 *seq.,* 257 *seq.,* 273

Coutant, M., Paris, ii. 226

Craig-Sellar, Mrs., i. 412 *seq.*

Crawford and Balcarres, Earl of, ii. 173

Cremer [Sir] W. R., i. 297

Crichton-Browne, Sir J., ii. 99

Cripps, Judy, i. 383 (*see* i. 396)

Cripps, Mrs. W. H. (*née* Potter): i. 373, 396. Letter to, on care of her children, i. 382

Critics, Spencer's experience of, i. 249, 267, 280; ii. 132, 138

Croft, W. C. (Liberty and Property Defence League), letter to, i. 298

Crookes, Sir William: theory of composition of elements, ii. 169 *seq.*

Cross, John W.: i. 113, 180, 258, 285; ii. 78; *Life of George Eliot,* i. 356; ii. 316. Letter to, ii. 78

Cross, Mrs. J. W. (" George Eliot," *q. v.*)

Cross, Miss Mary, ii. 75

Crucifixion, *tableau vivant* of, at St. Cloud, i. 99

terest in subject, i. 37; as a franchise qualification, i. 122; State agency, i. 344; ii. 126, 196, 224; Journalistic plebiscite concerning leading educationists, i. 345; London Liberty Club, i. 370; outcry against insufficient, i. 375; centralisation and uniformity, ii. 127, 196; Spencer's views not influenced by Rousseau, ii. 212 *seq.;* evolutionary conception, ii. 320

Education, Intellectual, Moral, and Physical, [collected essays by Spencer]: i. 75, 92, 96, 109, 113, 133 *seq.;* ii. 304, 320, 366; sixpenny edition, ii. 212; translations, i. 262; ii. 194, 207 *note*

Edward VII., King: ii. 216; absurd story of, when Prince of Wales, ii. 141

Egypt: visit and impressions, i. 271 *seq.;* crisis in, i. 297 *seq.*

Egyptians, Ancient: *Descriptive Sociology,* ii. 196

Elam, Dr., i. 249

Electric current, analogy in nervous action, i. 237

Elements, chemical: products of evolution, ii. 169 *seq.*

Eliot, George (*née* Marian Evans): i. 272; ii. 141; first meeting, i. 83; introduced by Spencer to G. H. Lewes, i. 83; on Spencer's ethics, i. 264; last meeting, i. 284; death and funeral, *ib.;* Spencer's relations with, i. 286, 356 *seq.;* her mental powers, i. 395; gives Mill's *Logic* to Spen-

cer, ii. 147; instigates Spencer to read Comte, ii. 321. Letter from, i. 285

Ellicott, Dr., Bishop of Gloucester, i. 250

Elliott, Sir Frederick, committee-man at Athenæum, ii. 255

Ellis, Mr., educationist, i. 163

Emerson, Ralph Waldo: i. 310 *seq.;* opinion of Spencer, i. 198

Engineer's Journal, i. 43

English: " bovine unintelligence," ii. 5; too stupid to generalise, ii. 6; national aggressiveness, ii. 16, 24, 121 (*see also* ii. 105); Spencer's prestige in, ii. 194; freedom, ii. 313

Equilibration, views of Tyndall and Spencer, i. 135 (*v.* ii. 335)

Escrick Park, i. 288

Essays (Spencer's collected), i. 109, 110, 147, 169, 301; ii. 67, 172, 304, 367

Ethical Lectures' Fund, ii. 144 *seq.,* 197 *seq.,* 381

Ethical Movement, ii. 198

Ethics: absolute, i. 77; genesis of moral sentiments, i. 195 *seq.;* and religion, i. 303; highest aim of the beneficent, ii. 19; differentiation from religion, ii. 19; ideal or absolute, in political affairs, ii. 27 *seq.;* social evolution, ii. 35 *seq.,* qualifications for teaching, ii. 147; Hector Macpherson on Spencer's work in, ii. 287; conception formerly current, ii. 312; evolutionary conception, ii. 362 *seq.;* conclusions concerning pri-

INDEX

vate conduct empirical, ii. 363

Ethics (periodical), ii. 381

Evans, Sir John, ii. 100

Evans, Marian (*see* Eliot, George)

Everett, Edward, i. 131

Eversley, Lord (Mr. Shaw Lefevre), ii. 225

Evolution: man the highest result, i. 81; Darwin's views, i. 113, 327; ii. 4; incompatible with spontaneous generation, i. 190 *seq.;* Cazelles' outline, i. 202; reply to criticisms on doctrine, i. 219; A. R. Wallace on altruism, i. 265; heredity, i. 360 *seq.;* W. H. Hudson's exposition, ii. 3 *seq.;* social state, ii. 35 *seq.*, 314 *seq.*, 352 *seq.;* religious ideas, i. 335 *seq.;* ii. 354 *seq.;* application to inorganic nature, ii. 156, 184; origin of elements, ii. 168 *seq.*, 184; equality of men excluded, ii. 213; filiation of ideas in relation to, ii. 314 *seq.*

Examiner, i. 221; ii. 373

Exhibition, the Great (1851), i. 81

Exhibition, International (1862), i. 136

Explanation, relativity of the conception, ii. 125

Eyre, Governor, ii. 192

" FACTORS of Organic Evolution," i. 329, 359

Facts and Comments (Spencer's last book): ii. 56 *note*, 186, 189 *seq.;* 197, 200 *seq.;* 234; opinion of friends and critics, ii. 205;

translations, ii. 206; "ultimate questions," ii. 234

Fairbairn, Dr. A. M., i. 289

Faraday, Michael: attitude to Comtism, i. 149

Fawcett, Henry, i. 397

Fawcett, Mrs., i. 369

Felton, C. C., i. 131

Ferri, Prof. Enrico: evolution and socialism, ii. 79

Ferry, Jules, French statesman, i. 266; ii. 374

Fetichism (*see* Animism)

Figaro, Le, ii. 70, 377

" Filiation of Ideas," ix., ii. 140 (Appendix B), 304 *seq.*

First Principles: i. 131 *seq.*, 136 *seq.*, 141 *seq.*, 159, 194, 202, 232, 268, 280, 318; ii. 366; second edition, i. 194; ii. 341, 366; J. S. Mill's appreciation, i. 141 *seq.;* French translation, i. 202; Tyndall's criticisms, i. 232; ii. 161 (*v.* ii. 335); position in scheme of Synthetic Philosophy, ii. 90 *seq.;* final revised edition, ii. 156, 183 *seq.;* ii. 366; scheme for omitted divisions, ii. 158 *seq.;* in relation to recent advances in physical science, ii. 170; ghost theory, ii. 193; independence of its two parts, ii. 210 *seq.* (*v.* i. 268), ii. 334; Hector Macpherson's criticism, ii. 286 *seq.;* filiation of ideas in, ii. 334 *seq.*

Fiske, John: i. 225; defence of Spencer in *Nation*, i. 198; lectures at Harvard on Spencer's philosophy, i. 206; proposes title " Cosmic Philosophy," i. 207

401

INDEX

Henzey, foreign origin of family so named, i. 1

Herald, New York, i. 300

Herbert, Hon. Auberon: i. 412; ii. 207; urged to write on social questions, ii. 60; individualistic propaganda, i. 401 *seq.;* scheme for better ventilation of houses, i. 404; Herbert Spencer, Lecturer, ii. 237. Letters to, i. 300, 401 *seq.,* 405; ii. 60 *seq.*

" Herbert Spencer on American Nervousness," i. 306

Herbert Spencer on the Americans, etc., i. 300

Heredity: use-inheritance, i. 360; ii. 45, 205; interbreeding of unlike races, ii. 16 *seq.;* limitation by sex, ii. 116

Herkomer, Sir Hubert von, R. A., painter of subscription portrait of Spencer, ii. 104, 108. Letters to, ii. 110 *seq.,* 112

Herschel, Sir John: on programme of Synthetic Philosophy, i. 126; Comtism, i. 148; aids reorganisation of *Reader,* i. 153; nebular hypothesis, ii. 157, 386 *seq.;* theory of the sun, ii. 331

Hertwig, Prof., ii. 54

Heyworth, Lawrence, M.P., i. 60, 70, 414

Highgate Cemetery: George Eliot's funeral, i. 285 *seq.;* Spencer's tomb, ii. 234

Hill, Dr. Alex., Master of Downing, Cambridge, ii. 240

Hillard, George S., i. 131

Hinton Charterhouse, Somerset-shire: Spencer's life at, i. 16 *seq.,* 45; Library, i. 372

Hirst, Dr. T. Archer, i. 219, 408; ii. 29

History: futility of, i. 80 (*v.* ii. 123) ; science of, repudiated by leading writers, ii. 352

Hobbes, Thomas: Spencer's knowledge of his writings, ii. 146; saying quoted, ii. 247

Hobhouse, Lord: ii. 100, 239; a greeting from, ii. 203

Hodge, F. H., i. 131

Hodgson, Richard, junr.: i. 282 *seq.* Letter to, i. 303

Hodgson, Shadworth, ii. 100

Höffding, Prof. Harold: Danish translator, i. 389; correspondence concerning correlation of mind and body, i. 235 *seq.*

Hoguet, M., ii. 226

Holland, Sir Henry: testimonial to Spencer, i. 117

Holme, Charles: i. 272; last visit to Spencer, ii. 227; executorship, ii. 228. Letter to, ii. 92

Holme, George, of Derby: i. 272; saves Spencer's life when a boy, i. 13, 234; his gratitude, i. 13; portrait sketch, i. 43; death, ii. 92; Spencer's tribute, *ib.* Letter to, i. 234

Holmes, Jane (*née* Brettell), Spencer's grandmother, i. 3

Holmes, John, Spencer's grandfather, i. 3

Holmes, Oliver Wendell, i. 372

Holt, Henry, American publisher, i. 198

405

INDEX

Huxley, Leonard, *Life and Letters of T. H. Huxley*, i. 132

Huxley, Prof. T. H.: on Spencer's boyhood, i. 15; friendship initiated, i. 83; ii. 318; introduces Spencer to Tyndall, i. 85; friendly relations and intercourse, i. 101, 108, 110, 219 *seq.*, 255 *seq.*, 316, 318; ii. 18; gives Spencer advice and criticism, i. 106, 108, 131 *seq.*, 161 *seq.*, 172, 190, 237, 356 *seq.*, 359, 367; New Year's dinners, i. 108, 318; controversy with Owen, i. 112; testimonial to Spencer, i. 118; ii. 279; attitude to Comtism, i. 148; reorganisation of *Reader*, i. 153; spontaneous generation, i. 191; "Administrative Nihilism," i. 197 *seq.*; International Scientific Series, i. 210, 248; Belfast lecture, i. 228; George Eliot's funeral, i. 284; jocose reference to photograph of Spencer, i. 284; Darwin's funeral, i. 296; President Royal Society, i. 315; views on heredity, i. 359 *seq.*; reads proofs of Spencer's Autobiography, i. 367; reply to W. S. Lilly, i. 369; State-education, i. 370; "The Struggle for Existence in Human Society," i. 374; combativeness, i. 376; banter, i. 377; ii. 263; house-building at Eastbourne, i. 388; land-question, ii. 27 *seq.*; ii. 213; Romanes lecture, "Evolution and Ethics,"

ii. 35; death, ii. 82; age of the Earth, ii. 166, 179; alleged influence of Rousseau on Spencer, ii. 213; saying about Spencer's deductive bent, ii. 264; literary composition, ii. 265; on the value of theory in scientific research, ii. 279; early discussion on development question recalled, ii. 318; hatred of deductive reasoning, ii. 326. Letters to: introductory, i. 85; *Psychology*, and congratulations on marriage, i. 101; foreign consulship, i. 119; *First Principles*, i. 131 *seq.*; loss of his son, *ib.*; plans for keeping the philosophy going, i. 166 *seq.*; a publisher's indiscretion, i. 303; X Club frivolity, etc., i. 333; criticism on "Factors of Organic Evolution," i. 360; suggested yachting cruise, i. 364; reply to Lilly, i. 369; death of his daughter, i. 373; London dissipations, i. 377; house-building, i. 288; reconciliation after estrangement, ii. 37; Lord Salisbury's Address, ii. 73 *seq.*; age of the Earth, ii. 178. Letters from: X Club frivolity, i. 333; use-inheritance, i. 360; Spencer's *Autobiography*, i. 367; reconciliation, ii. 37; Lord Salisbury's Address, ii. 74; Lord Kelvin and the age of the Earth, ii. 178

Huxley, Mrs. T. H.: i. 130, 279; on Boehm's bust of

unknown to Spencer, ii. 120

Jose, Mrs., i. 372, 414

Journal of Education, i. 345

Jowett, Benjamin, i. 132

Judd, Prof. J. W.: correspondence on volcanic phenomena, ii. 175 *seq.*

Judge, Mark, letter to, ii. 152

Justice, gratuitous administration, i. 322; ii. 68

" Justice " (Part IV. of Spencer's *Principles of Ethics*), i. 407, 412; ii. 43

KANAKAS, in Queensland, ii. 21

Kaneko, Baron Kentaro, Japanese statesman: i. 390; ii. 11 *seq.* Letters to: conservative policy for Japan, ii. 11; on Japanese policy with regard to foreigners, ii. 14 *seq.*

Kant, Immanuel: philosophy, i. 303 *seq.;* ii. 198; Spencer's knowledge of his writings, ii. 146; principle of individual action, ii. 313

Karnak, i. 274

Keatinge, M. W., letter to, ii. 127

Kelvin, Lord (Sir Wm. Thomson): metric system, ii. 94; method of reasoning, ii. 116; age of the earth and solar system, ii. 166 *seq.*, 178, 179; cosmic evolution, ii. 173; rigidity of earth's interior, ii. 174. Letter to, ii. 173

Kershaw, John Derby, i. 9

Key, Miss Lilian, ii. 131

Killick, Miss Edith: ii. 131; reminiscences of Spencer, ii. 227, 256, 260, 267 *seq.*

Kimberley, Earl of, i. 292

Kingsley, Rev. Charles: on programme of Synthetic Philosophy, i. 127; repudiation of " science of history," ii. 352

Kirchhoff, G. R., ii. 184, 331

Kirk Ireton, Derbyshire, records of Spencer family in parish register, i. 3

Kirkman, Rev. T., i. 249, 280

Knight, Charles, publisher, i. 79

Knight, Prof. William, ii. 100; article in *Bookman*, ii. 194

Knowledge, society for the repeal of taxes on, i. 88

Knowles, Herbert, poet, Spencer named after, i. 9

Knowles [Sir] James, Editor of *Nineteenth Century*, i. 278, 338; ii. 123

Krakatau, volcanic eruption, ii. 175 *seq.*

Krishnavarma, Shyamaji,founder of Herbert Spencer Lectureship, Oxford, ii. 237

LACAZE-DUTHIER, origin of annulose type, ii. 343

Lace Manufacture, Spencer's father's connection with, i. 5, 10

Laidlawstiel, i. 226

Laissez-faire, current conception, i. 212

Lamarck, heredity, i. 360

Land Nationalisation Society, i. 290

Land question: i. 76, 330; Spencer's change of views, ii. 22, 26 *seq.*, 120; discussion in *Daily Chronicle*, ii. 66

Land Restoration League, ii. 43

INDEX

Liberty: the idea and sentiment, ii. 61; result of removal of restraints, ii. 79

Liberty and Property Defence League, i. 323, 400 *seq.*; ii. 39

Libraries (*see* Free Libraries)

Lieber, Francis, i. 131

Life: gospel of relaxation, i. 306 *seq.*; æsthetic element in, *ib.*; a thing or a process, ii. 83; ultimate mystery, ii. 119; commencement of, on the Earth, ii. 182 *seq.*; conception of, as individuation, ii. 315; coordination of actions, ii. 318, 322

Life, the Science of (*see* Biology)

Lilly, W. S., i. 369; ii. 47

Limburg Stirum, Count (executor of Auguste Comte): pecuniary help declined by Spencer, i. 166

Linguistic culture, based on authority, ii. 306

Linnæan Society: Spencer's paper on plant circulation, i. 163; ii. 373

Linton, Lynn, Mrs.: i. 69; "Grundyometer" to Spencer, ii. 2; article on Prof. H. Drummond, ii. 72. Letters to, ii. 72, 129

Literature: patronage and talent, i. 51; concentration of feeling and idea, ii. 137

Literature (weekly review), ii. 132 *seq.*, 380

Littleton, Hon. S., i. 262

Littré, E. (editor of *La Philosophie Positive*), i. 205

Liveing, Prof. G. D., ii. 240

Liverpool University, proposal

for chair of sociology, i. 280

Loch, Lord, ii. 151

Locke, John: Spencer's knowledge of his writings, ii. 146

Lockyer, Sir J. Norman: i. 296; ii. 101; conversation with, on spectrum, ii. 168. Letter to, ii. 48

Lo-Feng-Luh, Sir Chih Chen, Chinese Minister: opinion of Spencer, ii. 148

Logic: uselessness of formal, ii. 149; an objective science, ii. 325

London: Spencer's plans for pure water supply, i. 82; dryness of air, i. 124; movement for resisting municipal encroachments, i. 400, 404; ii. 4, 39

London and Birmingham Railway (afterwards London and North Western Railway), Spencer's engineering work on, i. 29

London County Council: Spencer proposed as Alderman, ii. 4

London Liberty Club, i. 370

London Library, Spencer's connection with, ii. 255

London Ratepayers' Defence League, i. 404; ii. 4 *seq.*, 40

London Review, i. 152

London School of Economics, ii. 125

London University: honorary degree offered to Spencer, ii. 214

Longevity: proposed enquiry, ii. 116

"Lord Salisbury on Evolution," ii. 74, 380

411

INDEX

Lothian, Lady, i. 263
Lott, Edward: Spencer's portrait sketch of, i. 43; remonstrates with Spencer on excessive language, i. 63; on Spencer's favour with women, i. 71; objections to *Social Statics*, i. 77; Spencer's companion on excursions and travels, i. 92, 102, 143, 152, 192, 257, 291, 300; illness and death, i. 365 *seq.;* Spencer's appreciation of, i. 367. Letters to: "Proper Sphere of Government," i. 42; Wilson, editor of *Pilot*, i. 62; Shelley, i. 68; Goethe, *Wilhelm Meister, ib.;* Carlyle's *Cromwell, ib.;* Dickens' *Christmas Tale, ib.;* history and evolution, i. 80; Alex. Smith, Scotch poet, i. 87; impressions of France, i. 98; Darwin's *Origin of Species*, i. 127; political events (general election), i. 275; holiday movements, i. 288; a plan frustrated, i. 332; last good-bye, i. 365
Lott, Francis Edward: Spencer's executor, ii. 288; reminiscences, ii. 257, 267. Letter from, i. 95
Lott, Miss ("Phy"), i. 332, 341, 365
Loubet, M., French President: visit to England, ii. 216
Lowell, J. Russell, i. 131, 278
Lubbock, Sir John (now Lord Avebury): i. 142; ii. 228, 239. Letter from, ii. 200
Lushington, Vernon, Q.C., ii. 101
Lyell, Sir Charles: i. 86, 133,

153; ii. 309, 322; on programme of Synthetic Philosophy, i. 127; on Criticism, i. 148
Lynn, W. T., assists Spencer in revising essay on "Nebular Hypothesis," ii. 173
Lytton, Sir E. Bulwer (Lord): on Spencer's views on education, i. 78; offended by Spencer's condemnation of Afghan war, ii. 121

MACAULAY, LORD, Spencer on style of, i. 79
McClure's Magazine, ii. 88
McCosh, Dr., i. 328
Machinery, outcry against, i. 48, 122
M'Lennan, J. F., i. 252
MacMahon, P. A., F.R.S., ii. 101
Macmillan's Magazine, i. 238; ii. 166, 372
Macpherson, Hector: ii. 148; book on Spencer, ii. 141; offered "Reminiscences of Herbert Spencer" by a lady, *ib.;* review of Spencer's position as a thinker, ii. 281 *seq.* Letter to: Carlyle, ii. 93; proposed book on Spencer, ii. 93; "Reminiscences of Herbert Spencer," ii. 141
Magnus, Laurie, letter to, ii. 224
Magrath, Rev. Dr. J. R., ii. 241
Mahaffy, Dr. J. P.: compilation of *Descriptive Sociology*, Greeks, ii. 196 *note*
Mail and Express, New York newspaper, i. 409
Maine, Sir Henry S.: election

INDEX

Abbey, ii. 238; the Dean's reply, ii. 242; on the philosophic faculty in scientific research, ii. 280
Menabrea, Marquis, i. 244
"Mental Evolution," i. 197; ii. 373
Mentone, i. 261
Merry, Rev. Dr. W. W., ii. 241
Mesnil, M. du, ii. 75
Metaphysical Society, i. 191
Methodist Register Office, Spencer's birth and baptism entered at, i. 9
Metric System, Spencer's opposition to, ii. 94, 140
Miall, C. S., i. 49, 54, 58, 76
Midland Naturalist, i. 307
Miers, Prof. Henry A., ii. 241
Milan, i. 274
Miles, Mr., i. 273
Militancy: growth in teaching institutions, ii. 196; factor in social evolution, ii. 355 *seq.*
Militia, i. 70
Mill, John Stuart: i. 79; ii. 320; opinion of Spencer's *Psychology*, i. 106; "Universal Postulate," i. 106; ii. 146; consulted by Spencer about official appointment, i. 114; his testimonial, i. 116; ultimate test of truth, i. 156; ii. 319; interest in Spencer's success, i. 165; recommends French translator to Spencer, i. 169; death, and Spencer's obituary notice, i. 221; ii. 373; his educational standard, ii. 144; *Logic*, ii. 146, 320; omitted divisions of Spencer's programme, ii. 153; on philosophy in England, ii.

281; Hector Macpherson on his philosophic system, ii. 283 *seq.*; utilitarianism, ii. 287. Letters to, i. 140, 142; acknowledgment of sympathy, i. 114 *seq.*; liberty, i. 121; parliamentary reform, the franchise, etc., i. 122; *Principles of Psychology*, i. 150; the conduct of *The Reader*, i. 154, 156; political rights of women, i. 180 *seq.* Letters from: utilitarianism, i. 141; Comte, i. 149 *seq.*; aggressiveness of *The Reader*, i. 154 *seq.*; ultimate test of truth, i. 156 *seq.*, 160 *seq.*; Spencer's Biology, i. 200 *seq.* (*v.* i. 342; ii. 279)
Millais, Sir J. E., ii. 86, 102
Miller, Hugh, ii. 332
Milman, Dean, i. 88
Milne-Edwards [Henri], ii. 75, 317, 322, 356 *note*
Milnes, Monckton, [Lord Houghton, *q.v.*]
Mind: i. 229, 252, 260, 267, 282, 394; ii. 313, 374 *seq.*; change of control and policy, ii. 201 *seq.*
Minghetti, Sgr., i. 262
Minturn, R. B. (New York), i. 168
Mitchell, Dr. Chalmers, ii. 51
Mitchell, Mrs., of Laidlawstiel, i. 247
Mitchinson, Canon J., ii. 241
Mivart, Prof. St. George, i. 219, 228, 249
Monro, Dr. D. B., Oxford, ii. 241
Moorsom, Captain C. E.: Spencer's engineering chief, i. 29, 31; his opinion of

414

INDEX

Spencer quoted, i. 36; domestic life with, i. 39 *seq.;* endeavours to check Spencer's philosophic propensity, *ib.* Letter to, i. 39; letters to his niece, i. 45, 48

"Morals of Trade," essay on, i. 120 (*v.* 113); ii. 371

Mordan, A., Reigate, ii. 87

Morell [Dr. J. D.], i. 106

Morgan, Dr. C. Lloyd: ii. 101, 241; on Spencer's influence, ii. 279

Mori, Viscount Arinori, Japanese diplomat, i. 213; ii. 12

Morley, Rt. Hon. John: *Life of Cobden* quoted, i. 41; meetings with, i. 255 *seq.,* 286; ii. 97; Newcastle election, ii. 26; address of congratulation to Spencer, ii. 97, 101; correspondence with Spencer relating to obsequies, ii. 222 *seq.,* 228 *seq.; Life of Gladstone* quoted, ii. 247 *seq.* Letter to, martial law in South Africa, ii. 193

Morley, Samuel, M.P., i. 78, 298

Morning Leader, ii. 152 *seq.,* 381

Mosse, James, C.E., opinion of Spencer as engineering colleague, i. 29

Mottisfont, i. 410

Moulton (Sir J. Fletcher), i. 219, 281; ii. 171

Mozley, Mrs., advice to Spencer's father to join the Church, i. 11

Mozley, Rev. T.: *Reminiscences,* i. 327; ii. 375

Muirhead, Dr. John H., ii. 241

Municipalities, business enterprises, ii. 216

Murchison, Sir R., ii. 332

Murray, John, i. 404

Music: theory of origin, i. 109; needless expansion, ii. 138

Mysteries, mediæval, ii. 139, 249

Mystery, the ultimate, ii. 83, 92, 249

NADEN, CONSTANCE: Spencer's characterisation, i. 394

Napoleon, Louis: attitude to England, i. 112

Nation, The (American journal), i. 198, 393

National Portrait Gallery, ii. 86, 97

National Public School Association, i. 78

National Review, i. 105, 108, 136, 340; ii. 371

National Temperance Chronicle, i. 89, 370

Native Races: aggressions by civilised nations, ii. 121, 135

Natural Science, ii. 118, 380

Natural Selection: i. 360; the question of acquired characters, ii. 45 *seq.;* Lord Salisbury's view, ii. 73; partially recognised in *Social Statics,* ii. 314; factor in mental evolution, ii. 324; general doctrine of evolution, ii. 334; interpretation in general terms, ii. 339

Nature: non-moral character of, i. 374; merciless discipline, ii. 355

Nature: i. 219, 234, 283, 307; ii. 119, 175, 373 *seq.;* acquired characters contro-

415

INDEX

INDEX

INDEX

Spencer, Herbert: *Career —
Cont'd.*

jections to terms
"Positive" and "Cosmic," *ib. seq.;* reasons for selecting
"Synthetic," i. 208
(*v.* i. 225); International Scientific Series
started, i. 209 *seq.;
The Study of Sociology,* i. 211; reply to
Martineau, i. 212

1873. — Consulted
about Japanese institutions, i. 213; interest in disestablishment, i. 214; correspondence with Mr.
Gladstone concerning
criticism, *ib. seq.;*
cordial relations ensue, i. 217 (*v.* i. 222);
Descriptive Sociology
causes worry and trouble, *ib.* (*see* i. 230);
replies to criticisms, i.
218 *seq.;* obituary notice of Mill, i. 221;
reasons for not joining Royal Society, i.
222 *seq.;* British
Association Meeting,
Belfast, i. 227

1874.—*Principles of
Sociology* begun, i.
230; its destructive
nature, i. 231 *seq.;*
further revision of
First Principles, i.
232

1875.—Begins *Autobiography,* i. 234;
keeps away from Tyndall's wedding, i. 241;
election to Roman

Spencer, Herbert: *Career —
Cont'd.*

Academy, *ib.;* desires
it to be cancelled, i.
242; request withdrawn, i. 244; nomination for Lord Rectorships, Edinburgh
and Aberdeen, declined, i. 245 *seq.;*
invitation to Foreign
Office reception declined, i. 246 *seq.;*
first vol. of *Principles
of Sociology,* i. 250
seq., 253

1877.—Ill-health, i.
252; recuperates at
Ardtornish, i. 253;
"Ceremonial Institutions," *ib. seq.,* i. 257,
267; a bad time, i.
255; tries the social
distraction cure, i.
256; "Data of Ethics," i. 257, 262 *seq.;*
attends Lewes's funeral, i. 261

1879.—A holiday in
the Riviera, i. 261;
visit to Wilton, *ib.;*
"Political Institutions" begun, *ib.,*
i. 275; appreciation
from theologians, i.
269; visit to Egypt,
i. 271 *seq.;* intercourse
with celebrities, i.
279; proposal for
chair of Sociology at
Liverpool, i. 280; absurd rumours, i. 281

1880. — More encounters with critics,
i. 282 *seq.;* Tait's attack, i. 283; George

429

INDEX

INDEX

Spencer, H.: *Characteristics—Cont'd.*

Concentration, ii. 265

Conscientiousness, i. 32, 367

Consistency, ii. 30, 44

Conversational, ii. 256

Courteousness, ii. 255, 271

Criticism, sensitiveness to, ii. 35, 275; proneness to, ii. 273 *seq.*

Deductive tendency, ii. 56, 263, 307, 313, 338

Detachment, ii. 307

Distrust, ii. 270

Dogmatism, ii. 250, 263

Domesticity, ii. 255, 271

Ecclesiasticism, aversion from, ii. 354

Egotism, *v.* ii. 258

Erudition, ii. 144 *seq.*

Femininity, ii. 253

Filial affection, i. 177 *seq.*

Friendship, ii. 250 *seq.*

Health, concern for, i. 34, 102, 410

Honours, indifference to, i. 222, 242; ii. 40, 80, 105, 257

Ideality, ii. 307, 312, 314

Idleness, i. 396; ii. 261, 297, 308

Individualism (*see* Opinions, Social State)

Individuality, i. 23; ii. 309

Intellectual, ii. 143, 147, 261, 275, 307

Inventiveness, i. 19, 28, 30, 32, 33, 56, 59, 65, 107; ii. 249, 308, 311

Irritability, ii. **274**

Judgment, ii. 259

Spencer, H.: *Characteristics—Cont'd.*

Linguistics, aversion from, i. 17 *seq.;* ii. 306

Mathematical, i. 16 *seq.*, 28, 32 *seq.;* ii. 146, 174, 306

Memory, ii. 261

Method, ii. 266

Moral, ii. 44, 276

Music, ii. 131, 267

Nature, study, ii. 147

Optimism, i. 54, 56, 63, 92

Originality, i. 84, 226

Persistence, i. 64

Physical, ii. 110, 246 *seq.*

Political, ii. 3 (*see* Opinions)

Punctiliousness, i. 363

Principles, ii. 247

Radicalism, i. 45, 62 *seq.*

Reading, aversion to, ii. 247, 267

Restraint, impatience of, i. 16

Scepticism, ii. 217

Self-advertisement, aversion from, i. 213, 226; ii. 65 *seq.*, 96

Self-assertion, i. 21, 29

Self-confidence, i. 21 *seq.*, 31, 34; ii. 250, 307 *seq.*

Sincerity, i. 70 *seq.*, 177; ii. 269, 276

Singing, ii. 267

Social, i. 299, 381; ii. 253 *seq.*

Study, aversion from, i. 16 (*v.* reading)

Style, literary, i. 18, 50 *seq.*, 54, 71, 74 *seq.*, 79, 264 *seq.*, 307

433

INDEX

WADE, SIR WILLOUGHBY, ii. 102

Wales, Prince of (King Edward VII.), ridiculous statement concerning, ii. 141

Wales, Prince and Princess of: London University degrees, ii. 214

Walker, J. Hanson, ii. 113

Wallace, Alfred Russel: ii. 102; opinion of Spencer's biological writings, i. 200; Spencer's ethics, i. 265; Land Nationalisation Society, i. 290; Weismann controversy, ii. 52. Letter to, ii. 73

Waller, i. 255

Walshe, Walter H., i. 256

War: in social evolution, i. 375; ii. 77, 355 *seq.*

Ward, Prof. James: ii. 242; controversy with, ii. 184, 385

Ward, Lester F.: biological basis of Spencer's sociology, ii. 357 *note.* Letter to, on Spencer's relations to Comte, ii. 90 *seq.*

Ward, Wilfred, i. 340

Water Question, article by Spencer on, i. 82; ii. 369

Watkins, Rev. Prof.: appreciation of Spencer, i. 269

Watson, Prof., i. 303 *seq.*

Watson, William, ii. 136

Watts, George F., R.A., ii. 86

Watts, Isaac, *Divine and Moral Songs:* Spencer's text-book as a child, 9

Wealth: distribution during life approved, i. 407

Wealthy, lack of initiative, ii. 67

Webb, Sidney, ii. 69

Webb, Mrs. Sidney (*née* Beatrice Potter): ii. 102; last visit to Spencer, ii. 227. Letters to: "game-cure," i. 316; social pathology, i. 368; proposed portrait, i. 378; billiard story, i. 398; agnostics and believers, ii. 200; thoughts in illness, ii. 219

Weismann, Prof. A.: controversy respecting inheritance of acquired characters, ii. 45 *seq.*

Welby, Lady Victoria, ii. 102

Wells, H. T., R.A., ii. 87

Wemyss, Earl of, ii. 9. Letters to: reasons for not joining Liberty and Property Defence League, i. 323; anti-socialist movement, i. 400 *seq.;* railway nuisances, ii. 5; English stupidity, *ib.*

Werner, E. T. C.: i. 394; compiler of Chinese *Descriptive Sociology,* i. 394

Wesley, John: letter quoted, i. 2; converts Spencer's grandmother, i. 4

Wesleyan Methodism, associations of Spencer's family with, i. 2, 4, 7

Westerham, Kent, ii. 82

Westmacott, Mr. [son of Sculptor], i. 326

Westminster Abbey: i. 285 *seq.;* movement for memorial to Spencer in, ii. 237 *seq.*

Westminster Review: Spencer's contributions to, i. 83, 86 *seq.,* 108 *seq.,* 125; ii. 323, 369 *seq.;* review of Spencer's *First Principles,* i. 137

441

INDEX

"What is Electricity," i. 153; ii. 160, 164, 341, 372

Wheatley, Mr., i. 262

Whewell, William: *History and Philosophy of the Inductive Sciences*, ii. 282; Mill's criticism, ii. 319

Whipple, E. P., i. 131

Williams, Geoffrey S., ii. 238

Williams, Mr. [Sidney], i. 303

Williams and Norgate (Spencer's publishers), i. 165

Williamson, Dr., ii. 173

Wilks, Dr. Samuel, ii. 102

Wilson, Rev. Dr. James, editor of *Pilot*, i. 62, 384

Wilson, James, M.P., of the *Economist*, i. 62, 73, 120

Women: suffrage question, i. 180 *seq.;* outcry against wrongs of, i. 376; intellectual powers, i. 395 *seq.;* over-exaltation of, ii. 129

Worcester, i. 29; ii. 309

Working classes: political power, i. 122

Workman's Peace Association, i. 297

Wright, Prof. W. Aldis, ii. 242

Wright-Henderson, Rev. P. A., Oxford, ii. 242

Wroughton, Mr., i. 273

Wylde, Rev. M., i. 269 *seq.*

Wyman, Jeffries, i. 131, 198

X Club, i. 223, 256, 332 *seq.*, 377; ii. 23, 29 *seq.*, 199, 219

Yale College, i. 276

Youmans, Edward Livingston: introduction to Spencer, i. 128; personal intercourse, i. 136, 170, 260 *seq.*, 290; Civil War, i. 139 *seq.;* watches Spencer's interests in America, i. 143 *seq.*, 217 *seq.*, 230, 275, 371; raises fund to recoup Spencer's losses, i. 167; amanuensis to Spencer, i. 170; Spencer's drastic criticism of lectures, i. 171; organises Int. Scientific Series, i. 210, 248; founder and editor of *Popular Science Monthly*, i. 211, 230; lecture on Spencer, i. 227; introduction to Spencer's *Data of Ethics*, i. 263, 267; Spencer's obligations to, i. 290, 336 (*see* i. 315); Spencer's American visit, i. 301; conscientiousness, i. 367; Spencer's appreciation, i. 366, 271; ii. 88; death, ii. 370; Fiske's memoirs, ii. 64; interest in Spencer recalled, ii. 94. Letters to: Civil War, i. 139 *seq.;* publishing affairs, i. 144 *seq.;* change of views in *Social Statics*, i. 145 *seq.;* Comtism, i. 148; Count Stirum's donation, i. 166; holiday sightseeing, i. 171 *seq.; First Principles*, i. 172; spontaneous generation, i. 191; progress with the Philosophy, a forecast, i. 193 *seq.;* Hutton controversy, i. 195; Darwin and mental evolution, i. 197; Fiske's Harvard lectures on "Positive" philosophy, i. 206 *seq.;* making a fortune by

442

philosophy, i. 211; an opportunity for advertisement rejected, i. 213 *seq.; Descriptive Sociology* worries, i. 217 *seq.;* Huxley's condition, i. 219; author and publisher, i. 220; a tilt with Tyndall, *ib.;* lecture at Liberal Club, i. 226; Tyndall's Belfast address and its effect, i. 228 *seq.;* scheme for financial assistance, i. 230; *Popular Science Monthly* policy, i. 231; Bain and evolution, Romanes, i. 240; Dr. Elam's attack, i. 249 *seq.;* conversation with a bishop, i. 250; copyright, i. 251, 278; Tylor and McLennan, i. 252; *Data of Ethics,* i. 257; holiday companionship invited, i. 266; " devil-may-care " mood enjoined, i. 263; French clerical party, i. 265; reviews of *Data of Ethics,* i. 267; Mr. Guthrie's misrepresentations, *ib.;* reviewers' misconceptions about *First Principles,* i. 268; visit to Egypt, i. 271; Grant Allen and Critics; professorship of sociology, etc., i. 280; civilities with an old antagonist, i. 281; sundry critics, i. 282 *seq.,* 289; hardest bit of work finished, i. 296; the American visit, i. 300; Hughlings Jackson's researches, i. 302; Henry George, i. 305; " gospel of relaxation," i. 307; a Japanese translation, revision of *Essays,* i.

308; Drummond's book, election to French Academy, i. 309 *seq.;* Darwinism, i. 316, 317; Tylor, i. 317; Communism, *ib.; Edinburgh Review's* criticism, i. 318; political articles, i. 319, 324; proposed parliamentary candidature, i. 322; *Pall Mall Gazette's* couplet, i. 326; Boehm's bust, *ib.;* permanent work resumed, *ib.;* personal inquiries, i. 327; Irish Obstruction, i. 330; friends breaking up, i. 332; a " dreadfully destructive " chapter in " Ecclesiastical Institutions," i. 335; " Religious Retrospect and Prospect," i. 337 *seq.;* Harrison's controversy, i. 339 *seq.; Autobiography,* i. 343; reprinting the Harrison controversy, i. 347 *seq.;* relations with George Eliot, i. 357; " Factors of Organic Evolution," i. 359, 362; International copyright, i. 363; consolation in illness, i. 366; a last greeting, i. 370; " What is Electricity," ii. 160; nebular hypothesis, ii. 164, 172. Also i. 162, 164, 275. Letters from: publishing affairs, i. 133, 143 *seq.;* Civil War, i. 138 *seq.,* 277; *Social Statics,* i. 145 *seq.;* Abbot controversy, i. 190 *seq.;* a " little thrust " from the *Nation,* i. 198; false report of Bain's death, i. 251; Harrison's controversy, i. 345 *seq.,* 348; Spencer's

)0